Dialectics of the Self

Dialectics of the Self

Transcending Charles Taylor

Ian Fraser

imprint-academic.com

Published in the UK by
Imprint Academic, PO Box 200, Exeter EX5 5YX, UK

Published in the USA by
Imprint Academic, Philosophy Documentation Center
PO Box 7147, Charlottesville, VA 22906-7147, USA

ISBN 978 184540 0453
A CIP catalogue record for this book is available from the
British Library and US Library of Congress

Contents

Acknowledgements

I would like to thank Lawrence Wilde for his insightful comments on the manuscript, and for his support and encouragement throughout the project. Anthony Freeman, Managing Editor of *Imprint Academic*, deserves thanks for his understanding, and David Boucher for backing the book. Gary Browning and Howard Williams have been supportive over a number of years for which I am especially grateful. Joan Melia also merits a mention for her infectious love of Joyce's *Ulysses*. I am grateful to Nottingham Trent University for granting me sabbatical leave and the library staff there, particularly Terry Hanstock, for their excellent provision of interlibrary loans. The technical wizardry of Paul Green was impressive and greatly appreciated. Audrey Bradshaw, Keith and Mary Fraser, and Carol and Vincent Murphy, have helped in indirect ways that they may not even realise, which is all the more reason for mentioning them here. My Brother, Keith Fraser, requires a further mention, along with my nieces Danielle and Laura Fraser, in memory of our unforgettable, epiphanic night in Istanbul. Molly has kept me company for the entire project, and that necessitates a posthumous recognition of similar exploits by Strider and Tigger. Sharon Garratt deserves heartfelt praise for her patience and support. As a transcending testament to the power of dialectics, I dedicate the book to the memory of Frank Fraser, for developing one form of his aesthetic self in his superb photography, and also for being my Father.

Portions of the book have appeared elsewhere. Chapter Two is a revised version of my 'Charles Taylor's Catholicism', *Contemporary Political Theory*, 4, 3, 2005. Chapter Three is a revised version of my 'Charles Taylor on Transcendence: Benjamin, Bloch and Beyond', *Philosophy & Social Criticism*, Vol 29, 3, 2003. Chapters One and Seven feature some of the sections from my 'Charles Taylor, Marx and Marxism', *Political Studies*, Vol 51, 4, 2003. I would like to thank the anonymous referees of those journals for their helpful comments and suggestions, and Paul Kelly in particular in relation to the *Political Studies* article. Many thanks also to Ruth Abbey for providing a stimulating basis for debate in relation to the Catholicism piece. The usual disclaimers apply.

Emphases in quotations in the book are always in the original unless otherwise stated. Terms in square brackets are my amendments and insertions unless otherwise stated.

Introduction

All I know is that I'm not a Marxist (Karl Marx).[1]

A spectre haunts Charles Taylor's conception of the self — the spectre of Marxism. One of the most prominent thinkers to identify this Marxist presence was Isaiah Berlin who, in 1994, five years after the publication of *Sources of the Self*,[2] wrote a brief introduction to one of the first comprehensive evaluations of Charles Taylor's work.[3] While seeing him as a teleological Christian and Hegelian, Berlin also stressed how Taylor is influenced 'in a fascinating fashion' by 'Marxist ideas'.[4] This emanates, he suggests, from Taylor's emphasis on the possibility of human flourishing only if society is liberated from oppression, exploitation and domination, which derive from modern capitalism and which have their roots in various formations in the past. He argues that, for Taylor, such liberation is only possible with the creation of a rational society where individuals pursue their ends on their own and as part of a community. Berlin suggests this 'Marxist' desire is impossible because of the multiplicity of values that are pursued by different societies and cultures and that often conflict or are incompatible with each other.[5] Any notion of a common humanity, as he assumes Taylor to approve of, is therefore unrealistic. In his response to Berlin, Taylor ignores the Marxist epithet but does mention the 'sad story of Bolshevism' and urges that

[1]   Quoted by Engels in a letter to Conrad Schmidt August 5, 1890 in Karl Marx & Frederick Engels, *Collected Works*, Volume 49, London, Lawrence & Wishart, 2002, p. 7.

[2]   Charles Taylor, *Sources of the Self: The Making of the Modern Identity*, Cambridge, Cambridge University Press, 1989.

[3]   Isaiah Berlin, 'Introduction', to James Tully (ed.), *Philosophy in an Age of Pluralism: The Philosophy of Charles Taylor in Question*, Cambridge, Cambridge University Press, 1994, pp. 1–3.

[4]   Berlin, 'Introduction', pp. 1–2.

[5]   Berlin, 'Introduction', pp. 2–3.

we keep the aim of human liberation and fulfilment 'before our eyes' rather than assume we have achieved them with 'cheap substitutes, like Leninist "democracy"'.[6] However, Taylor maintains that there is still a possibility for a more humane and liberated society even though the aforementioned disasters have been realised in pursuit of the goals he obviously endorses. Against Berlin, he believes that we should still continue to struggle for a 'mode of life' where conflicting demands 'could be reconciled' even where other conflicting demands persist.

Despite Berlin's observation, there has been little written about Taylor's relationship to Marx, Marxism and the notion of the self.[7] Such an omission is strange, because Taylor has a long history of sympathy, albeit critical, with the more humanist side of Marx's and Marxists' writings. We should not forget that he was one of the founders of the New Left in Britain, and began the journey of rethinking and re-evaluating Marxism's continued relevance to contemporary debates concerning a more humane society and pursuit of the good life. From the late 1950s onwards, he wrote a number of articles and chapters, which explicitly engaged with Marxism in one form or another.[8] Over this thirty-year period, he can be seen as adopting a sympathetic and immanent critique of Marx and Marxism in which he teases out problems or unanswered questions and then explores them in relation to his own political philosophy. Such a project is certainly of great service in re-vitalising Marxist theory from under the shadows of Stalinism and a supposedly triumphant

---

[6]   Charles Taylor, 'Charles Taylor Replies', in James Tully (ed.), *Philosophy in an Age of Pluralism: The Philosophy of Charles Taylor in Question*, Cambridge, Cambridge University Press, 1994, p. 214.

[7]   Nicholas H. Smith, in his impressive study of Taylor's work, does offer a discussion of Taylor's relation to Marx and Marxism but only briefly. See his *Charles Taylor. Meanings, Morals and Modernity*, Cambridge, Polity, 2002, pp. 180–83.

[8]   See Charles Taylor, 'Marxism and Humanism', *New Reasoner*, 2, 1957; 'The Ambiguities of Marxist Doctrine', *The Student World*, 2, 1958; 'Marxism and Empiricism', in Bernard Williams & Alan Montefiore (eds.), *British Analytical Philosophy*, London, Routledge & Kegan Paul, 1966; 'From Marxism to the Dialogue Society', in Terry Eagleton & Brian Wicker (eds.), *From Culture to Revolution*, London & Sydney, Sheed & Ward, 1968; 'Socialism and Weltanschauung', in Leszek Kolakowski & Stuart Hampshire (eds.), *The Socialist Idea: a Reappraisal*, London, Weidenfeld & Nicholson, 1974; *Hegel*. Cambridge, Cambridge University Press, 1975; 'Marxist Philosophy', in Brian Magee (ed.), *Men of Ideas: Some Creators of Contemporary Philosophy*, London, BBC Publications, 1978; 'Marxism and Socialist Humanism', in Robin Archer *et al* (eds.), *Out of Apathy: Voices of the New Left Thirty Years On*, London, Verso, 1989.

capitalism. Indeed, it was one of the factors for constituting the New Left itself. Most of the early pieces developed and re-iterated similar themes that were drawn together in his first major study *Hegel*, which was first published in 1975. Three years later, he was prominent enough to be chosen by Bryan Magee to discuss Marxist theory as part of the 'Men Of Ideas' series televised by the BBC.[9] However, by 1989, in the year *Sources of the Self* was published, Taylor was about to settle his account with Marx and Marxism in a retrospective essay, 'Marxism and Socialist Humanism'[10], in which he considered the position of the New Left thirty years after its inception. Throughout this piece, he certainly desires to distance himself from his Marxist past, even though he does note some positive aspects in that tradition. Ten years later, the break with Marxism becomes more overt with his eventual declaration for the Catholic religion as *his* preferred framework within which to pursue the good.[11] It is interesting to note here that Stuart Hall, a co-founder of the New Left, referred to Taylor in his younger days as a 'sort of Catholic Marxist'[12], which might suggest that Catholicism and Marxism are not mutually exclusive — at least not for Taylor.

As Taylor is quite rightly seen, in the words of Richard Rorty, as 'among the dozen most important philosophers writing today, anywhere in the world', then his long engagement with Marxism certainly warrants attention'.[13] Indeed, if Berlin could detect the presence of 'Marxist ideas' in Taylor's work *five* years after the publication of *Sources* and his retrospective essay, then an analysis of his engagement with Marx and Marxism on the conception of the self and of its moral and political possibilities in modernity seems even more pertinent. This book is an attempt to do just that. I therefore offer an immanent and transcendent critique of Taylor's notion of the self, through which I will demonstrate the continued relevance of the humanist Marxist tradition he came from but ultimately rejects. This rejection is not total, as we shall see throughout the course of this book, because certain elements of Marx and Marxism continue to haunt his work. I will therefore be engaging in an analy-

---

[9]   Taylor, 'Marxist Philosophy'.
[10] Taylor, 'Marxism and Socialist Humanism'.
[11] Charles Taylor, 'A Catholic Modernity?', in James. L. Heft (ed.), *A Catholic Modernity?* Oxford, Oxford University Press, 1999.
[12] Robin Archer *et al* (eds.), *Out of Apathy: Voices of the New Left Thirty Years On*, London, Verso, 1989, p. 28.
[13] Quoted in James. L. Heft, 'Introduction' to James. L Heft (ed.), *A Catholic Modernity?* Oxford, Oxford University Press, 1999, p. 3.

sis of Taylor's own sympathetic and immanent critique of Marx and Marxism to expose those aspects where he shares similarities and where he has been far too dismissive of that tradition.

I begin in Chapter One by outlining Taylor's notion of the self in order to offer a comparison with Marx's discussion of the self. I show that Taylor has, by his own admission, a core aspect of Marxism in his notion of the self which is the affirmation of ordinary life, while other aspects — the social self, self-interpretation, language and dialogue — also find resonance in Marx's writings. Taylor operates with a universal/particular notion of the self, which is reflected in Marx's dialectical understanding of the self as abstract and concrete. The dialectical nature of the self in capital means that people find their identity being imposed from outside at the same time they attempt to assert their own identity or human essence. The self therefore becomes a split or alienated self as we try to assert our human essence, and attempt to make our existence conform to our essence in our struggles in and against the class system of capital. I argue that Taylor pays too little attention to this imposition of identity by capital and the struggles involved against it.

Taylor's emphasis on a religious self, and his own Catholic vision as an orientation towards the good, is the subject of Chapter Two. After an initial discussion of the complex role of religion in relation to Marxism, I then critically explore the nature of Taylor's Catholicism across the following themes: the transcendent, difference, unconditional love, and his endorsement of the sixteenth century Jesuit project of Matteo Ricci as an exemplar for modern day Catholics. I show his arguments to be contradictory and ultimately to undermine his preference for difference across diverse belief systems, thereby exposing his restrictive theism

Chapter Three takes further Taylor's difficulty in articulating his notion of the transcendent that emerged in the previous Chapter, and which he sees as crucial for his vision for a better society. I show that he previously endorsed the Marxist writers Walter Benjamin and Ernst Bloch in 1989 for offering a transcendent philosophy but chose, for some unspecified reason, not to develop this in his work. I rectify this by displaying how a notion of the transcendent can emerge from the Marxist tradition that Taylor ultimately rejected, whilst recognising the boundaries that must arise given Taylor's restrictive theism, and the ultimate atheism of Benjamin and Bloch.

One way Taylor suggests we can be brought into an awareness of the transcendent is through epiphanic art, so in Chapter Four I critically assess Taylor's emphasis on the notion of epiphany as a moral source and as a crucial moment in the making of the self. I show how Taylor appropriates the Joycean epiphany and exalts it as theistic. However, this not only goes against the non-theistic way the epiphany was used by James Joyce, whom Taylor still endorses as a main purveyor of epiphanic art, but it closes off the epiphany from non-theistic sources of the good. I therefore suggest that in privileging theistic epiphanies over non-theistic epiphanies Taylor again undermines his commitment to openness and diversity.

In his discussion of art, Taylor offers an appreciatively critical assessment of Adorno in this area. In Chapter Five I seek to examine and contrast the positions of both writers, and ultimately expose similarities and differences whilst also trying to defend Adorno against Taylor. Taylor praises Adorno's attack on instrumentalism and also supports his pessimism, but in the end rejects Adorno's position for its lack of theism and subjectivism. I therefore explore the richness of Adorno's non-theistic approach to religion through art, and examine his understanding of the subject-object relation in aesthetic theory and practice to critique Taylor's own position.

Modern Social Imaginaries (2004) is Taylor's most recent statement on his examination of the modern identity, which builds on and expands themes that have been considered in the previous Chapters. In Chapter Six I offer a critical and extended assessment of this work, which attempts to identify the shared self-understandings or social imaginaries of Western modernity. Taylor sees the social imaginary of Western modernity as a moral order of society that is shaped by social forms such as the market economy, the public sphere and the self-government of people, and results in what he calls 'multiple modernities'. My main argument against him here is that he pays insufficient attention to the role of class struggle in history in the development of his social imaginaries.

Chapter Seven responds to Taylor's challenge to Marxism to say more about the personal level of the individual, and to offer a Marxist theory of art, human and aesthetic experience. To this end, I further examine and develop Marx's own vision of the self in the non-alienated society, where, as Taylor approvingly notes, there is a vision of humans socially expressing themselves as though they were artists. I defend a conception of the aesthetic self, which is dialectical in its mediation between universals and particulars, and suggest that it is in movements and ideas that oppose capital, and in their desire for a more humane world, that we can see the realm of the aesthetic emerging. I show that Taylor's own desire for the aestheticisation of the self, for the contemplative life for all, is therefore a forlorn quest without putting in place measures that allow time for that development. I contend that this must be premised on a reduction in necessary labour time and a commitment to radical democracy, both crucial measures that were pre-figured by Marx. However, to achieve this means not only transcending Charles Taylor, but also transcending the constraints of capital itself.

Chapter One

The Self

One is. But this is not enough; indeed it is the very least.[1]

One of Taylor's major criticisms of Marxism is that, if it is to be a more relevant theory, it must say something extra about the personal level of the individual.[2] Such a criticism is not only important for Marxism, but has increased significance for Taylor himself, in that his major work *Sources of the Self* sets out to consider this personal level. I respond to Taylor's challenge in this Chapter by agreeing that he certainly has a valid point here, although he does not really consider those passages where Marx actually does this. Consequently, what I will show is that in developing his own notion of a situated self, particularly, but not exclusively, in *Sources of the Self*, Taylor bears an interesting comparison with Marx on this issue. To this end, I begin by outlining Taylor's own discussion of the self to compare with Marx, and then illustrate how the self becomes manifest in an alienated form with the development of capitalist society. I show that Taylor recognises the alienated form of the self that capitalism produces through his own discussion of Marx, but fails to follow this to the logical conclusion that capitalism must be transcended for alienation to cease.

Taylor on the Self

Taylor begins his monumental study of the self by considering the 'inextricably intertwined themes' of 'selfhood and the good'.[3] He notes when considering these themes, how too much of moral phi-

---

[1]   Ernst Bloch, *Literary Essays*, California, Stanford University Press, 1998, p. 1.
[2]   Charles Taylor, 'Marxist Philosophy', in Brian Magee (ed.), *Men of Ideas: Some Creators of Contemporary Philosophy*, London, BBC Publications 1978, p. 52.
[3]   Charles Taylor, *Sources of the Self*, Cambridge, Cambridge University Press, 1989, p. 3.

losophy has emphasised the right to do something rather than what good life we ought to pursue. His conception of the self therefore sets out to rectify this problem by asking what makes life worth living?[4] We answer such a question through our moral and spiritual intu-itions within which we engage in '"strong evaluation"' of what is right or wrong. On the one side, these moral intuitions are instinctive responses, but on the other side, they also recognise, albeit implic-itly, the moral claims concerning others.[5] Taylor wants to explore the 'moral ontology' or '"background picture"' that lies behind these moral intuitions, which we draw on to substantiate our moral claims.[6] One such universal claim that Taylor thinks is undeniable, is that humans should be respected, which means that suffering should be avoided, autonomy enhanced and dignity emphasised where it involves commanding, what he calls, attitudinal respect, which refers to looking up to someone rather than respecting some-one's rights.[7] Such a sense of dignity can be found in a self as a 'householder, father of a family, holding down a job, [and] provid-ing for my dependants', which means that it is woven into the important notion of the affirmation of ordinary life.[8] Taylor argues that the affirmation of ordinary life 'is a term of art, meant roughly to designate the life of production and the family' both of which are 'central to our well-being'.[9] For Taylor, the affirmation of ordinary life is seen as 'one of the most powerful ideas in modern civilisation', and it is worth mentioning straight away here that he cites Marx-ism's 'apotheosis of man the producer', 'who finds his highest dig-nity in labour and the transformation of nature, in the service of life', as a crucial part of that idea.[10] For Taylor, the affirmation of ordinary life implies that there is a certain worth and dignity to life, which is expressed in the way we live our lives.[11] It is here, in this affirmation, that we can find the higher life in the way of living ordinary life through production, reproduction, work and the family. For Taylor, then, Marxism is clearly and positively cited as advancing the affirma-tion of ordinary life, and is therefore at the core of his notion of the self.

---

[4]   Taylor, *Sources of the Self*, p. 4.
[5]   Taylor, *Sources of the Self*, p. 7.
[6]   Taylor, *Sources of the Self*, pp. 8–9.
[7]   Taylor, *Sources of the Self*, p. 15.
[8]   Taylor, *Sources of the Self*, pp. 15–16.
[9]   Taylor, *Sources of the Self*, pp. 13–14.
[10] Taylor, *Sources of the Self*, pp. 14 & 215.
[11] Taylor, *Sources of the Self*, p. 23.

On this basis, Taylor considers the question of identity in the formulation of: 'Who am I?' Answering this question indicates that our
identity is defined by the commitments and identifications that pro-
vide the framework within which we can determine what is good or
bad, or ought to be done, or ought to be supported or opposed.[12] It is
not answerable, Taylor suggests, by simply giving one's name and
genealogy. By 'taking a stand' in this way individuals either identify
themselves as, say, an Armenian or Québécois or commit themselves as a Catholic, or anarchist, for instance, but in doing so they
are using a framework within which they can determine where they
stand on a particular issue of what is good or valuable to pursue. If
they lost this commitment or identification then they would be 'at
sea', in that they would not know what the significance of things was
for them over a number of important issues. The most extreme form
of this loss is an identity crisis where people become disorientated,
not in the sense that they do not know who they are, but in the sense
that they do not know where they stand. For Taylor, this link
between identity and orientation is essential, because to know who
you are is oriented in a moral space within which you accord value to
what is good, bad, worth doing and not worth doing.[13] We make
'qualitative distinctions' and 'strong evaluations' in this moral
space, which give us an identity that we ought to be true to, fail to
uphold, or give up when necessary.[14] An identity therefore orients
us, and provides a framework within which we give things meaning. For Taylor, such frameworks are inescapable and anyone who
denies this is to be regarded as 'pathological' or 'deeply disturbed'.[15]
It follows, then, that human beings are selves in the sense that they
'are beings of the requisite depth and complexity' that have an identity where they make qualitative distinctions in a moral space.[16] He
therefore rejects any notion of the self that emanates from psychology and sociology, as they do not link identity with a notion of the
good.[17] For Taylor, we define a self or identity by the way in which
things have significance for a person. Identity therefore develops
'through a language of interpretation' that a person comes to accept
as a 'valid articulation of these issues'.[18] The self is not an object in the

---

[12] Taylor, *Sources of the Self*, p. 27.
[13] Taylor, *Sources of the Self*, p. 28.
[14] Taylor, *Sources of the Self*, pp. 29–30.
[15] Taylor, *Sources of the Self*, p. 31.
[16] Taylor, *Sources of the Self*, p. 32.
[17] Taylor, *Sources of the Self*, pp. 32–33.
[18] Taylor, *Sources of the Self*, p. 34.

sense that it can be studied separately from the way people interpret it, but is rather partly constituted by these self-interpretations, which are articulated within a 'language community'.[19] Consequently, one is a self only in relation to other selves. Who a self is occurs within an 'interchange of speakers' where the self is defined by where it speaks from, as part of a family, as acquiring a particular social status, and as a member of a moral and spiritual space within which the most important relations are played out. The self engages in conversations with others, shares a common language, and discovers what its conception of the good life will be in 'webs of interlocution'.[20] In this way, it defines itself in displaying where it is speaking from and to whom. Identity, then, involves a stand on moral and spiritual matters and some reference to a defining community. It follows, therefore, that for Taylor, selves exist only in a certain moral space that considers the nature of the good, so any notion of an abstract or neutral self separate from these concerns must be rejected.[21] On this basis, Taylor wants to avoid the mistaken assumption that the modern individual is the taken for granted starting point, whereas in reality the starting point of our first self-understanding of our identity was as a tribe member, or Father or son.[22] It follows therefore that 'to be an individual is not to be a Robinson Crusoe, but to be placed in a certain way among other humans'.[23] As we shall see shortly, this is exactly the point Marx makes against Adam Smith's and David Ricardo's Robinsonade understanding of an individual.

Taylor's notion of the self is also engaged in a process of change and becoming as it centres itself not simply with who we are, but where we are going, and where we have come from.[24] In determining our place in relation to the good, we understand ourselves in a narrative in which we see our lives as in a story and so give an account of the self.[25] As part of this account, Taylor notes that agents attribute differential worth or importance to certain goods. Some goods are considered to be higher than others, and as such he refers

[19]   Taylor, *Sources of the Self*, p. 35.
[20]   Taylor, *Sources of the Self*, p. 36.
[21]   Taylor, *Sources of the Self*, pp. 49–50.
[22]   Charles Taylor, *Modern Social Imaginaries*, Durham & London, Duke University Press, 2004, p. 64.
[23]   Taylor, *Modern Social Imaginaries*, p.65
[24]   Taylor, *Sources of the Self*, p. 47.
[25]   Taylor, *Sources of the Self*, pp. 51–52.

to these as 'hypergoods'.[26] However, he recognises that hypergoods pose problems for his theory because they invariably result in conflict.[27] For instance, someone may rank your hypergood at a lower rank in their own moral schema. Despite this, he argues that hypergoods have often arisen as a movement on from earlier inferior views, and this presents a path along the road to a higher moral consciousness in a Nietzschean 'transvaluation of values'. So the new hypergood offers a standard with which to judge other ordinary goods and also radically alters our view of their value.[28] These other supposedly inferior goods do not disappear though, and as such become a source of tension. To overcome this tension, Taylor argues that we need practical reasoning, which does not say a position is correct absolutely, but only that one position is superior to another.[29] For example, he argues that when someone realises that a love which seemed ephemeral initially, but is now realised to be deep over time, then that is a superior position to the one before. This does not mean that all argument and discussion now ceases because moral growth could actually be challenged by a competing interpretation, which might show that the person was perhaps deluded and now comes to realise that was the case. It follows then that we need to recognise the contingency of our hypergoods, but at the same time we can, according to Taylor, hope that articulating our hypergoods can lead to forms of reconciliation by recognising the varied range of goods we live by.[30] Even where reconciliation is impossible, he maintains that the great inner conflict this causes, although risky, is 'at least putting an end to the stifling of the spirit and to the atrophy of so many of our spiritual sources which is the bane of modern naturalist culture'. Indeed, Taylor suggests that the main reason that he wrote *Sources* was precisely to offer a liberation of the spirit from this stifling.[31]

For Taylor, another crucial aspect of our identity, which he terms authenticity, is a moral ideal of being true to oneself in the process of self-fulfilment.[32] By moral ideal, he means an indication of what a better or higher life might be not in terms of haphazard choices, but in terms of offering a 'standard of what we ought to desire'. Endors-

[26]   Taylor, *Sources of the Self*, p. 63.
[27]   Taylor, *Sources of the Self*, p. 64.
[28]   Taylor, *Sources of the Self*, p. 65.
[29]   Taylor, *Sources of the Self*, p. 72.
[30]   Taylor, *Sources of the Self*, p. 107.
[31]   Taylor, *Sources of the Self*, p. 520.
[32]   Charles Taylor, *The Ethics of Authenticity*, Cambridge, Mass, Harvard University Press, 1992, pp. 15–16.

ing such an ethic of authenticity means using reasoned arguments about ideals, seeing how they can be put into practice, and believing that these arguments really can make a difference.[33] He argues that humans must do this in their own way of being, and in contact with their inner nature, in the knowledge that it could be lost either to conformity or instrumentality.[34] Being authentic means people being true to their own originality, which they can discover and then articulate. For Taylor, this is the powerful force that is the background to the modern ideal of authenticity and to the aims of self-fulfilment and self-realisation. Moreover, this leads to another crucial aspect of the self that has developed with the ideal of authenticity, and that is the need for recognition.[35] Taylor argues that when we try to work out our identity, we do so through dialogue with others in a process of recognition.[36] He maintains that recognition on the intimate level of personal relationships has a powerful function in forming identities, just as on the social level it has shaped the politics of equal recognition.[37]

Taylor realises that this pursuit of the ideal of authenticity can certainly take debased forms in terms of narcissism or self-absorption, but that does not mean we should reject the ideal.[38] On the contrary, he urges us to tread a path not between the boosters and the knockers of modernity, or along some sort of trade off between both positions.[39] Rather, he wants us to steer the developments of modernity to their most fruitful outcomes, whilst avoiding the slide to their more debased forms.[40] To do so, means engaging in a 'work of retrieval through which this ideal can help us restore our practice',[41] and expose how the 'more self-centred modes of self-fulfilment betray the ideal of authenticity'.[42] On this basis, he argues that subjectivism, the view that moral positions are ungrounded in reason and instead mere preferences of individuals, must be rejected, as must any account of modernity that sees people imprisoned in mod-

---

[34] Taylor, *Ethics*, p. 23.
[35] Taylor, *Ethics*, pp. 28–29.
[36] Taylor, *Ethics*, pp. 45–46.
[37] Taylor, *Ethics*, pp. 47–48. Cf. Charles Taylor, 'The Politics of Recognition', in his *Philosophical Arguments*, Cambridge, Mass, Harvard University Press, 1995, p. 231.
[37] Taylor, *Ethics*, p. 49.
[38] Taylor, *Ethics*, pp. 4 & 23.
[39] Taylor, *Ethics*, pp. 22–23.
[40] Taylor, *Ethics*, p. 12.
[41] Taylor, *Ethics*, p. 23.
[42] Taylor, *Ethics*, p. 105.

ern culture by the system, be it capitalism, industrial society, or bureaucracy.[43]

In trying to understand further Taylor's notion of the self as we have discussed above, it is helpful to consider Ruth Abbey's suggestion that he has a two-dimensional approach to the self, which focuses on its historical and ontological dimensions.[44] She suggests that, for Taylor, the ontological aspects of the self which do not change are — self-interpretation in that we have an understanding of who 'we' are, which is itself informed by what others think of us; the fact that humans are animals with language; and the dialogical aspect of selfhood, in that we have an ongoing dialogue with others. The historical aspect is the way that Taylor charts the change of the self throughout history. Abbey notes how some commentators[45] have seen this two-dimensional approach to the self as strange and contradictory, because it seems to offer essentialist notions of the self which conflict with Taylor's historicist notion of the self as a changing phenomenon over time.[46] In contrast, she argues that Taylor's two-dimensional approach is viable because he is acknowledging facets common to all humans while at the same time emphasising the different ways in which these features — self-interpretation, language and dialogue — are experienced.[47] In this account, the self must therefore be understood as a universal and a particular. The universal facets of the self in terms of self-interpretation, language and dialogue manifest themselves in many different forms of identity, which are themselves continually evolving through further self-interpretation. What I will now show is that Taylor's discussion of the self has a relatively strong resonance in Marx's own writings; a resonance which Taylor failed to explore.

Marx on the Self

For Marx, the key to understanding any notion of the self emerges out of his developmental method of properly grasping the abstract

---

[43] Taylor, *Ethics*, pp. 18 & 23.

[44] Ruth Abbey, *Charles Taylor*, New Jersey, Princeton University Press, 2000, p. 56.

[45] F.A. Olafson, 'Comments on *The Sources of the Self*', *Philosophy and Phenomenological Research*, LIV (I), 1994; H. Rosa, 'Goods and Life–Forms: Relativism in Charles Taylor's Political Philosophy', *Radical Philosophy*, 71 (May/June), 1995; O. Flanagan, *Self Expressions: Mind, Morals and the Meaning of Life*, New York, Oxford University Press, 1996.

[46] Abbey, *Charles Taylor*, p. 57.

[47] Abbey, *Charles Taylor*, p. 71.

and the concrete. In his early work on Hegel both in the *Critique of Hegel's Doctrine of the State* (1843) and the *Economic and Philosophical Manuscripts* (1844), Marx rebuked the latter for beginning his analysis with abstract concepts rather than real subjects.[48] In doing so, Hegel 'abstracts from nature and real man' and is therefore 'completely indifferent to all real determinateness'.[49] It follows then that for Marx, to grasp properly this real determinateness, we must avoid abstract theorising separately from it. Such an abstract/concrete dichotomy is what Marx perceives to be a fundamental flaw in Hegel's philosophy, because instead of understanding things as themselves, Hegel instead understands things as emanations of abstract concepts. Marx develops this further in relation to his critique of Ludwig Feuerbach where he now begins to give an indication of how the self should be understood. In the *Theses on Feuerbach* (1845), for instance, Marx berates Feuerbach for not realising that 'the essence of man is no abstraction inherent in each single individual', rather, 'in its reality it is the ensemble of the social relations'.[50] For Marx, Feuerbach therefore puts forward only an 'abstract-*isolated*-human-individual' that is divorced from the 'historical process'. Feuerbach fails to realise that the 'abstract individual which he analyses belongs in reality to a particular form of society'.[51] In making this point, Marx is drawing the distinction between abstract and concrete or socially situated moments of the self, and this, as we shall see, forms the cornerstone for understanding the self in his writings. What is important to stress here is that Marx is not saying we should reject any notion of an abstract self. Rather, what he is saying is that the self should be understood not *just* as abstract but also as abstract *and* concrete, that is, socially situated. As Ernst Bloch notes, Marx 're-fuses to stop with man understood as an abstract genus, without

[48]   Karl Marx, *Critique of Hegel's Doctrine of the State*, in Karl Marx, *Early Writings*, Harmondsworth, Penguin, 1992, p. 80. Karl Marx, *Economic and Philosophical Manuscripts*, in Karl Marx, *Early Writings*, Harmondsworth, Penguin, 1992, p. 383. For the argument that Marx misrepresents Hegel here see Ian Fraser, 'Two of a Kind: Hegel Marx, Dialectic and Form', *Capital & Class*, 61, 1997 and *Hegel and Marx: The Concept of Need*, Edinburgh, Edinburgh University Press, 1998, Ch. 2

[49]   Marx, *Economic and Philosophical Manuscripts*, p. 383.

[50]   Karl Marx, *Theses on Feuerbach*, in Karl Marx & Frederick Engels *Collected Works*, Volume 5, London, Lawrence & Wishart, 1976, p. 4.

[51]   Marx, *Theses on Feuerbach*, p. 5. Cf. Karl Marx & Frederick Engels, *The German Ideology*, in Karl Marx & Frederick Engels, *Collected Works*, Volume 5, London, Lawrence & Wishart, 1976, pp. 39 & 41.

specific articulation to class and history'.[52] In this way, Bloch continues, Marx, unlike Feuerbach, manages to avoid the 'empty connection' between a 'particular individual' and the 'abstract genus man'.[53]

Some twelve years later, Marx was to develop this argument more explicitly in the *Grundrisse* (1857-58). In his discussion of his method in the Introduction to that work, he makes the distinction between general and determinate abstractions.[54] General abstractions are where we abstract from concrete social circumstances to focus on a common universal element amongst phenomena. Determinate abstractions are when we analyse the movement from the general to the concrete or particular form. One illustration of the power of Marx's method here is in his example of understanding the notion of the individual in contrast to that of Smith and Ricardo.[55] Marx argues that both Smith and Ricardo remain at the level of general abstraction by having a concept of the individual as an isolated hunter and fisherman that exists throughout time. But the general abstraction they make is based on their own assumptions about human nature rather than on the forms individuals take in particular historical circumstances. For Marx, Smith's and Ricardo's independent individual is projected back into the past as an ideal, rather than as a result of the end of feudal relations and the development of capitalism. Marx asserts that the more we look back into history the more we see an individual as being 'dependent' and 'belonging to a greater whole'.[56] This is exemplified in the movement from the family to the clan and then to different communal forms of organisation through the inter-relations of the clans. With the onset of 'civil society' in the eighteenth century, individuals suddenly appear as 'isolated' and preoccupied with pursuing only their self-interest. Smith and Ricardo, then, belong amongst the 'unimaginative conceits of the eighteenth century Robinsonades' by positing as a norm the rare exception of an isolated individual producing outside society.[57] Indeed, even when this rarity occurs it is normally where an individual is, like Crusoe, cast into the wilderness, but already possesses aspects of 'civilised' society in terms of the products he salvages

[52]   Ernst Bloch, *On Karl Marx*, New York, Herder and Herder, 1971, p. 74.
[53]   Bloch, *On Karl Marx*, pp. 74–75.
[54]   Karl Marx, *Grundrisse*, Harmondsworth, Penguin, 1973, p. 85. Cf. Fraser, *Hegel and Marx: The Concept of Need*, p. 32.
[55]   Marx, *Grundrisse*, p. 83. Cf. Fraser, *Hegel and Marx: The Concept of Need*, p. 33.
[56]   Marx, *Grundrisse*, p. 84.
[57]   Marx, *Grundrisse*, pp. 83–84.

from the ship and the social relations he has previously formed. As C.L.R. James observes, Defoe's Crusoe was a British bourgeois and he brought such behaviour to the island in all his activities.[58] For Marx, therefore, a human being is a 'political animal, not merely a gregarious animal, but an animal which can individuate itself only in the midst of society'.[59] Marx, then, rejects any notion of an abstract self separate from its concrete form. Selves must be understood in their social setting as part of a community and as historically developed in different ways. The Robinsonade nature of Smith's and Ricardo's notion of the individual, which they assume as a general abstraction true for all time, must therefore be rejected as 'twaddle'.[60]

It follows from Marx's method that we need to understand the self dialectically as a general and determinate abstraction. We need to have an understanding of a self in its determinate form in concrete circumstances in a certain historical epoch from which we can make general abstractions. It is important that the general and determinate are not held distinct, but that there is a dialectical movement from one to the other. Moreover, as Marx notes, the general abstraction itself, although trying to focus on a common element, 'splits into different determinations. Some determinations belong to all epochs, others only to a few. [Some] determinations will be shared by the most modern epoch and the most ancient'.[61] The emphasis must be on understanding these moments as contradictions in a unity, where they are distinct and united at the same time. Conceptually, we can hold these two moments of general and determinate apart, but we must understand how they link with and inform each other if phenomena are to be properly understood. For Marx, then, as is the case for Taylor, the emblematic figure of Crusoe as the starting point for understanding individuals must be rejected. Selves must be understood in their social setting as part of a community and as historically developed in different forms. It is therefore surprising given Taylor's Marxist background that he chose not to allude to Marx over this issue, especially given his reference to Crusoe.

If the social aspect and historical development of the self is also captured by Marx, then what of the three ontological aspects of the self identified by Abbey as crucial for Taylor's notion of the self? As regards the issue of self-interpretation, there are some passages in

[58] C.L.R. James, 'Letters to Literary Critics', in Anna Grimshaw (ed.), *The C.L.R. James Reader*, Oxford, Blackwell, 1992, p. 236.
[59] Marx, *Grundrisse*, p. 84.
[60] Marx, *Grundrisse*, p. 84.
[61] Marx, *Grundrisse*, p. 85. Term in square bracket in the original.

Marx's writings that show an awareness of this important aspect of identity formation. In *The German Ideology*, Marx notes how 'individuals have always and in all circumstances 'proceeded from themselves' but due to their needs 'they *had to* enter into relations with one another'.[62] In doing so, Marx argues, they entered into these relations as 'what they were' — they 'proceeded from themselves' — but in their development they become 'determined by the development of all the others with whom' they have 'directly or indirectly associated'.[63] In this way, Marx continues, the 'history of a single individual cannot possibly be separated from the history of preceding or contemporary individuals, but is determined by this history'. So Marx clearly has an understanding of individuals that have a knowledge of themselves, which is itself conditioned by other selves in the development of that understanding. To be sure, this is not to suggest that Marx is offering an extended analysis of the self here as Taylor does, but it is to suggest an awareness by Marx of this self-interpretive aspect of individuality that Taylor sees as crucial to identity formation. What then of language and dialogue?

For Taylor, as we have seen, the fact that humans are language users not only gives us a vocabulary to make evaluations between what is moral and what is not, but also allows us to be dialogical in our interaction with other selves in the formation of our identity. In *The German Ideology*, Marx makes some pertinent comments in relation to language that find some resonance in Taylor's approach. Marx argues that 'language *is* practical, real consciousness that exists for other men as well, and only therefore does it also exist for me'.[64] Marx traces the emergence of language through the development of immediate self-consciousness, which initially has limited connection with people outside. As a growing self-consciousness, it then realises the 'necessity of associating with the individuals around' it, and language is a crucial mediation in that process. As Marx says in the *Grundrisse*, 'the development of language' presupposes 'individuals living together and talking together', which proves he has an awareness of the dialogical nature of language that Taylor wants to emphasise in identity formation.[65]

Taylor also sees language as crucial for making strong evaluations on moral matters, as we saw earlier. Indeed, this is also why he was

---

[62]   Marx & Engels, *The German Ideology*, p. 437.
[63]   Marx & Engels, *The German Ideology*, p. 438.
[64]   Marx & Engels, *The German Ideology*, p. 44.
[65]   Marx, *Grundrisse*, p. 84.

critical of Marx and Marxism for not saying enough about moral arguments. Even so, Taylor himself was clearly aware of the power of Marx's critique against the inhumanity of capital, and it was this aspect of Marx's work that obviously influenced him in his involvement in the New Left. What Marx shows is that capitalism tends to negate rather than realise our human essence, and while he, at times, explicitly eschewed moral discourse[66], his works also contain many moral approbations about the injustices of capital. Indeed, Norman Geras affirmed the ethical basis to Marx's arguments in his extensive investigations into this topic,[67] and from which he himself urged for greater moral discourse for a critique of capitalism and for thinking about socialism.[68] So the type of moral discourse that Taylor sees as crucial for making evaluations about the good were being articulated within the Marxist tradition. Additionally, recent works have attempted to show and explore this ethical basis in Marx's writings more extensively,[69] and also the ethical basis to the thought of certain Marxists after Marx.[70] However, Taylor is correct to say that even more work needs to be done in this area by Marxists themselves, and this book is a further contribution to that aim. In one sense, then, he is to be commended for bringing that issue to prominence, both by his sympathies with Marx's humanist critique, and with his own development of his notion of the self and the good.

The Self in History

I mentioned earlier how Ruth Abbey correctly depicts Taylor as having a two-dimensional understanding of the self in historical and ontological terms, and I have tried to indicate the similarities in relation to Marx. As Abbey also points out, Taylor's own history of the modern self focuses mainly on the cultural realm with an examination of the major historical works of philosophy and poetry and literature, and with only minimal attention given to how changes in production, the effects of technology and so on, have forged the

---

[66] Marx & Engels, *The German Ideology*, p. 247.
[67] Norman Geras, 'The Controversy About Marx and Justice', *New Left Review*, 150, 1985, pp. 47–85 & 'Bringing Marx to Justice: An Addendum and Rejoinder', *New Left Review*, 195, 1992, pp. 37–69.
[68] Geras, 'Bringing Marx to Justice, p. 69.
[69] Lawrence Wilde, *Ethical Marxism and its Radical Critics*, London, Macmillan, 1998.
[70] Lawrence Wilde, (ed.), *Marxism's Ethical Thinkers*, Basingstoke, Palgrave, 2001, and see my contribution to that volume which explores the ethical basis of the work of Marcuse, 'Herbert Marcuse: Essence and Existence'.

modern identity.[71] As regards the historical aspect of the self that Taylor develops in *Sources*, he offers a brief, but important, discussion of historical explanation that has implications for Marxism that I want to consider here.[72] In his discussion, Taylor confesses that his account of the making of the modern identity lacks a 'plausible diachronic-causal story', because to do so would be far too ambitious in one work.[73] He contends, therefore, that he is not asking what brought the modern identity about, but is instead offering an 'interpretation of the identity (or of any cultural phenomenon which interests us) which will show why people found (or find) it convincing/inspiring/moving, which will identify what can be called the "idées-forces" it contains'.[74] Despite the fact that he realises these two approaches can be taken separately, he also realises that this cannot be done entirely given that they both influence each other.[75] For Taylor, understanding the force of an idea means understanding how it became so essential to a society in history. On this basis, he attacks 'over-simple and reductive variants of Marxism' or 'vulgar Marxism', whose answer to the diachronic question of what were the 'precipitating conditions' that brought the modern identity about is the 'breakdown of the previous ("feudal") mode of production, and the rise of the new ("capitalist") one'.[76] Taylor thinks such an answer is 'implausible' because it neglects the sheer power of, for example, 'religious or moral or legal-political ideas' in this process.[77] Indeed, certain Marxists, he mentions Althusser and Balibar, even when they do not neglect this point, 'rely on some incomprehensible "structural" determination that bypasses human motivation altogether', and offer a 'picture of human motivation' that is 'unbelievably one-dimensional'.

Taylor is, of course, correct about the sterility of the structural Marxism of Althusser but, as he notes himself, this is a vulgar variant of Marxism, which by definition implies that there could be a more enlightened answer to the diachronic question. Taylor chooses not to explore this, despite a few pages later mentioning a Marxist who was totally opposed to structuralist Marxism and Althusser in particular:

[71]   Abbey, *Charles Taylor*, pp. 73–74.
[72]   Taylor, *Sources of the Self*, Ch. 12.
[73]   Taylor, *Sources of the Self*, p. 203.
[74]   Taylor, *Sources of the Self*, pp. 202–203.
[75]   Taylor, *Sources of the Self*, p. 203.
[76]   Taylor, *Sources of the Self*, pp. 202–203.
[77]   Taylor, *Sources of the Self*, p. 203.

the historian E.P. Thompson.[78] Indeed, the criticisms Taylor is making here are already present in Thompson's *The Poverty of Theory*,
written in 1978, where he castigates Althusser's 'constructions of the
"theory of history" [that] afford no terms for *experience*, nor for process when it is considered as human *practice*'.[79] The role of agency,
crucial to Thompson's account of the making of the working class, is
thereby reduced to the mercy of structural constraints. Taylor therefore prefers to perpetuate one strand of Marxism to have his debate
with, whilst in the same breath mentioning a Marxist who is totally
opposed to such an approach, and who could support his own
argument from within the humanist Marxist tradition.

Taylor reiterates that given the scope of his enquiry he is limiting
himself to the interpretive question, which, he realises, can be seen as
idealist in 'some Marxist circles'.[80] As he points out, this can only be
seen as a valid criticism if studying the main ideas alone was enough
to answer the diachronic-causal question.[81] For Taylor, nobody,
except perhaps a 'vulgar Hegelian', has held or would support such
a view. Vulgar Marxism, then, offers the 'opposite absurdity' to idealism by disallowing any casual role '*at all*' to the force of ideas.
Moreover, and even worse, this vulgar Marxism ignores the third
possibility out of these extremes, which implies that 'one has to
understand people's self-interpretations and their visions of the
good, if one is to explain how they arise'. For Taylor, this means not
collapsing the first task into the second or vice versa.

Taylor then decides that he does need to say what he thinks on this
issue of diachronic causation, despite the fact that his main focus will
be on interpreting the development of the modern identity. He
argues that the ideas that he is interested in such as 'moral ideals,
understandings of the human predicament, concepts of the
self...exist in our lives through being embedded in practices'. He
explains that a practice is 'more or less any stable configuration of
shared activity, whose shape is defined by a certain pattern of dos
and don'ts'. Practices become articulated by ideas as 'patterns of dos
and don'ts', and they range across all areas of life from the family to
national politics and religious communities, to name but a few. For
Taylor, these changes in self-understandings that were connected
with a diverse number of practices, such as 'religious, political, eco-

---

[78] Taylor, *Sources of the Self*, pp. 206–207.
[79] E.P. Thompson, *The Poverty of Theory and other Essays*, London, Merlin, 1978,
       p. 98.
[80] Taylor, *Sources of the Self*, pp. 203–204.
[81] Taylor, *Sources of the Self*, p. 204.

nomic, familial, intellectual, artistic', intertwined with each other to bring the modern identity onto the historical stage.[82] As an example, he notes the relation between the Lockean notion of '"possessive individualism"' and the economic practices of capitalist, market society'. However, he warns that this relation must not be seen in a unidirectional causal manner, where the self-understanding paved the way for the extension of market relations. He argues that it is also necessary to note how the extension of the market 'made it natural for people to see themselves this way'. So 'the causal arrow runs in both directions', and moreover, the balance between the two directions can alter over time. For example, he suggests that possessive individualism emerged prior to the extensive development of market relations in the industrial revolution, but this direction was often reversed when the new ideas of the elite filtered into the whole of society.[83] On that basis, he cites the expulsion of the peasantry from the land as being prior to, and a cause of, the acceptance of atomistic self-consciousness by many of their descendants today. This is despite the attempts at those thrown off the land engaging in acts of resistance and solidarity at the time, which have been documented by writers such as the aforementioned E.P. Thompson in his seminal *The Making of the English Working Class*, and whom Taylor mentions in this regard.[84] Indeed, Taylor notes how the emergence of capitalism is 'one example of a general process by which certain practices of modernity have been imposed, often brutally, outside their heartlands'. Nevertheless, he concludes by admitting that this development will only figure in his analysis 'at the boundaries,' as it concerns the historical causation issue, whereas he is focusing on the interpretive question whilst 'trying to articulate the modern identity in its various phases'. Accordingly, he warns the reader that he is not offering an historical explanation, but adds, despite this, that he himself should still keep the historical developments 'in mind' throughout his discussion.

Such an attempt by Taylor to limit the account of the making of the modern identity to the cultural realm, with causal-historical developments somewhere in the background, has led to the charge that

---

[82] Taylor, *Sources of the Self*, p. 206.
[83] Taylor, *Sources of the Self*, pp. 206–207.
[84] Taylor, *Sources of the Self*, p. 207.

his account of the self is therefore incomplete.[85] Taylor himself acknowledges that he is full of 'uncertainty and hesitation' in making this distinction, but still clings to it.[86] Such incompleteness in his account is evinced for our purposes here in that he recognises, without actually stating it, the role of class struggle in the development of capitalism, and the expulsion of the peasantry off the land. Marx himself referred to this process as primitive accumulation, and it was responsible for the important formation of proletarian identity.[87] As Marx points out, the move from feudalism to capitalism saw the transformation of the immediate producers into wage-labourers and the transformation of the social means of subsistence and production into capital.[88] Primitive accumulation is therefore nothing more than the 'historical process of divorcing the producer from the means of production'.[89] Its primitive nature arises because it 'forms the pre-history of capital' as capitalism develops out of the dissolution of feudalism. The proletariat, then, is now 'free' in the sense it is 'free' to sell its labour-power wherever it wants, and is no longer tied to the regime of the guilds with their restrictive labour regulations or serfdom. As Marx notes, any guarantees afforded by the previous feudal arrangements are swept aside, as the producers are 'robbed' of their own means of production, and 'hurled onto the labour market as free, unprotected and rightless proletarians'[90] who have 'nothing to sell except their own skins'.[91] Marx argues that the creation of the proletariat was due to the dissolution of the bands of feudal retainers, and the forced expulsion of people from the land towards the end of the fifteenth and the beginning of the sixteenth century.[92] The size of the proletariat meant that it could not be readily absorbed into the embryonic factory system. Moreover, the proletariat, trying to accustom themselves to a new way of life through 'inclination' and 'force of circumstances', became, 'in massive quantities', 'beggars, robbers and vagabonds' in order to survive. In the sixteenth century, therefore, 'bloody legislation' was used against the proletariat through-

---

[85] See Quentin Skinner, 'Who are "We"? Ambiguities of the Modern Self', *Inquiry*, 34, 1991, p. 145. Cf. Mark Redhead, *Charles Taylor. Thinking and Living Deep Diversity*, Oxford, Rowman & Littlefield, 2002, p. 200.
[86] Charles Taylor, 'Comments and Replies', *Inquiry*, 34, 1991, p. 239.
[87] Karl Marx, *Capital*, Volume 1, Harmondsworth, Penguin, 1988, Part Eight.
[88] Marx, *Capital*, Volume 1, p. 874.
[89] Marx, *Capital*, Volume 1, p. 875.
[90] Marx, *Capital*, Volume 1, pp. 875–876.
[91] Marx, *Capital*, Volume 1, p. 873.
[92] Marx, *Capital*, Volume 1, p. 896.

out Western Europe to stop its vagabondism. As Marx observes, the law treated this new proletariat by making them '"voluntary" criminals', as it was assumed they could work under the old conditions of feudal relations even though they no longer existed. For Marx, the whole legislative process and horrific nature of punishments such as whipping, branding and general torture, was a terrorist device that was crucial for disciplining the proletariat for wage-labour.[93] As he records, the vicious nature of this expropriation 'is written in the annals of mankind in letters of blood and fire'.[94] Consequently, for Marx, the 'history of all hitherto existing society is the history of class struggles' where oppressor and oppressed engaged in an 'uninterrupted, now hidden, now open fight', which resulted in either revolution or the 'common ruin of the contending classes'.[95] He argues that the bourgeois society that emerged from feudalism had not abolished class antagonisms, but had instead 'established new classes, new conditions of oppression, new forms of struggle in place of the old ones'.[96] The class struggle continues in a modern bourgeois society where the new bourgeoisie engage in the 'naked, shameless, direct, brutal exploitation'[97] of the 'modern working class — the proletarians'.[98] Marx explains further how, with the development of industry, the working class expands and unites and draws other classes under its orbit.[99] Through class struggle, the proletariat forms itself into a class, albeit being subject to bourgeois attacks using competition, for instance, to undermine unity.[100] Class struggle, then, is at the heart of the making of the modern identity and warrants far more attention than Taylor accords it given the negation of the self in capitalism. On that basis, I now want to discuss how such a negation results in an alienated self.

[93] Marx, *Capital*, Volume 1, p. 899.
[94] Marx, *Capital*, Volume 1, p. 875.
[95] Karl Marx & Friedrich Engels, *The Communist Manifesto*, Harmondsworth, Penguin, 1987, p. 79.
[96] Marx & Engels, *Communist Manifesto*, p. 80.
[97] Marx & Engels, *Communist Manifesto*, p. 82.
[98] Marx & Engels, *Communist Manifesto*, p. 87.
[99] Marx & Engels, *Communist Manifesto*, pp. 88–89.
[100] Marx & Engels, *Communist Manifesto*, p. 90.

The Alienated Self

When Marx examined the fate of subjects constituting themselves in nineteenth century industrial capitalism the true horrors of the system were encapsulated in his theory of alienation.[101] Marx argues that workers are alienated in four particular ways. First, there is the alienation of the worker from the product that he or she creates. This is because that product belongs not to the worker but to a capitalist. The worker has no control over the production process in which commodities are created because he or she does not own the means of production. Second, there is alienation from the productive activity itself. Work can often be boring and repetitive and not a fulfilling activity and this alienates humans from their capacity to express their creativity through their work. Third, there is alienation from other individuals in the labour market in particular and in society in general as people are forced to compete against each other. This inevitably leads to alienation between people as they see each other as hostile and contrary to each other's interests. Finally, there is alienation from our species-being, that is, the distinguishing characteristic of what it is to be human and which serves as the main distinction between humans and nonhuman animals. Marx argues that humans have capacities that animals do not. For instance, human essence is not pre-inscribed for individuals because through their productive activity they can choose what they want to do or to be but an animal has no such choice. A beaver has to build its dam, a rabbit its burrow and so on. Humans in contrast can reflect and decide on what to do. In capitalism, therefore, where the means of production are in private hands, we, as human beings, are alienated from our capacity to determine ourselves. Trying to determine ourselves in capitalism is incredibly difficult due to the fact that we have to sell our labour-power in order to exist.

It is also important to link Marx's alienation thesis to his theory of fetishism as developed in volume one of *Capital* in his discussion of the commodity. There he argues that capital makes the social relations of human beings to one another assume 'the fantastic form of a relation between things'.[102] This arises due to the nature of commodity production, which involves the separation of workers from controlling what they produce. Commodities then take on fetishised forms that appear to be devoid of any social content and so hide the antagonistic basis of production between workers and the owners of

[101] Marx, *Economic and Philosophical Manuscripts*, pp. 322–344.
[102] Marx, *Capital*, Volume 1, p. 165.

capital. So the critique of the all-pervasive fetishisation of social relations in capitalist society is fundamental in beginning the process of
overcoming alienation.

Taylor himself is also aware of the alienating effects of capitalism,
which emerges in his early engagement with Marx in *Hegel*. Taylor
sympathises with the young Marx who he sees as the heir to the radical Enlightenment, first in his belief that humans shape nature and
society to their own purposes, and second in his critique of the inhumanity of existing society.[103] Taylor notes that, for Marx, transforming nature also means transforming one's self, but in a class society
this transformation results in alienation, because the products
humans create, which are meant to be part of their essence, are actually an 'alien reality' that stand in opposition to them.[104] As Taylor
argues, Marx's notion of alienation clearly indicates the expressivist
nature of his thought. Humans express themselves through their
labour and interaction with nature. The loss of this expression is not
simply 'deprivation' but 'self-diremption', and overcoming this is
not simply a path to happiness but a way to regaining 'wholeness
and freedom'. For Taylor, Marx is continuing with the main theme of
most expressivist thought, in that he indicts any society that puts
possession before expression. As Taylor realises, in an alienated
world where the emphasis is on possession, human powers become
detached and take the form of property, which is a 'poor, distorted
substitute for genuine recovery'. In a class society, humans are therefore not in control of their own expression, so the positive aspect of
Marx's expressivism is to regain this control over our lives and
achieve real freedom.

Some fourteen years later in *Sources*, Taylor's worry about the
alienating effects of industrial capitalism also appears. In a further
elaboration on his theme of the affirmation of ordinary life, he talks
of the family as developing historically into a unit, which protects its
members from the harshness of the industrialised world.[105] Whilst
not denying that elements of family sentiment preceded industrialisation, he argues that it was with the onset of the latter and the
'growth of a capitalist, mobile, large-scale, bureaucratic world' that
the family became a '"haven in a heartless world"'. The family, then,
'filled a crying need' for the 'newly industrialised workers' which
developed into our seeing 'love, family—or at least "relation-

---

[103] Charles Taylor, *Hegel*, Cambridge, Cambridge University Press, 1975, p. 547.
[104] Taylor, *Hegel*, p. 548
[105] Taylor, *Sources of the Self*, p. 292.

ships" — as central human fulfilments.[106] By Taylor's own admission, therefore, there is almost a denial of self that is produced in capitalism and which results in alienation.

Taylor also realises the connection between alienation and fetishism, when he positively cites Lukács' interpretation of the latter as reification in his attack on instrumentalism and the spatialisation of time.[107] Indeed, we should not forget that for Lukács fetishism or reification was at the core of Marx's critique of capitalist society[108], and he saw it as permeating all aspects of social life.[109] Moreover, it is in Taylor's discussion of instrumentalism that he comes closest to endorsing Marxist arguments in this area, because he also recognises that there is a loss of meaning attached to instrumental understandings of society, a loss which Taylor himself wants to win back.[110] Moreover, along with Lukács and Marx, Taylor also sympathises with Marcuse, Adorno, and Horkheimer, for their opposition to the ways in which commercial-industrial-capitalist society forces people to see and experience the world in a mechanistic, instrumental manner, resulting in atomised individuals. Indeed, Taylor explains how Marx's theory of capitalism exposes its 'quasi-coercive' nature, which 'has the inevitable effect of destroying or marginalizing purposes of intrinsic value'. To this end, Taylor endorses Marx's claim in the *Communist Manifesto* that with the development of capitalism '"all that is solid melts into air"'. For Taylor, as for Marx, this results in a 'loss of resonance, depth, or richness in our human surroundings; both in the things we use and in the ties which bind us to others'. The fetishistic nature of capitalist society is, according to Taylor, therefore reflected in the 'shoddy, replaceable commodities with which we now surround ourselves'.

As Taylor realises, the political consequences of this process are also dire. He points out that for Marx, the experience of capitalism translates publicly into unequal power relations that expose the sham of political equality.[111] Indeed, Taylor accepts that this too is a form of alienation, because people do not feel their voices are heard

---

[106] Taylor, *Sources of the Self*, p. 293.

[107] Taylor, *Sources of the Self*, pp. 464 & 478. Georg Lukács, *History and Class Consciousness*, London, Merlin, 1990, p. 90.

[108] Lukács, *History and Class Consciousness*, p. 171. Cf. John Holloway, *How to Change the World Without Taking Power*, London, Pluto, Expanded Edition, 2005, p. 51.

[109] Lukács, *History and Class Consciousness*, pp. 91 & 100. Cf. Holloway, *How to Change the World*, pp. 56–57.

[110] Taylor, *Sources of the Self*, pp. 500–501.

[111] Taylor, *Sources of the Self*, p. 502.

or even count in the face of oppressive instrumental political institutions.[112] Not surprisingly, voter apathy and 'citizen alienation' prevail which results in people not identifying with the system that governs them and brings forth fragmentation and atomism.[113] As Taylor correctly recognises, any democratic initiatives that emerge from communities are weakened by the operations of the market and a bureaucratic state, which means that people come to see themselves atomistically and 'less and less bound to their fellow citizens in common projects and allegiances'.[114] He argues that this results in a sort of partial politics focused around specific rather than generic issues that would unite a majority of people.[115] So even though there can be a lot of democratic initiatives over single issue politics, Taylor still thinks that they lack any coherent overall programmes that a democratic majority can agree on and implement.[116] On this basis, Taylor quite rightly castigates American politics, for example, as 'abysmal', and candidates themselves as 'self-serving' with their hollow promises that are never kept.

Overall, then, Taylor clearly asserts the need for autonomy, dignity and a more meaningful non-alienated life in the affirmation of ordinary life, but how does that relate to the '"heartless world"' of capitalism? For Marx, of course, capital can negate our autonomy and reduce people's dignity through the incessant search for surplus value. His account of the brutality and inhumanity inflicted on ordinary people in the pursuit of profit is one of the most damning indictments of the capitalist system. Taylor, though, does not fully explore why the need for a '"haven"' is required from this '"heartless world"' of capitalism. This is strange because it is clear that he has great problems with the way capitalist society dehumanises people, but he seems to neglect how the dialectical nature of the self in capital means that people find their identity being imposed in an alien fashion from outside, at the same time they attempt to assert their own identity or human essence. He therefore pays too little attention to this imposition of identity by capital and the struggles involved against it. The dialectical movement of the abstract and concrete moments of the self must lead us to examine the forms the self takes in capital. As we try to assert our human essence and attempt to make our existence conform to our essence in our struggles in and

[112] Taylor, *Ethics*, pp. 8–10.
[113] Taylor, *Ethics*, pp. 115–117.
[114] Taylor, *Ethics*, pp. 112–113.
[115] Taylor, *Ethics*, p. 113.
[116] Taylor, *Ethics*, p. 115.

against capital, the self becomes a split self. Consequently, Taylor's lack of attention to class struggle is a glaring gap in his elucidation of the self. While it is implicitly present in his notion of the affirmation of ordinary life with his emphasis on humans as producers, he does not take this further to examine the nature of class identities that emerge in this process. This is even more strange given the emphasis he puts on the notion of dignity, which capitalism does so much to undermine and alienate. As we have seen, he does recognise the link between class and alienation, but he does not further explore this issue as being of fundamental importance in ensuring that people can have a fulfilled life.[117] This exposes a severe weakness in his own work, namely, that he does not follow to the logical conclusion that capitalism needs to be overcome in order for alienation to end. In this sense, what Taylor misses is that the 'drama of alienation is dialectical', because it is through the inhuman forms of alienation that people build the human world and offer the possibility of a different one.[118] Alienation is a dynamic concept which implies change because 'alienated activity not only produces "alienated consciousness", but also the "consciousness of being alienated" and therefore 'indicates the appearance of a *need* for the supersession of alienation'.[119] Capitalism, then, through class struggle, must be transcended for alienation to cease.

Interestingly enough, in an interview with Taylor in 2001, Ruth Abbey questioned him over his lack of attention to what she referred to as economic matters, and suggested that one reason for this was that it was partly a response to the Marxist preoccupation with class to the neglect of ethics and culture.[120] Taylor agreed with this assessment, but in doing so offers a one-sided understanding of the Marxist tradition. As I pointed out earlier, there is an important normative dimension to Marx's work. Moreover, as we have just seen, Taylor endorses writers such as Lukács, Adorno, Horkheimer, and Marcuse in relation to their critiques of fetishism and alienation, and

---

[117] As Skinner correctly points out, Taylor 'has almost nothing to say about Marx's insight that a major source of alienation from our true identities may lie in the character of our daily commitments themselves'. See Skinner, 'Who are "we"?', p. 142.

[118] Henri Lefebvre, *Critique of Everyday Life*, London & New York, Verso, 1992, pp. 169–170.

[119] István Mészáros, *Marx's Theory of Alienation*, London, Merlin, 1970, p. 181. Cf. Bertell Ollman, *Alienation*, Cambridge, Cambridge University Press, 1976, pp. 131–132.

[120] Ruth Abbey, 'The Articulated Life: An Interview with Charles Taylor', *Reason in Practice*, 1, 3, 2001, p. 7.

they also had a great deal to say about ethics and culture, as did Bloch and Benjamin to add another two.[121] Indeed, it is their explorations of the human condition that led these writers to turn to culture in the first place given its increasing importance within the capitalist system.[122]

A further point to make against Taylor here is the apparent dichotomy he sees between class and culture. As the Marxist historian E.P. Thompson points out, 'class is a cultural as much as an economic formation',[123] and should also be understood as a historical phenomenon and a relationship rather than a thing.[124] As such, class relates to real people in real situations and occurs when people, through common experience, come together with shared interests that stand in opposition to the interest of others. Historically, class itself, and class-consciousness for that matter, is therefore premised on the notion of class struggle.[125] People come together in their struggle against exploitation and in doing so become aware of themselves as a class and develop class-consciousness. In this sense, Thompson emphasises how too much attention has been paid to class, often seen wrongly as static and ahistorical, rather than to the more universal concept of class struggle.[126] Class struggle, then, must be the focus to pinpoint the emergence of class as a historical and social process. Thompson's dynamic understanding of class means that we need to examine the nature of class struggle to try and identify moments of working class formation. Alongside this process is the possible emergence of class-consciousness, which is the way in which class experiences are 'handled in cultural terms: embodied in traditions, value systems, ideas, and institutional forms'.[127] Class, then, is part of culture rather than separate from it as Taylor suggests.

---

[121] Terry Eagleton makes a similar point, with a longer list, against anti-Marxist cultural theorists in his *After Theory*, London, Penguin, 2004, p. 30.
[122] Cf. Eagleton, *After Theory*, p. 31.
[123] E.P. Thompson *The Making of the English Working Class*, Harmondsworth, Penguin, 1970, p. 13.
[124] Thompson, *Making of the English Working Class*, pp. 9–10.
[125] E.P. Thompson, 'Class and Class Struggle', in Peter Joyce (ed.), *Class*, Oxford & New York, Oxford University Press, 1995, p. 136.
[126] Thompson, 'Class and Class Struggle', pp. 134 & 136.
[127] Thompson, *Making of the English Working Class*, p. 10.

Conclusion

Taylor's demand for a greater discussion of the personal level within Marxism is to be welcomed, and I have shown that his conception of the self reveals a number of interesting comparisons with Marx's notion of the self. However, Taylor does not really engage with Marx on this issue, which is remiss given that Marx had a notion of the individual as social rather than just abstract, and which Taylor would endorse. Furthermore, the affirmation of ordinary life, which Taylor sees as a crucial aspect of the self, is a part of the expressivist humanist Marxist tradition. Similarly, there are aspects of Marx's thought that resonate in Taylor's own two-dimensional notion of the self and particularly in the ontological aspects of self-interpretation, language and dialogue.

In relation to the constitution of the self in social reality, Taylor recognises, and abhors, as does Marx and the Marxists mentioned by Taylor himself above, the alienating and fetishistic effects of capitalism on human beings. Unlike Marx, Taylor does not recognise that the dialectical nature of the self in a relation of class struggle means that capitalism must be overcome for alienation to cease. Finally, his contention that Marxists have concentrated on class to the detriment of ethics and culture is also a misrepresentation of the Marxist tradition, and breaks the real links that exist between class, ethics and culture. I will return to some of these issues in Chapters Six and Seven, but I now want to consider a crucial aspect to Taylor's thought and his notion of the self, and that is his emphasis on the importance of religion and, in particular, his Catholicism.

Chapter Two

Catholicism

We do not then set ourselves opposite the world with a doctrinaire principle, saying: "Here is the truth, kneel down here!" It is out of the world's own principles that we develop for it new principles.[1]

The religious dimension to Taylor's notion of the self and the theistic basis to *Sources* have caused a great degree of controversy amongst commentators on his work.[2] In a seminal examination of this issue, Michael Morgan has ably shown that Taylor, in his emphasis on God as a source of the good, re-establishes the plausibility of the divine-human relationship as a crucial feature of the self.[3] Indeed, Taylor's mapping of the development of the modern identity shows that religious belief has and still plays a crucial part in orienting us towards the good. However, his own theism becomes apparent in *Sources* in two particular instances. One is when he says his 'hunch' is that the significance of human life should be articulated and understood theistically rather than non-theistically.[4] Another is at the end of the book where he suggests that his 'hope' for a better world is 'implicit in Judaeo-Christian theism (however terrible the record of its adherents in history), and in its central promise of a divine affirmation of the human, more total than humans can ever attain unaided'.[5] The book concludes on this note leaving the possibility of a future work

[1]   Karl Marx, Letter to Arnold Ruge, 1843, in David McLellan (ed.), *Karl Marx. Selected Writings*, Oxford, Oxford University Press, 2000, p. 44.

[2]   For a representative example see Michael L. Morgan, 'Religion, History and Moral Discourse', in James Tully (ed.), *Philosophy in an Age of Pluralism: The Philosophy of Charles Taylor in Question*, Cambridge, Cambridge University Press, 1994, p. 50. n. 3.

[3]   Charles Taylor, *Sources of the Self: The Making of the Modern Identity*, Cambridge, Cambridge University Press, 1989, pp. 92–93, 533. n. 6. Morgan, 'Religion, History and Moral Discourse', pp. 50 & 53.

[4]   Taylor, *Sources of the Self*, pp. 517–518.

[5]   Taylor, *Sources of the Self*, p. 521.

to show how this might be achieved. That future work emerged in 1996 when Taylor received the Marianist Award from the Catholic religious order the Society of Mary, and then presented a lecture entitled, 'A Catholic Modernity?', which explored the nature of his religious faith.[6] This lecture was important because it was the first time Taylor had the opportunity to discuss openly his Catholicism after *Sources* in which his theism was relatively implicit, and he admits that he had to keep his religious views tacit in his previous philosophical writings for two reasons. The first was to 'persuade honest thinkers of any and all metaphysical or theological commitments' to consider his arguments irrespective of their own belief systems.[7] The second reason is that theistic arguments are generally not welcome in a predominantly secularist academic world.[8] Given the hostility that was shown even towards his implicit theism by some commentators, one can readily understand Taylor's caution,[9] but now he was free to air his views and to put his case for Catholicism. This is an important moment in the development of Taylor's work, so I now critically examine the nature of his Catholicism as explicated in 'A Catholic Modernity?' in particular, but also drawing on his other writings that are relevant. I show that four main themes lie at the heart of Taylor's Catholicism, namely: the transcendent, difference, unconditional love, and his endorsement of the sixteenth century Jesuit project of Matteo Ricci as an exemplar for modern-day Catholics. I argue that all these themes have distinct weaknesses that ultimately undermine the viability of his Catholicism. Moreover, what also emerges from this analysis is that the apparent contingent nature of his theism that he attempted to stress in *Sources*, is shown to be far more restrictive than he realises and is indeed the Achilles heel of his own orientation to the good. This is not to dismiss out of hand Taylor's concerns on this issue. On the contrary, I will openly engage with the importance of religious and spiritual fulfilment as crucial moments of the self here and in subsequent chapters. However, to begin with, I want briefly to consider the issue of religion or a spiri-

---

[6]　Charles Taylor, 'A Catholic Modernity?', in James. L Heft (ed.), *A Catholic Modernity?* Oxford, Oxford University Press, 1999.

[7]　Taylor, 'A Catholic Modernity?', p. 13.

[8]　Taylor, 'A Catholic Modernity?', pp. 118–119.

[9]　For a notable and vociferous example see Quentin Skinner, 'Who are "We"? Ambiguities of the Modern Self', *Inquiry* 34, 1991, and also his 'Modernity and Disenchantment: Some Historical Reflections', in James Tully, (ed.), *Philosophy in an Age of Pluralism*, Cambridge, Cambridge University Press, 1994.

tual dimension in relation to Marx and Marxism and Taylor's response to it.

Marxism and Religion

The role of religion in the history of Marxism is certainly a complex one. Marx's infamous dictum that religion is the *'opium* of the people'[10] has generally been held as an indication of his contempt for that doctrine as Stalinists interpreted and used it to attack believers.[11] Even so, as Denys Turner notes, 'it is a decidedly ambiguous remark, full of hidden complexities'.[12] Indeed, a sympathetic reading of Marx here shows how he was pointing out how the poor and dispossessed would long for the promise of a better world in the hereafter given their wretched existence in class-based societies. As Marx states, *'religious* suffering is at one and the same time the *expression* of real suffering and a protest against real suffering'.[13] As such, Marx recognised the spiritual longing that religion encapsulated in people's hope for a better world. It is therefore interesting that Taylor himself observes that Marx was not wholly dismissive about the role of religion in society.[14] In his discussion of the Enlightenment, Taylor notes how the latter exposed the notion of a cosmic order ordained by God that allotted people to their station in life forever as a sham. Instead, society was now seen as the instrument of human beings who wanted to achieve happiness and who were not prepared to accept their 'fate' as peasants, say, as the old cosmic order might have ordained. A new 'consciousness of inhumanity' was called forth by the Enlightenment along with the determination to combat it.[15] Taylor argues that Marx takes up this radical critique of inhumanity, and that his principal target for the existence of exploitation and oppression is not the old religion, but the 'new, atomistic, utilitarian Enlightenment philosophy' itself as reflected in classical political economy. That said, Taylor's obvious unease with the his-

---

[10] Karl Marx, *A Contribution to the Critique of Hegel's Philosophy of Right: Introduction*, in Karl Marx, *Early Writings*, Harmondsworth, Penguin 1992, p. 244.

[11] Francis Wheen, *Karl Marx*, London, Fourth Estate, 1999, pp. 57–58.

[12] Denys Turner, 'Religion: Illusions and Liberation', in Terrell Carver (ed.), *The Cambridge Companion to Marx*, Cambridge, Cambridge University Press, 1991, p. 320.

[13] Marx, *A Contribution to the Critique of Hegel's Philosophy of Right*, p. 244.

[14] Charles Taylor, *Hegel*. Cambridge, Cambridge University Press, 1975, p. 548.

[15] Taylor, *Hegel*, p. 548.

tory of atheist Marxism in practice cannot be doubted. For example, he is keen to emphasise that the 'history of despotic socialism' or twentieth century communism is Janus faced because the actual desire to emancipate humanity can turn itself into contempt for the masses.[16] He cites the example of Elena Ceausescu who, shortly before her death after the Romanian revolution, expressed her disappointment in the masses for not realising what her husband had done for them, which implies that humanism in the hands of certain Marxists translates into anti-humanism and tyranny.[17] Similarly, the calls for justice and the righting of wrongs actually turns into hatred for anyone involved with these injustices. Taylor's point here is that secular philosophies that have tried to replace the Christian faith, such as Marxism, have scarcely led to better results and have in many cases been much worse.[18]

Whilst Taylor recognises these weaknesses in Marxism, he also accepts that it is undeniable that Christianity has resulted in similar atrocities. In his own defence of Christianity, he argues that where it has been undermined in the past with an example such as the Inquisition, Christians like himself should see this as both 'humbling' and 'liberating'.[19] The 'humbling' aspect is a result of secularists who show the dark side of Christian beliefs. The 'liberating' aspect originates in Christians recognising the truth in such a criticism and judging them accordingly. He says that such a criticism does not mean Christians have nothing more to say.[20] Rather, the Voltairean right to express differences and to defend those who oppose your own view is a freedom that has its own Christian meaning. For Taylor, this Christian meaning is the 'freedom to come to God on one's own'. However, if we were to compare the history of religion with the history of Marxism, as Taylor does, it is certainly possible to come up with a parallel story to his own. For instance, Marxists of the humanist variety have been, and still are, appalled at the Inquisition type practices that have been applied in Marx's name in Stalinist states. So, following Taylor, they can be 'humbled' by this but also find it 'liberating' that others may, in the Marxist meaning, come to Marxism 'on their own', just as Taylor hopes many will come to God on

---

[16]   Taylor, 'A Catholic Modernity?', pp. 32–33.
[17]   Taylor, 'A Catholic Modernity?', p. 33.
[18]   Taylor, 'A Catholic Modernity?', pp. 17–18.
[19]   Taylor, 'A Catholic Modernity?', p. 18.
[20]   Taylor, 'A Catholic Modernity?', p. 19.

their own.[21] He is quick to reiterate that just as religion generates 'dangerous passions' so too does the exclusive humanism of which the even more humanist Marxism is a part. This leads him to put forward the important Christian idea of the transcendent. A main theme of my argument against Taylor will be that there is a Marxism transcending capital within which the possibilities of a flourishing aesthetic self become possible. For now, I offer an examination of the main tenets of Taylor's own religiously informed orientation to the good, beginning with the transcendent.

The Transcendent

The notion of transcendence is at the core of Taylor's Catholicism and he attempts to put forward this idea by arguing that life does not exhaust the 'point of things'.[22] While the full life is to strive for the benefit of humankind, 'acknowledging the transcendent means seeing a point beyond that'. For Taylor, then, this emphasis on transcendence means 'aiming beyond life or opening yourself to a change in identity'.[23] What worries Taylor about contemporary society is that a 'spiritual lobotomy' seems to have occurred, which denies any consideration of the transcendent and instead focuses solely on human flourishing in the here and now. As I mentioned above, he refers to this position as exclusive humanism, although without informing us which thinkers fall under this rubric.[24] Taylor's concern, therefore, is to re-assert the importance of transcendence in emphasising that 'more than life matters',[25] and he goes so far as to assert that 'humans have an ineradicable bent to respond to something beyond life'.[26]

---

[21] It is interesting to note that Marxist Christians such as Andrew Collier who has tried to show the complementarities between Christianity and Marxism, not least in that both share a commitment to those who are oppressed, has also stressed that Marxists and Christians should not throw stones at each other in glass houses in relation to the atrocities committed both in the name of Marxism and Christianity. Instead, they should confess their sins and endeavour not to repeat them. See Andrew Collier, *Christianity and Marxism. A Philosophical Contribution to their Reconciliation*, London, Routledge, 2001, p. 126.

[22] Taylor, 'A Catholic Modernity?', p. 20.

[23] Taylor, 'A Catholic Modernity?', p. 21.

[24] Taylor, 'A Catholic Modernity?', p. 19.

[25] Taylor, 'A Catholic Modernity?', p. 24.

[26] Taylor, 'A Catholic Modernity?', p. 27.

However, Taylor's notion of the transcendent is far from adequate as fellow Catholic Rosemary Luling Haughton points out.[27]

In the first instance, she accuses Taylor of seemingly privileging the transcendent afterlife over the here and now. Moreover, she suggests that pursuing whatever it is that we are longing for in such terms as transcendence and beyond life can only lead to 'theological and spiritual dead ends'. Taylor is sensitive to this criticism and admits that he is actually uncomfortable with using the term transcendence as it does not quite capture exactly what he wants to say.[28] He recognises that the term transcendence is both 'abstract' and 'evasive', but he used the term because he wanted to say something general which could appeal to all people, not just Christians, in indicating how we need to get beyond the narrow focus on the exclusively human. He therefore further explains the notion of transcendence in two ways that he suggests are both complementary and in tension.[29] He realises that the emphasis on human flourishing on the one hand, and an emphasis on spiritual transcendence on the other, can lead to a kind of dualism where such oppositions have been used to deny life, as in the case of Catholic guilt about sex for instance. He clearly wants to avoid such a dualism and suggests that we therefore 'tack back and forth' between these two moments of human flourishing on the one hand and going beyond life on the other. Again, he is aware that trying to describe this process 'evades our language' to a great extent and offers Haughton's own term of 'bewilderment' to try and give some description of this process, whilst recognising how inadequate that notion might ultimately be. Now this is a big admission by Taylor, because he is suggesting that he has no substantial vocabulary to express the transcendent dimension that exclusive humanism denies, but transcendence is crucial for his Catholicism and is what he says distinguishes the latter from exclusive humanism. At the core of his Catholic vision therefore is a notion of the transcendent that Taylor cannot fully articulate.

---

[27] Rosemary Luling Haughton, 'Transcendence and the Bewilderment of Being Modern', in James L. Heft (ed.), *A Catholic Modernity?*, Oxford, Oxford University Press, 1999, p. 77.

[28] Charles Taylor, 'Concluding Reflections and Comments', in James L. Heft (ed.), *A Catholic Modernity?*, Oxford, Oxford University Press, 1999, pp. 105–106.

[29] Taylor, 'Concluding Reflections and Comments', pp. 109–110.

The gravity of Taylor's failure here should not be underestimated because articulation itself plays a crucial role in his ethical theory.[30] For Taylor, articulation involves explicating the '"background picture" lying behind our moral and spiritual intuitions'.[31] In doing this, he continues, 'we assume and draw on in any claim to rightness, part of which we are forced to spell out when we have to defend our responses as the right ones'.[32] Articulation therefore acts as a source of empowerment because it brings us into contact with moral sources that have the 'capacity to inspire our love, respect, or allegiance'.[33] Taylor's notion of transcendence, then, should also generate these qualities but of course cannot because it remains unarticulated. Indeed, for Taylor, the failure to articulate a moral source is damaging because it means losing contact with the good and thereby strikes at what it means to be human.[34] So the failure to articulate transcendence severely weakens Taylor's Catholicism as an orientation to the good. Moreover, such a weakness is exacerbated further when he returns to the issue of transcendence four years after giving the Marianist lecture.[35] Instead of addressing the articulation problem, he prefers to consider the status of transcendence in societies today. Again, the silence on this important matter for the viability of his Catholicism is deafening.

The final and quite damaging flaw in his notion of the transcendent is that it also contains a contradictory element, as Jeffrey Stout correctly points out.[36] Stout notes how Taylor errs in stating, as he does above, that acknowledging the transcendent means aiming beyond life or opening yourself to a change in identity. Stout quibbles with Taylor's 'or' here by suggesting that it is certainly possible for a person to change identity and thereby aim for a transcendence of one's self without having a belief in a transcendent God. Indeed,

[30] For an excellent account of the various roles articulation plays in Taylor's thought see Ruth Abbey, *Charles Taylor*, New Jersey, Princeton University Press, 2000, pp. 41–47.

[31] Taylor, *Sources of the Self*, p. 8.

[32] Taylor, *Sources of the Self*, p. 9.

[33] Taylor, *Sources of the Self*, p. 96.

[34] Taylor, *Sources of the Self*, p. 97.

[35] See Charles Taylor, 'A Place for Transcendence?', in Regina Schwartz (ed.), *Transcendence. Philosophy, Literature and Theology Approach the Beyond*, New York & London, Routledge, 2004. The essay was first published in French as 'Une Place pour le Transcendance', in Pierre Gaudette (ed.), *Mutations Culturelles et Transcandance*, Québec, Laval Théologique, in 2000. Thanks to Ruth Abbey for informing me about this essay.

[36] Jeffrey Stout, 'Review' of *A Catholic Modernity?*, *Philosophy in Review*, 21, 6, 2001, p. 426.

as Stout further indicates, the possibility of self-transcendence can certainly avoid Taylor's claim that with exclusive humanism the human spirit is stifled. Consequently, Stout accuses Taylor of offering an 'external critique' of exclusive humanism in that he 'does not give humanists a reason, grounded in their own commitments, for changing their minds about transcendence'. Instead, he wants to show humanists that the position they hold will be seen as 'spiritually stifling' even to them, but given the possibility of transcending one's self through a change in identity this is something Taylor specifically fails to do. A humanist could just as easily point to moments of self-transcendence that are of the greatest spiritual fulfilment but which do not point to God. I will take up this issue more specifically in Chapter Four when I examine the notion of epiphany that Taylor sees as a crucial source for putting us in contact with the transcendent, but which in his hands, I suggest, operates under a restrictive theism.

Difference

Taylor argues that for him Catholicism is encapsulated in the phrase: 'Go ye and teach all nations'.[37] He argues that the way this instruction has been traditionally understood is to subsume other points of view and beliefs under the banner of Catholicism. For Taylor, this must be resisted. Instead, he goes back to the origins of Catholicism by taking the original word *katholou* as meaning both 'universality and wholeness' or 'universality through wholeness'. In doing so, he wants to stress the importance of achieving wholeness not through making people into good Catholics, but in recognising diversity.[38] For Taylor, God weaves his life into human lives in many different forms, so we can only achieve Redemption through Incarnation and

---

[37] Taylor, 'A Catholic Modernity?', p. 14. Ruth Abbey, 'Turning or Spinning? Charles Taylor's Catholicism: A Reply to Ian Fraser', *Contemporary Political Theory*, 5, 2, 2006, p. 165, suggests that there is 'no basis for [my] claim that Taylor sees his Catholicism as being encapsulated in [this] phrase' because he then renders it problematic by asking how this injunction should be understood. But asking a rhetorical question about a statement does not undermine it. As I point out above, 'go ye and teach all nations' for Taylor, is a call for Catholic diversity against Catholic universalism even though the phrase may suggest otherwise. The problem is Taylor does not practice what he preaches as my subsequent examples of his discussion of Catholicism and Buddhism will show.

[38] The emphasis on diversity also permeates his discussion of William James in Charles Taylor, *Varieties of Religion Today. William James Revisited*, Cambridge, Mass & London, Harvard University Press, 2002.

oneness by recognising this diversity as a 'unity-across-difference' rather than a 'unity-through-identity'. This, he says, is 'true Catholicism' and is itself encapsulated in the life of God as Trinitarian (i.e. Father-Son-Holy Ghost), which implies that human diversity itself is therefore the way in which we are made in the image of God.[39] For Taylor, then, a Catholic principle 'is no widening of the faith without an increase in the variety of devotions and spiritualities and liturgical forms and responses to Incarnation'.[40] He recognises that the history of the Catholic Church has often failed to respect this principle, but maintains that at times it has, citing the example of the Jesuit missions in China and India at the start of the modern era. Indeed, he specifically mentions Matteo Ricci's Jesuit mission in sixteenth-century China as a positive example of this form of evangelisation and that I consider later. Taylor argues that the task for Catholics in the modern world is to examine modern civilisation to find out 'what it means to be a Christian here' and discover 'our authentic voice in the eventual Catholic chorus'. The fact that this takes place at a time of so many different forms of Christian life is a blessing, because it allows the journey to wholeness to take place by recognising the need to 'complement our own partiality', and to avoid any notion of narrowness in one's beliefs. Taylor therefore urges that there should be no 'particular outlook' dominating and this will allow us 'to live the gospel in a purer way, free of that continual and often bloody forcing of conscience' that typified the dark side of Christianity for many centuries.[41] By being free to come to come to God on one's own, therefore, one can hear better the 'barely audible voice' of the Holy Spirit.[42]

Much of Taylor's argument here can be seen as re-emphasising a diverse and open Catholicism that emerged from the second Vatican council in the 1960s.[43] In his recent examination of the work of William James in *Varieties of Religion Today*, Taylor himself positively notes how Vatican II led to a 'new predicament', which involved a recomposition and redefinition of the Christian faith in different

[39] Taylor, 'A Catholic Modernity?', pp. 14–15.
[40] Taylor, 'A Catholic Modernity?', p. 15.
[41] Taylor, 'A Catholic Modernity?', p. 18.
[42] Taylor, 'A Catholic Modernity?', p. 19.
[43] For a useful overview of Vatican II and its implications for the Catholic faith see the selection of essays in Adrian Hastings, (ed.), *Modern Catholicism. Vatican II and After*, London & New York, SPCK & Oxford University Press, 1991, and for a more recent assessment Robert A. Burns, *Roman Catholicism After Vatican II*, Washington, D. C, Georgetown University Press, 2001.

ways.[44] For Taylor, this 'new predicament' is to be celebrated because it allows for a diverse range of beliefs that exist not only side by side but can also intermingle with each other.[45] For example, he suggests, in what could be a reference to himself, that some people may see themselves as Catholic but reject some of its crucial dogmas, or they even incorporate aspects of Buddhism with Christianity.[46] There is therefore a dialogical nature to Taylor's Catholicism that is emphasising 'unity-across-difference' rather than 'unity-through-identity'.

However, this dialogical process is not without problems, as we shall now see when Taylor begins to articulate how his Catholicism relates to different belief systems in 'A Catholic Modernity?' Interestingly, given the example above, Taylor offers a brief comparison between Christianity and Buddhism on the issue of transcendence, but in doing so reveals that his attempt to offer Catholicism as difference actually results in the subsuming of other belief systems under the Catholic banner. As we have seen, Taylor argues that acknowledging the transcendent means in Christian terms aiming beyond life or opening yourself to a change in identity. In Buddhism, for example, he notes, how this change is a radical one in that it is a movement from 'self to 'no self' (*anatta*)', but he then adds that the 'Christian faith can be seen in the same terms: as calling for a radical decentering of the self, in relation with God'. What therefore appeared to be different between Catholicism and Buddhism can, according to Taylor, now be seen as the 'same'. In that sense he thinks he achieves unity-across-difference, but such an elision does seem problematic because a 'decentred self' is precisely that, 'decentred', whereas a 'no self' is not 'decentred' at all, it is what it says: a 'no self'. Indeed, for the Buddha the 'world is empty of a Self and anything belonging to a Self', which led him to posit the notion of '"Emptiness"'.[47] Furthermore, whereas for the Buddha the 'no self' is 'without object',[48] Taylor's 'decentred' self is decentred in relation to the 'object' of God. The Buddhist 'no self' therefore has no object

---

[44] Taylor, *Varieties of Religion Today*, p. 107.
[45] Taylor, *Varieties of Religion Today*, pp. 106–107.
[46] Taylor, *Varieties of Religion Today*, p. 107.
[47] Quoted in E. Lamotte, 'The Buddha, His Teachings and His Sangha', in Heinz Bechert, & Richard Gombrich, (eds.), *The World of Buddhism*, London, Thames & Hudson, 1984, p. 49.
[48] Quoted in Rupert Gethin, *The Foundations of Buddhism*, Oxford and New York, Oxford University Press, 1998, pp. 76–77. Cf. Paul Williams with Anthony Tribe, *Buddhist Thought*, London & New York, Routledge, 2000, pp. 49–50.

or other being to relate to, which is in stark contrast to Taylor's decentering of the self in relation with God.[49] So difference between Catholicism and Buddhism remains and unity is not thereby achieved as Taylor would like to believe.

Taylor runs into further difficulties with his unity-across-difference approach in that he contradicts his own edicts on relating different belief systems to each other. This arises in his emphasis on the biblical Christian notion of 'agape', which encapsulates God's will that humans should flourish.[50] Again he compares this to Buddhism where 'Enlightenment doesn't just turn you from the world; it also opens the flood-gates of *metta* (loving kindness) and *karuna* (compassion)', and it is the latter that he equates with Christian 'agape'. So Taylor clearly equates Christian 'agape' with the Buddhist notion of 'karuna' just as he mistakenly suggested the Christian 'decentred self' can be seen in the 'same terms' as the Buddhist 'no self'. Now, some years earlier, Taylor himself had specifically warned against this type of exercise.[51] He argued that in considering different belief systems one should respect the other view and in doing so attempt to understand it. He cautions that doing so 'means precisely not trying to reduce it to some common denominator, not trying to fudge the differences with Christianity, because often the power of this other faith resides in what differentiates it from mine'. Ultimately, argues Taylor, 'we have to come to be able to understand — and therefore also admire — spiritualities which are nevertheless not ours'. But this 'fudging', this reducing to a 'common denominator' is exactly what Taylor is engaging in with his consideration of Buddhism and Christianity and his reduction of 'karuna' to 'agape'. However, as sensitive Catholic theologians such as van Beeck have noted in considering the relation between Christianity and Buddhism, Christians should not understand Buddhism in a way to understand their own faith but should instead understand Buddhism on its own terms.[52] He bemoans, for instance, the case of seeing parallels between Christ and Buddha because this is 'entirely the product of a

---

[49] Cf. William E. Connolly, 'Catholicism and Philosophy: A Nontheistic Appreciation' in Ruth Abbey, (ed.), *Charles Taylor: Contemporary Philosophy in Focus*, Cambridge, Cambridge University Press, 2004, p. 174, who quite rightly states that 'as I receive Buddhism, its proponents do not place an intelligent, personal God at the apex of being'.

[50] Taylor, 'A Catholic Modernity?', p. 22.

[51] Charles Taylor, 'Charles Taylor Replies', in James Tully (ed.), *Philosophy in an Age of Pluralism*, Cambridge, Cambridge University Press, 1994, p. 229.

[52] Franz Joseph, S. J. van Beeck, *Catholic Identity After Vatican II. Three Types of Faith in the One Church*, Chicago, Loyola University Press, 1995, p. 98. n. 16.

Christian theologian's effort to come to terms with his own faith' instead of appreciating Buddhism on its own terms. The same criticism can therefore be applied to Taylor because it is such a coming to terms with his own Catholicism that leads him to 'fudge' differences and seek 'common denominators' between his belief system and that of Buddhism. So his unity-across-diversity either fails in its task as in the case of the 'decentred self' and a 'no self' or it succumbs to a unity-through-identity approach that Taylor himself rejects outright. However, it has been suggested that these examples are not enough on their own to justify this claim that Taylor is subsuming other belief systems under the Catholic banner.[53] But these are the only examples available where Taylor is explicitly engaging in religious comparison, and the point is that when he does, he undermines his call for religious diversity.

Jeffrey Stout has detected a further problem for Taylor here in that Buddhism itself comes in many different forms, which may be non-theistic or even call into question the importance of metaphysical commitments to spiritual practice.[54] For Stout, these different types of Buddhism therefore aspire to a different type of transcendence of self that resists explication in the metaphysical terms Taylor otherwise associates with the transcendent—something 'beyond life'. Indeed, one could go further. Taylor's assumption about the importance of something 'beyond life' for Buddhism, ignores the fact that the Buddha's path to *nirvana* where suffering ceases also results in the ending of the cycle of death and rebirth.[55] Moreover, the path to salvation and enlightenment is precisely to stop this endless cycle of rebirth, which is the product of desire and is itself the cause of suffering. As the Buddha himself said on reaching *nirvana*: 'I have lived the pure life; what had to be done has been done; henceforth there will be no further rebirth for me'.[56] Far from pointing to something 'beyond life' as Taylor would like to suggest, the Buddha is instead pointing to this life and the end of suffering in the here and now. Across a number of issues then, Taylor's emphasis on Catholicism as difference seems problematic. The unsatisfactory attempt to elide aspects of Buddhism and Catholicism, in particular, transgresses Taylor's own caveat on 'fudging' and looking for 'common

[53] Abbey, 'Turning or Spinning?', p. 165.
[54] Stout, 'Review' of *A Catholic Modernity?*, p. 426.
[55] Richard Gombrich, 'Introduction: The Buddhist Way' in Heinz Bechert, & Richard Gombrich, (eds.), *The World of Buddhism*, London, Thames & Hudson, 1984, p. 9.
[56] Quoted in Lamotte, 'The Buddha, His Teachings and His Sangha', p. 53.

denominators', and so reduces his Catholicism as difference to a flawed Catholicism of identity.

Unconditional Love

Another core aspect of Taylor's Catholicism is his suggestion that we need to have faith in a Christian spirituality which offers 'love or compassion that is unconditional—that is, not based on what you the recipient have made of yourself' because we are beings 'in the image of God' that, due to the Trinity, means a 'standing among others in the stream of love'.[57] We must therefore 'open ourselves to God' and thereby transcend exclusive humanisms, according to Taylor. Such an opening to God's grace therefore means affirming human flourishing that is itself God's will and that, as I mentioned earlier, Taylor calls 'agape'.[58] He admits this is a matter of faith rather than a guarantee, but it is faith in Christian spirituality that is unconditional love or the fact that you are a being in the image of God.[59] Taylor says that it makes a big difference if you think this kind of love is possible for human beings, and that he thinks it is, *only* to the extent that we open ourselves to God', (my emphasis) which by definition goes beyond exclusive humanism.

With his emphasis on unconditional love stated, Taylor then considers the weaknesses he detects in exclusive humanisms, which he suggests lack this unconditional love. On a positive note, he praises the unprecedented levels of solidarity and benevolence that pervade modernity and which he admits are also a part of exclusive humanism.[60] Despite this, he suggests that a lot of these sentiments are in fact fickle and subject to the media focus on the latest high profile cause.[61] When the focus changes, he contends, the cause is then forgotten for a new one. He argues that this fickleness is due to the solidaristic efforts being driven by a sense of moral self worth which, he assumes, gives us a degree of satisfaction and superiority when we consider others. Additionally, he also recognises how even philanthropic actions driven by high religious ideals can result in this superiority aspect.[62]

[57]   Taylor, 'A Catholic Modernity?', p. 35.
[58]   Taylor, 'A Catholic Modernity?', p. 22.
[59]   Taylor, 'A Catholic Modernity?', p. 35.
[60]   Taylor, 'A Catholic Modernity?', pp. 30–31.
[61]   Taylor, 'A Catholic Modernity?', p. 31.
[62]   Taylor, 'A Catholic Modernity?', p. 32.

A further criticism he makes here is that 'lofty humanism' and a solidarity driven by high religious ideals are both Janus faced. One side is predisposed to act to do some good. The other side becomes disappointed in the people that are supposed to be getting help. The philanthropy that was meant to help people eventually succumbs to 'contempt, hatred and aggression'. Lofty humanism, then, sets high standards to forge towards, but in its wake encourages 'force, despotism, tutelage and ultimately contempt'.[63] He again notes how such sentiments were prevalent in the religion that the Enlightenment critique exposed. However, for Taylor, the issue of belief is not important because where these high ideals are held, either by exclusive humanists or religious supporters, they result in an 'ugly dialectic' because they are not 'tempered, controlled and ultimately engulfed in an "unconditional love" of the beneficiaries'.

Taylor notes a further criticism of exclusive humanism, which he also sees as occurring within certain religious movements such as the Christian Right. He argues that in the search for justice, the level of indignation over trying to right a wrong often results in hatred towards the perpetrators and inevitably leads to a feeling of superiority. So even though the initial motive was to seek justice, this turns into its opposite and we become generators of hatred and injustice.[64] For Taylor, then, adherents of exclusive humanism do not realise how problematic it is to rely on self-worth to keep us on our mettle and human worth to drive us forward to do good. Exclusive humanists do not seem to realise how such motivations 'can slide into something trivial, ugly, or downright dangerous and destructive'. He reiterates that much of what he has just discussed was a part of Christendom and not just exclusive humanism, but he proposes that his way out from this dilemma, which he admits is a matter of faith rather than a guarantee, is faith in Christian spirituality, which is unconditional love or the fact that you are a being in the image of God.

Taylor presents two forms of giving and helping above, which result in a superior air and/or utter contempt towards the beneficiaries. He himself thinks he avoids this through his emphasis on unconditional love, which for him is only possible if we open ourselves up to God. One individual that he does put forward as an exemplar for offering unconditional love is Mother Theresa.[65] From

---

[63]   Taylor, 'A Catholic Modernity?', p. 33.
[64]   Taylor, 'A Catholic Modernity?', p. 34.
[65]   Taylor, *Sources of the Self*, p. 517.

a position of Christian spirituality, Taylor praises Mother Theresa for extending help to the 'irredeemably broken'. For Taylor, individuals like Mother Theresa are 'exceptional people' whom he calls for short 'saints'.[66] He argues that in doing so he is giving a 'Christian "spin"' to the things which seem to point to God, e.g. extraordinarily saintly people', and his own experience of prayer.[67] While he admits that all the above can be given a non-theistic 'spin', his own preferred account is theistic. On that point let me give a non-theistic account. When, like Taylor, I look at the world and see individuals, theists or non-theists, undertaking extraordinary benevolent acts I admire them whilst recognising that they are also fallible human beings. Taylor, instead, has to spin doctor them into paragons of virtue who are purveyors of unconditional love. The problem with this is that it accepts uncritically the practices of these people that might not be as 'saintly' as Taylor supposes. In the case of Mother Theresa, she can either be interpreted in a positive light as the embodiment of unconditional love,[68] or she can be seen far more problematically given her extreme form of Catholicism, hostility to Vatican II,[69] and the possibility that her treatment of the poor and sick was far from benign.[70] Now, it is not enough to suggest here that Taylor has picked a bad example and could therefore get a better one. What I am suggesting is that the process of Christian 'spin' he is engaged in is problematic because it offers an uncritical interpretation of the acts of others. It blinds him to the fact that they are human beings who can have weaknesses just like everyone else. A more realistic reading of the saintly experience may be gleaned from Elizabeth Stuart, a Christian Feminist, who argues that in the case of a female saint 'we might recognise, celebrate and tap into her energy as manifested in particular actions or ways of being, whilst also acknowledging that not all of her life was about flourishing, that some of it may have been about withering of herself and others'.[71] Taylor's extreme position means that he cannot allow for this because he assumes that saints engage only in acts of unconditional love.

[66] Taylor, 'Charles Taylor Replies', p. 226.
[67] Taylor, 'Charles Taylor Replies', p. 227.
[68] Malcolm Muggeridge, *Something Beautiful for God: Mother Theresa of Calcutta*, London, Fontana, 1971.
[69] Christopher Hitchens, *The Missionary Position: Mother Theresa in Theory and Practice*, London, Verso, 1995.
[70] Susan Shields, 'Mother Theresa's House of Illusions. How She harmed her Helpers as well as those they "Helped"', *Free Inquiry* 18, 1, 1997/98.
[71] Elizabeth Stuart, *Spitting at Dragons. Towards a Feminist Theology of Sainthood*, London & New York, Mowbray, 1996, p. 133.

Even when we do examine studies on giving there is little evidence to support Taylor's extreme position here. One offering from the 1970s is that of Manser and Cass, who argued that the Judeo-Christian concept of love of one's neighbour is at the core of people's desire to help others.[72] However, the majority of more recent studies on giving do not see the love of God as a motivating factor at all. Some suggest that altruism is the main motivating factor,[73] but as this is not necessarily linked to God it does not help Taylor's position anyway. Others have suggested that motives are always mixed,[74] which does not help Taylor's position either. So on the whole there is little evidence amongst studies on giving to support Taylor's contention that a truly benevolent act is only possible if you open yourself up to God.

The extremity of Taylor's position also reveals another problem in that it shows him to have the superior air he tried to assign to lofty humanism and those adopting a high religious standpoint. Taylor would have to declare that multiple examples of giving, even if they were deemed altruistic, are inferior compared to giving premised on the love of God. At one stroke then, those of us who do not open ourselves up to God are incapable of unconditional love whereas those who do are. Such a holier than thou attitude, which Taylor would no doubt like to reject out of hand, actually emerges in his Catholicism. Just why non-theists are incapable of unconditional love is unclear. Let us say as a hypothetical example we have a theist and a non-theist both working in the Third World to help the poor. Let us assume that they both do so not for anything for themselves, but simply for the unconditional love they offer to fellow human beings who are suffering. How is the love offered different between the theist and the non-theist? Taylor would no doubt say that the non-theist is susceptible to the problems of lofty humanism mentioned earlier, but

---

[72] Gordon Manser, & Rosemary Higgins Cass, *Voluntarism at the Crossroads*, New York, Family Service Association of America, 1976, p. 35.

[73] Kristen Renwick Monroe, *The Heart of Altruism. Perceptions of a Common Humanity*, Princeton, Princeton University Press, 1996; E.G. Clary, & M. Snyder, 'A Functional Analysis of Altruism and Prosocial Behaviour: The Case of Volunteerism', *Review of Personality and Social Psychology*, 12, 1991; J.M. Piliavin, & H.W. Charng, 'Altruism: A Review of Recent Theory and Research', *Annual Review of Sociology*, 16, 1990.

[74] Mike W. Martin, *Virtuous Giving*, Bloomington & Indianapolis, Indiana University Press, 1994, pp. 123–124; Paul G. Schervish, & John J. Havens, 'Social Participation and Charitable Giving: A Multivariate Analysis', *Voluntas*, 8, 3, 1997, pp. 236–240; Joan Mount, 'Why Donors Give', *Nonprofit Management & Leadership*, 7, 1, 1996, pp. 7–8.

exactly the same can be said for the theist as well, as Taylor himself realises. If they both do not descend into this 'ugly dialectic' as Taylor calls it, then he is still committed to denying that the love offered by the non-theist is unconditional. Is it therefore not slightly arrogant of Taylor to tell the non-theist that although her actions and motivations are exactly the same as the theist, they must be conditional and thereby inferior? So there is a superior air in Taylor's loading of the dice in the favour of theists, which also undermines the supposed openness of his Catholicism.

William Connolly has also detected such a lack of openness in Taylor's Catholicism due to his apparent hostility to non-theistic sources of the good.[75] Connolly does not think this fully undermines Taylor's Catholicism and advocacy of diversity because there are 'openings and breaks that hold considerable promise' there, which indicate that he could come to appreciate non-theistic sources of the good.[76] However, what we have just seen above is that on the issue of unconditional love at least, no such respect is possible because, as Taylor explicitly states, unconditional love is 'only' possible if we adopt a theistic perspective. There is a clear indication then that Taylor appears to give a privileged position to his theism, which is evinced in the case of unconditional love, despite his attempt in *Sources* to couch it in the manner of a 'hunch'. However, Ruth Abbey suggests that Taylor's claim here is more of a 'suspicion' rather than a firm conclusion, especially given his recognition of non-theistic sources of the good,[77] but the absolutism of Taylor's 'only' indicates where *his own* Catholicism lies on this issue. Moreover, as Abbey herself comments, Taylor's tendency to repeat the claim means 'the less convincing it becomes to present it as a hunch'.

It is also pertinent to note here that Abbey herself has taken Connolly's concern over Taylor's negativity towards non-theistic sources of the good, and related it to his discussion of William James in *Varieties of Religion Today*, which appeared after Connolly's piece was published.[78] Whilst she notes that there is evidence for arguing

---

[75] Connolly, 'Catholicism and Philosophy', pp. 171–172. Cf. Mark Redhead, *Charles Taylor. Thinking and Living Deep Diversity*, Lanham, Rowman & Littlefield, 2002, *Charles Taylor*, p. 3.

[76] Connolly, 'Catholicism and Philosophy', p. 181.

[77] Abbey, 'Turning or Spinning?', p. 170.

[78] Ruth Abbey, 'Introduction: The Thought of Charles Taylor', in Ruth Abbey (ed.), *Charles Taylor*, Cambridge, Cambridge University Press, 2004, pp. 20–23. In the article version of this Chapter I suggested that Ruth Abbey in her 'The Primary Enemy? Monotheism and Pluralism' in James Boyd

against such an interpretation of Taylor, she concludes by saying that 'right at the point where religious unbelief is not the other to be externalised, objectified, or abjected but rather embraced as an enrichment of the self, Taylor pulls away' and decides that 'James had to be someone who ultimately situated himself on the side of faith'.[79] As Abbey correctly points out, Taylor realises that this could be dismissed as a '"bit of a believer's chauvinism"', but in doing so he 'seems to vindicate some of Connolly's critical remarks', and this gives further support for my own claim that he is operating with a restrictive theism.[80] Additionally, this also casts doubt on Stephen K. White's attempt to depict Taylor's theism as a weak, rather than strong, ontology.[81] Incidentally, White had also said in a previous article, which he now rejects, that Taylor was a 'border runner between strong and weak ontology'.[82] However, as Abbey indicates, White ignores or neglects how Taylor's theism fires his pluralism and this again implies a strong ontology.[83] For me, of course, the strong ontology of his theism undermines Taylor's claim for plurality as I try to argue here.[84]

If more evidence were needed on the restrictive nature of his theism, then it is furnished by his further use of the apparently tentative 'hunch' in *Sources*, that re-appears in his most recent work *Modern Social Imaginaries*.[85] As I pointed out in the discussion of transcendence earlier, Taylor argues that humans have an ineradicable bent to respond to something beyond life, which for him is God. When he considers this issue again and asks whether this human-transcen-

White, (ed.), *How Should We Talk about Religion?*, South Bend, Indiana, University of Notre Dame Press, 2004, utilised Connolly's argument here in order to defend Taylor against the charge of not offering due respect to non-theistic moral sources. However, she was actually reporting what Connolly was attempting to do rather than defending Taylor. See Abbey, 'Turning or Spinning?', p. 173, n. 3.

[79] Abbey, 'Introduction: The Thought of Charles Taylor', pp. 22–23.

[80] Abbey, 'Introduction: The Thought of Charles Taylor', p. 23. Taylor, *Varieties of Religion Today*, pp. 59–60.

[81] See his *Sustaining Affirmation. The Strengths of Weak Ontology in Political Theory*, Princeton & Oxford, Princeton University Press, 2000, Ch. 3.

[82] See his 'Weak Ontology and Liberal Political Reflection', *Political Theory*, 25, 4, 1997, p. 506.

[83] Abbey, 'Turning or Spinning?', pp. 172–173.

[84] Abbey describes this as the 'most important thread running through [my] critique of Taylor', even if she disagrees with it. Abbey, 'Turning or Spinning?', p. 172.

[85] Charles Taylor, *Modern Social Imaginaries*, Durham & London, Duke University Press, 2004, p. 51. The main themes of this work will be discussed in Chapter Six.

dent aspect is indeed 'inescapable', or whether we can put it behind us, he confesses that he himself has 'strong hunches' on these questions, but chooses not to develop his point further. When Abbey herself mentions Taylor's point here she misses out the adjective 'strong', which makes Taylor's position appear more open than it really is.[86] On inspection then, the adjective 'strong' is certainly an even more explicit indication of his restrictive theism, and must undermine any contention that he is expressing such notions only tentatively.

A further problem with Taylor's conception of unconditional love is that when it is given to beneficiaries, they are a means to an end—loving God—rather than an end in themselves. Taylor's position is so extreme here that we must remember that all acts of giving, if they are to avoid falling into the 'ugly dialectic', must be linked to God. Conditionality, such as doing benevolent actions for greater self-worth, which Taylor thinks is present in lofty exclusive humanism and some religious groupings, must be rejected. When we examine Taylor's own position in this instance, we find that conditionality is also present because it is not caring for people for their own sake, but only as vehicles for showing your love of God. The offer of unconditional love is therefore actually conditional on loving God. Whilst it has been conceded Taylor's edict seems tautological, given that offers of unconditional love are conditional upon loving God, it has also been suggested that it is not tautological at all because what is unconditional is not the 'source of the love' but rather its 'extent'.[87] The unconditional love of parents towards their children, for example, following the logic of my critique of Taylor, would be contradictory, because the love is conditional upon the individuals being the parents' children. In reality, the parents' love for their children is unconditional irrespective of their talents or failures as it is just based on who they are, although it is conditional on the child belonging to the particular parent or parents in some manner. This, though, is what I have just been arguing in that the unconditionality of love in this case is if the children are in some way related to the parents (source), *and* if it is given by accepting the children for what they are (extent). Both aspects are necessary. As I pointed out above, in the example of a Mother Theresa figure (parent) 'helping' the poor (children), she is meant to do so unconditionally by recognising their status as human beings. In reality, Taylor's extreme position means that

[86]   Abbey, 'Turning or Spinning?', p. 174. n. 11.
[87]   Abbey, 'Turning or Spinning?', pp. 170–171.

her love for the poor is conditioned by the need for her to show her love to God. The parent/child relation is direct, whereas in the Mother Theresa example the poor are a mediation on the path to loving God.

An additional problem also arises when we consider the dangers present in offering love or compassion that is unconditional, and cannot therefore be based on the 'worth realised in you just as an individual'.[88] For Taylor, the love must therefore be directed at an 'other' with no strings attached as it were, otherwise all the problems mentioned above about contempt and superiority can begin to emerge. Now while this 'can' happen, as Taylor suggests, it does not mean it 'will' happen. For example, a woman escaping domestic violence by seeking shelter in a women's refuge may regain her self-esteem and be fired by an ambition to help other women who have been abused. As this involves her own worth, which has developed from her own experiences, Taylor thinks it 'can' descend into contempt or a superior air towards the women she will be trying to help. While this is certainly a possibility it also might not be the case as Taylor's 'can' indicates. Her belief in the rights of women could have a positive effect in inspiring women to escape domestic violence and also support other women in distress.

Taylor's conception of unconditional love in his Catholicism is therefore problematic in a number of areas. His religious spin doctoring means he has an uncritical and thereby unrealistic approach to those he considers capable of unconditional love. His emphasis on unconditional love also ignores the fact that the extreme theistic form of giving Taylor desires finds little support across a number of studies on that issue. It is also self-contradictory because it is conditional on the love of God. It further ignores the fact that self-worth as a motivating factor for helping need not lead into contempt or a superior air over others. Additionally, the attempt by Taylor to maintain that only theists are capable of unconditional love brings in a superior air to his Catholicism, which he was so critical of in lofty humanism. Moreover, Taylor's hostility to non-theistic sources of the good is evident in his emphasis on the possibility of unconditional love 'only' from within a theistic perspective.

---

[88] Taylor, 'A Catholic Modernity?', p. 35.

A Modern Exemplar? Matteo Ricci

Another core aspect of Taylor's Catholicism, as we noted earlier, and which he admits does seem 'strange' and 'outlandish', is his clarion call to 'try to do for our time and place what Matteo Ricci was striving to do four centuries ago in China'.[89] In short, Taylor suggests this involves asserting the Catholic principle stated earlier of 'no widening of the faith without an increase in the variety of devotions and spiritualities and liturgical forms and responses to incarnation'. Now when a major philosopher pinpoints an individual as, in the words of one of his fellow Catholics, 'the emblem of his argument for inculturation',[90] then we must take him at his word and carefully examine the nature of Ricci's mission and his approach to differing belief systems. My contention here, then, will be two-fold. First, Ricci's mission of widening the faith was not as Taylor assumes. Indeed, Taylor offers us no historical references or evidence about the nature of Ricci's mission to support his argument, which is a little strange given the latter is his exemplar for modern-day Catholicism. To this end, I examine the nature of Ricci's mission below to reveal it is not at all as open to difference as Taylor suggests. Second, I show how Taylor runs into further difficulties when he begins to backtrack on this aspect of Ricci's approach and instead suggests he was using it to consider modernity without preconceptions. Before that, it is worth pointing out straight away that Taylor's Catholic principle of propagation only with diversity is itself illogical in practice. Let us suppose that Taylor was to have a conversation with a Protestant about his Catholicism and the Protestant was so impressed by Taylor's 'best account' that he decided to become a Catholic. Taylor would certainly have widened the Catholic faith, but it would not have resulted in diversity because Protestantism would have lost one of its recruits. By definition then, Taylor would not want the Protestant to become a Catholic, which clearly shows the illogical nature of his edict. However, it has been objected that this example is 'unconvincing' because the real issue for religious pluralism is about increasing diversity rather than increasing numbers.[91] The point here though is to show the contradictory nature of Taylor's edict if followed to the letter. Additionally, it has been suggested in an admittedly 'contestable' reading of his position, that

[89] Taylor, 'A Catholic Modernity?', p. 15.
[90] William M. Shea, '"A Vote of Thanks to Voltaire"' in James L. Heft (ed.), *A Catholic Modernity?* Oxford, Oxford University Press, 1999, p. 44.
[91] Abbey, 'Turning or Spinning?', p. 166.

Taylor is committed to diversity because in 'A Catholic Modernity?' he is full of 'doubts and hesitations', which is indicated by the question mark in the title.[92] For me, the text reads more of someone who has, after a very long time, finally been able to come clean about his religious beliefs and is excited by the opportunity to do so, which accounts for the more open way it is written, and leads him to be more exposed to critique.

Further problems arise for Taylor when we consider his endorsement of Matteo Ricci as an exemplar for modern-day Catholicism. In his history of the Jesuits, Jean Lacouture notes how Ricci followed in the footsteps of Francis Xavier who, disillusioned with the hellfire and damnation approach to preaching the gospel, emphasised the importance of immersing oneself in the culture of the Other in order to achieve 'active exchange and mutual fertilisation'.[93] For Lacouture, what was distinctive about this approach was that the 'key to conversion was in discovery of and respect for the Other' and conversion itself was also 'self-conversion, or at least self-adaptation to fit the contours of another culture'.[94] A dialogue or exchange therefore takes place to achieve what Lacouture calls a 'cultural symbiosis', which modern-day Jesuits refer to as 'inculturation', or in Lacouture's term 'acculturation'.[95] To this end, Xavier advocated that the missionary's aim in China was to detail the affairs of the country, say how they had been received and establish 'what opportunities this country offers for the propagation of our Holy Faith'.[96] It was left to Ricci to take up this quest.

The emphasis on 'information, intelligence gathering and understanding as conditions for the progress of the faith' would certainly seem to fit in with Taylor's own preference for only propagating the Catholic faith whilst allowing for diversity. But as Lacouture himself admits, the propagation of the faith is 'fundamental' for Ricci, which would seem to undermine the supposedly open approach of 'acculturation'. Moreover, the fact that Lacouture can say that Ricci's aim was to 'conquer China' through his intelligence suggests something more than 'acculturation'. This will become clear as we now examine Ricci's mission in China, the ultimate goal of which was subsumption and not a respect for difference as Taylor assumes and so desires as a model for his modern-day Catholicism.

[92]   Abbey, 'Turning or Spinning?', p. 167.
[93]   Jean Lacouture, *Jesuits*, London, Harvill Press, 1996, p. 105.
[94]   Lacouture, *Jesuits*, p. 126.
[95]   Lacouture, *Jesuits*, p. 137.
[96]   Lacouture, *Jesuits*, p. 179.

To propagate the Holy Faith Ricci certainly attempted to inculturate himself into Chinese culture. He learnt Chinese and adopted the appearance of a Buddhist monk.[97] He attempted to gain the confidence of the Chinese by allowing them to borrow books, by his use of cartography, and in showing them the prisms, sundials and clocks that he constructed.[98] Lacouture informs us that these tactics were part of a strategy in 'winning the Chinese to Christianity', which again suggests subsumption rather then the 'unity-across-difference' that Taylor supposes Ricci's mission to be about.[99] These tactics resulted in a 'meagre' forty conversions, and Ricci duly received a letter from his friend Father Costa in Rome asking the reason why. In his reply, Ricci confirmed that 'it is with this object that we have come here'.[100] He further maintained that 'at this moment we are not in China to reap or even sow but simply to clear the forest', although the 'Chinese are not so wanting in intelligence that a single one of them is misled as to our final intentions'. That Ricci's ultimate aim was the 'unity-through-identity' that Taylor opposes therefore seems abundantly clear.

Ricci's strategy of dressing himself in the clothes of those he would like to convert to Catholicism further reveals the 'unity-through-identity' nature of his mission. Initially, he adopted the garb of a Buddhist monk, which, as it turned out, was a mistake because monks were held in general contempt due to the history of monasticism that involved beggary and thieving.[101] He therefore changed his appearance from Buddhist monk to a Confucian, exchanging his brown robe for a habit of dark red silk.[102] He also now had servants and was carried about on a palanquin, and not only looked the part of a Confucian scholar, but also played it, all with the aim of getting the Catholic religion accepted. As Jacques Gernet notes, Ricci 'did not wish to reveal himself as what he was: a priest who had come to preach the true God to Pagans'.[103] This was further

[97] Lacouture, *Jesuits*, pp. 186 & 188; Alain Woodrow, *The Jesuits. A Story of Power*, London & New York, Geoffrey Chapman, 1995, pp. 71–75.
[98] Lacouture, *Jesuits*, pp. 194–195; Woodrow, *The Jesuits*, pp. 71–72; David Mitchell, *The Jesuits. A History*, London, Macdonald Futura, 1980, pp. 155–156.
[99] Lacouture, *Jesuits*, p. 195.
[100] Quoted in Lacouture, *Jesuits*, p. 223.
[101] Lacouture, *Jesuits*, p. 196; J.C.H. Aveling, *The Jesuits*, London, Blond & Briggs, 1981, p. 182.
[102] Lacouture, *Jesuits*, pp. 200–201.
[103] Jacques Gernet, *China and the Christian Impact. A Conflict of Cultures*, Cambridge, Cambridge University Press, 1985, p. 17.

evinced in his attitude to Confucianism and its principle of the Taiji, which is the origin of the cosmos.[104] Ricci in his work *The True Meaning of the Master of Heaven* stated that 'we have judged it preferable in this book, rather than attack what they [Confucius scholars] say, to turn it in such a way that it is in accordance with the idea of God, so that we appear not so much to be following Chinese ideas as interpreting Chinese authors in such a way that they follow our ideas'.[105] Ricci's interpretations of Confucian ideas, then, were to 'make them say something other than what they really mean' to win the Chinese over to Christianity and not to ensure diversity as Taylor's Catholic principle suggests.[106]

Another aspect of Ricci's approach, which suggests subsumption under the Catholic banner rather than diversity, was the fact that his main target for conversion was the Emperor. This was because the Emperor had ultimate authority and would thereby ordain Catholicism throughout China.[107] Even on his deathbed Ricci 'babbled ceaselessly of his desire to convert the Chinese and their emperor'.[108] So the best way to propagate the Catholic faith was to go straight to the place where it would have the greatest possibility of dissemination over all the people, which would certainly not result in the increase in the variety of devotions that Taylor's Catholic principle desires.

Finally, we noted earlier how Taylor himself attempted to draw positive parallels between aspects of Christianity and Buddhism, but Ricci himself was completely hostile to Buddhism.[109] Lacouture notes how Ricci's diatribes against Buddhism were 'often expressed angrily, almost contemptuously'.[110] This is not surprising because, as Jonathan Spence reports, Buddhism was the 'central rival' to Ricci's Christian teaching and is why he spent so much of his time trying to 'demolish' the arguments of Buddhist believers.[111] Similarly, Gernet also notes how Ricci 'poured ridicule' upon central Buddhist beliefs such as transmigration and by 'giving an incorrect interpretation to the Buddhist thesis of the unreality of the self and the general phenomena, he advanced the claim that the only princi-

[104] Gernet, *China and the Christian Impact*, pp. 26–27.

[105] Quoted in Gernet, *China and the Christian Impact*, p. 27.

[106] Gernet, *China and the Christian Impact*, pp. 26–27.

[107] Lacouture, *Jesuits*, p. 207; Gernet, *China and the Christian Impact*, pp. 15–16.

[108] Jonathan D. Spence, *The Memory Palace of Matteo Ricci*, London, Faber & Faber, 1985, p. 161.

[109] Lacouture, *Jesuits*, p. 199; Cf. Spence, *The Memory Palace of Matteo Ricci*, p. 160.

[110] Lacouture, *Jesuits*, p. 202.

[111] Spence, *The Memory Palace of Matteo Ricci* , p. 250.

ple of Buddhism was nothingness'.[112] So Taylor's endorsement of Ricci's approach sits uneasily with his proffering of the Catholic principle of widening the faith whilst allowing for diversity. It is therefore not surprising to note that in a response to fellow Catholic George Marsden, who also questions Taylor's use of the Ricci project but mainly in terms of strategy,[113] Taylor begins to backtrack. For instance, Taylor suggests that Ricci's attempt to "go native!" and begin with an appreciation of what was good in Chinese civilisation 'must have been somewhere in my mind'.[114] However, Taylor's claim here seems somewhat questionable, especially as he also contradicts himself later when he says, again in response to Marsden, that he 'wasn't really thinking about' this facet of Ricci's mission.[115] Taylor's change of tack is even more undermined because, as we have seen, it is the inculturation approach that Ricci is renowned for and furthermore it was the use of this approach that Taylor explicitly endorsed for what modern-day Catholics should be doing in terms of his emphasis on unity-across difference. Despite this, Taylor now maintains that the point of using the example of Ricci was mainly to 'think more fruitfully' about society because we are both too close and too far from it to understand it properly.[116] In explaining this further, Taylor argues that what the Ricci image offers is a way to consider modernity 'without preconceptions' and allow 'ourselves to be both enthused and horrified by its different facets'.[117] One main problem, says Taylor, is that in describing our current age we do so in 'terms of what it is not' and instead we need to have a 'kind of Ricci-distance' to understand it better. For Taylor, this involves not only focusing on the present but also the past, because it is a store house for 'many spiritual forms, modes of prayer, devotion, of common life that could help us revivify the love and service of God in the present'.[118] Taylor is quick to caution that the latter can only be useful as long as he and his fellow Catholics do not claim that they have the '"*right* answer", which somewhere got lost and whose existence condemns whatever came after'. In this way, Taylor thinks that his

---

[112] Gernet, *China and the Christian Impact*, p. 78.

[113] George Marsden, 'Matteo Ricci and the Prodigal Culture', in James L. Heft (ed.), *A Catholic Modernity?* Oxford, Oxford University Press, 1999, pp. 85–86; Cf. Haughton, 'Transcendence and the Bewilderment of Being Modern', pp. 76–77.

[114] Taylor, 'Concluding Reflections and Comments', p. 106.

[115] Taylor, 'A Catholic Modernity?', p. 118.

[116] Taylor, 'A Catholic Modernity?', p. 106.

[117] Taylor, 'Concluding Reflections and Comments', p. 107.

[118] Taylor, 'A Catholic Modernity?', p. 108.

Catholicism will remain open and tolerant and is therefore less likely to slip into its more authoritarian and negative forms.

Taylor's persistence in using Ricci as a role model for modern-day Catholics therefore means that he still inherits the weaknesses that we have identified earlier. Ricci's approach was riddled with pre-conceptions in that he was always looking for a way to subsume the 'Other' under the Catholic banner, and, in the case of Buddhism in particular, he was downright hostile and dismissive. Now, again it is not just the case that Taylor has picked a bad example here. The point is that proselytising was the main reason for Ricci's mission and his attempt to understand Chinese society and its different faiths was to achieve that end. Ricci did have the 'right answer' and that was the authority of Catholic doctrine as laid down by the Catholic Church. His mission therefore was to get this doctrine accepted throughout Chinese civilisation.

A further problem for Taylor here is in the course of action he wants Catholics to take. Taylor suggests that Catholics need, like Ricci, to understand the world better by getting some distance from it, by not having preconceptions, by not having the 'right answer' and by drawing on the positive spiritual moments of the past to enlighten their 'service of God in the present'.[119] However, a number of problems arise here. The first point to note is that Taylor and his fellow Catholics do have a major preconception when they look at the world and that is they see it as having been created and influenced by God. As we saw earlier in the discussion of unconditional love, Taylor sees certain things in the world as a manifestation of God's existence. Such manifestations are also presumed to be good as God is again presumed to be incapable of evil. It is therefore difficult to see how Taylor can say he can look at the world without pre-conceptions given these pretty large and questionable assumptions.[120] Second, it should also be noted how in comprehending the world Taylor thinks he and his fellow Catholics do so with one aim in mind and that is to serve God in the here and now. In the section on unconditional love, I argued Taylor was making the latter conditional on loving God. In this instance he is subordinating the

---

[119] Taylor, 'A Catholic Modernity?', p. 108.
[120] Abbey, 'Turning or Spinning?', p. 168, misinterprets me here by saying that I see 'looking at modernity without preconceptions', as synonymous with 'facing the world without any ideas at all', which cannot apply to Taylor, but the latter is Abbey's phrase not mine. My point is that Taylor's desire for a 'more open minded attitude' is undermined by such preconceptions despite what he might suggest to the contrary.

lives and actions of individuals to serving God and at one stroke
undermining any notion of an autonomous self. If our good actions
are evidence of God's love in the world then those actions are being
directed by another and not by the person carrying them out. In
Sources of the Self, Taylor attempts to deny this by suggesting that 'internalising moral sources', of which God is one such source, is
accomplished by 'free, reasoning subjects' who have their own 'inner powers of constructing or transfiguring or interpreting the
world'.[121] They most certainly do but in doing so they are not carrying out their own will but the will of God. Michael L. Morgan has
attempted to defend Taylor here by arguing that the 'self and God
are related directly and not mediately, through the moral law',
which means that the 'self is not overwhelmed or belittled'.[122] 'Somehow', Morgan continues, 'the self remains autonomous and
becomes fulfilled even as it opens itself to the impact of the other'.
But it is this 'somehow' that is the crux of the issue, and it is not
answered by Taylor. Indeed, Morgan has to help Taylor out here by
suggesting that Martin Buber's *I and Thou* could be a useful resource
for an autonomous rendering of the divine-human relationship.[123]
What is interesting is that Taylor responds to Morgan by merely
thanking him 'for the interesting discussion of Buber', and makes no
attempt whatsoever to develop the issue of the autonomy of the self
in relation to God,[124] despite the fact, as we have seen, that when he
looks at the world he sees it as the will of God manifesting itself in the
benevolent actions of human beings. People are thereby reduced to
conduits of God's will and are not autonomous in their actions, as
Taylor would suggest. They may internalise God as a moral source
and use that to reason about the world, but ultimately it is God's
reasoning and not theirs.

When he further explores the divine-human relation in *Varieties of
Religion Today*, Taylor asserts that there are two aspects to religious
practice in relation to God that he thinks should complement each
other.[125] On the one side is what he calls 'devout humanism' where
there is an 'inner' relation to God where people focus their lives on
him through trust.[126] On the other side is 'a religious practice that
stresses the demands made by God...which consists in following the

[121] Taylor, *Sources of the Self*, pp. 454–455.
[122] Morgan, 'Religion, History and Moral Discourse', p. 57.
[123] Morgan, 'Religion, History and Moral Discourse', p. 59.
[124] Taylor, 'Charles Taylor Replies', p. 226.
[125] Taylor, *Varieties of Religion Today*, pp. 15–16.
[126] Taylor, *Varieties of Religion Today*, p. 15.

Law, or God's commands...without necessarily relying for guidance on one's own inner sense of these things'.[127] But this does still not get Taylor off the hook as regards the autonomy of the individual in relation to God. 'Devout humanism' again appears free because it emphasises the internalisation of God's thought, but in reality it is, again, God's thought not theirs. The second type of religious practice is quite blatantly following God's will and not the will of the individual involved. So the divine-human relation remains shrouded in a distinct lack of autonomy of the self that Taylor fails to recognise. As Fergus Kerr has pointed out, Taylor does not respond to Isaiah Berlin's criticism that Christianity is determinist and as such negates human autonomy.[128] It is certainly the case that such criticism sits uncomfortably with Taylor's own emphasis on autonomy elsewhere, most notably in his essay 'Atomism'.[129] Why, though, did Taylor himself not respond to the divine/autonomy issue in relation to Morgan's important point above, especially as he is re-emphasising the importance of the divine/human relation? This is not to say that I am claiming that 'religious belief renders autonomy impossible',[130] but it is to suggest that I consider the possibility extremely difficult for the reasons I have mentioned in relation to Taylor.

Overall, then, the Ricci project that Taylor wants modern Catholics to embrace is deeply flawed. The unity-across-difference that Taylor suggests Ricci displays is not only illogical in practice, but is also really the unity-through-identity approach that Taylor is so hostile to. Despite the supposed emphasis on 'acculturation', the ultimate aim for Ricci was conversion and a subsumption of Confucianism under the Christian banner. With this itself being internally problematic, and given his intolerance of Buddhism, it is incredibly difficult to think of a figure who can be less suited to Taylor's modern-day Catholic project. Additionally, the attempt by Taylor to walk away from this aspect of Ricci's mission and suggest that it was mainly about attaining some distance from society only results in further problems. Taylor does have preconceptions when examining the world and does not account for the lack of autonomy that appears to be involved in the divine-human relationship.

[127] Taylor, *Varieties of Religion Today*, p. 16.
[128] See Fergus Kerr, *Immortal Longings*, London, SPCK, 1997, pp. 154–155, cited in Abbey, *Charles Taylor*, pp. 32–33.
[129] Abbey, 'Turning or Spinning?', pp. 171–172. Charles Taylor, 'Atomism', in his *Philosophy and the Human Sciences: Philosophical Papers II*, Cambridge, Cambridge University Press, 1985.
[130] Abbey, 'Turning or Spinning?', p. 171.

Conclusion

In his concluding comments at the end of *A Catholic Modernity?*, Taylor pleads with those who are critical of his views to 'calm down, and listen' and not to dismiss them out of hand.[131] This is what I have tried to do in a spirit of openness in this Chapter, but having listened to his first full and explicit enunciation of the nature of his Catholicism[132] it is clear that severe doubts still remain. In his emphasis on Catholicism as difference he has picked an unsuitable role model in Matteo Ricci's Jesuit missionary work, which was more about subsumption or 'unity-through-identity' rather than 'unity-across-difference'. Indeed, Taylor's own Catholic principle of widening the faith only with increases in spiritual diversity has been shown to be illogical. Moreover, Taylor himself further undermines the diversity aspect by reducing aspects of Buddhism to Catholicism and thereby ignoring his own warnings not to 'fudge' or find a 'common denominator' between different belief systems. His notion of unconditional love, which he thinks is only possible if we open ourselves up to God, has little support in studies on giving, leads Taylor to assume a superior air and a lack of respect to non-theistic sources of the good, is conditional on loving God, and ignores the powerful role self-worth can have in motivating people to engage in benevolent actions which need not fall into contempt towards the beneficiaries. Finally, he has no substantial vocabulary to articulate his conception of the transcendent which itself is also contradictory. Overall, then, Taylor's theism dressed in the cloak of his Catholicism is revealed to be far more restrictive as an orientation to the good than he realises. As I mentioned at the outset and have shown here, his theism is the Achilles heel of his moral theory, and this will be evinced further in Chapter Four when I consider his emphasis on epiphanic art as a crucial moral source. For now, in the next Chapter, I attempt to offer a more viable notion of transcendence from the humanist Marxist tradition that Taylor chose to leave behind, but whose ghost still haunts his work.

---

[131] Taylor, 'Concluding Reflections and Comments', p. 125.
[132] Abbey, 'Turning or Spinning?', pp. 164–165, makes the fair point that this is only 'partly true' as Taylor may have far more to say on the topic given the relative brevity of 'A Catholic Modernity?'. She does agree, however, that 'it certainly provides the fullest and most explicit statement of Taylor's work to date'.

Chapter Three

Transcendence

I cannot be grasped in the here and now. For my dwelling place is as much among the dead as the yet unborn. (Paul Klee)[1]

In 1989, the year his magisterial study of the making of the modern identity, *Sources of the Self*, was published, Charles Taylor also wrote an essay in which he stated the following:

> Walter Benjamin ... sees the art and philosophy he is struggling for not in terms of self-expression but in terms of something beyond. Indeed, very specifically he brings in theology and religion ... Of course there are other people at that end of the spectrum ... for example, Ernst Bloch. That is the end of the spectrum for which I am strongly pleading today.[2]

Taylor was therefore positively citing Benjamin and Bloch for offering a transcendent 'something beyond us' philosophy that he clearly endorses,[3] but when we examine *Sources of the Self* we find that both thinkers do not figure as prominently as one might expect given the above affirmation of their approach. Bloch is not mentioned at all and Benjamin only fleetingly.[4] To be sure, *Sources* is not trying to be prescriptive in offering a way 'beyond', but is mapping out the 'various facets of the '"modern identity"'.[5] As we have seen in the previous Chapter, it is in his 'A Catholic Modernity?' that Taylor takes up the issue of transcendence, which implies either a change in identity or aiming beyond life rather than just focusing on human flourishing in the present. However, it was clear there that he found it difficult to

[1]   Quoted in Susanna Partsch, *Paul Klee*, Cologne, Midpoint Press, 2001, p. 7.
[2]   Charles Taylor, 'Marxism and Socialist Humanism', in Robin Archer *et al* (eds.), *Out of Apathy: Voices of the New Left Thirty Years On*, London, Verso, 1989, p. 69.
[3]   Taylor, 'Marxism and Socialist Humanism', p. 69.
[4]   Charles Taylor, *Sources of the Self: The Making of the Modern Identity*, Cambridge, Cambridge University Press, 1989, pp. 463, 478–479.
[5]   Taylor, *Sources of the Self*, p. 3.

articulate his notion of the transcendent, despite suggesting that we should 'tack back and forth' between these two positions to avoid any dualism. What is surprising therefore is that, given these difficulties, his discussion of transcendence pays no reference whatsoever to the work of Bloch and Benjamin whom he had fulsomely praised seven years earlier. Indeed, it is even more remiss given that he was one of the founders of the New Left who argued for a full rethinking of Marxism's contribution to moral issues. If Taylor wanted to keep his religious views quiet for fear of bias and in an attempt to reach a wide audience then maybe the Marxist label that would necessarily attach itself to endorsing Benjamin and Bloch was also seen as an unnecessary hindrance. Interestingly enough, in Taylor's early writings in the 1960s when he was establishing himself as a major thinker, he observed how Marxist arguments had severe difficulties in being accepted into the academic world of university life.[6] However, there could be another reason which links back into his restrictive theism.

In the 1989 essay, Taylor is fulsome in his praise for Benjamin and Bloch because they rejected the 'militantly atheist' stream of Marxism and emphasised the importance of transcendence.[7] Bloch and Benjamin are therefore to be commended, according to Taylor, for bringing in theology and religion to understand our spiritual experiences and revitalise Marxism. This was because the atheist aspect of Marxism had resulted in 'sterility and spiritual death', which 'has no place for the Benjamins and Blochs'. Taylor, then, seems to be emphasising the spiritual aspect to the thought of both of these thinkers despite the fact that they do consider themselves as 'materialists'. Indeed, he recognises that this is a 'mysterious area' of thought because of the presence of 'theistic', 'non-theistic', 'materialist and non-materialist views'. On that basis, it is also interesting that Vincent Geoghegan has found it useful to strike up a dialogue between Bloch and Taylor to explore the issue of postsecularism, although he seems unaware of Taylor's comments in the quotation above.[8] Geoghegan argues that Bloch's perspective is actually '"objective" atheism', which is 'diametrically opposite' to Taylor's

---

[6]   Charles Taylor, 'Marxism and Empiricism', in Bernard Williams & Alan Montefiore (eds.), *British Analytical Philosophy*, London, Routledge & Kegan Paul, 1966, p. 228.

[7]   Taylor, 'Marxism and Socialist Humanism', p. 69.

[8]   Vincent Geoghegan, 'Bloch: Postsecular Thoughts', in Lawrence Wilde (ed.), *Marxism's Ethical Thinkers*, London, Palgrave, 2001, pp. 62–67.

'"objective" theism'.[9] However, when he explains Bloch's atheism further, Geoghegan seems to undermine this opposition by stating that: 'Bloch's recognition of the inexhaustible plenitude of being renders any distinction between atheism and theism a mere semantic quibble'.[10] This is because, according to Geoghegan, Bloch recognises that 'at the fundamental level the atheist and the theist are united in a perception of the richness and mystery of the universe'.[11] This surely then must be what unites Taylor and Bloch and why Taylor could praise Bloch's work in the first place, although recognising this should not hide the fact that what Bloch, and Benjamin for that matter, are engaged in is a materialist understanding of religion as an expression of the moral development of mankind, and as a way of expressing our innermost yearnings and fears. This results in the apparent tension noted by Geoghegan above in Bloch's thought in particular.

Following on from the discussion of Taylor's Catholicism in the previous Chapter, it is clear that Taylor is claiming that there is a realm of experience that is generally ignored by materialists, and which he thinks that only by adopting a theistic perspective can we illuminate this realm and enrich our identity. Against this, Bloch and Benjamin, whilst appreciating the richness and mystery of the world, are suggesting that we can make sense of our spiritual emotions without resorting to theism. The dividing line between their atheism and Taylor's theism is that they do not believe in a personal God who intervenes in the world as Taylor does. So the atheism/theism opposition is ultimately not a mere semantic quibble on the issue of a belief in God. As Michael Löwy points out, Bloch and Benjamin are part of a messianic/libertarian philosophical tradition that 'radically contradicts all worship of an infallible Leader' or an 'autocratic Messiah', and he adds that 'nothing is further from their spiritual approach than religious worship of a charismatic saviour'.[12] That is the defining line beyond which their Marxist materialist spiritual approach cannot go. So given Taylor's ultimate belief in God, this may be the reason why Taylor chose not to develop a notion of transcendence from their writings. Even so, Taylor clearly thought Benjamin's and Bloch's exploration and expression of going beyond

[9]   Geoghegan, 'Bloch: Postsecular Thoughts', p. 62.
[10] Vincent Geoghegan, *Ernst Bloch*, London, Routledge, 1996, p. 103.
[11] Geoghegan, *Ernst Bloch*, p. 102.
[12] Michael Löwy, *Redemption and Utopia. Jewish Libertarian Thought in Central Europe. A Study in Elective Affinity*, Stanford, Stanford University Press, 1992, p. 202.

ourselves was well worth considering, and this is encapsulated in Geoghegan's interpretation of the blurring of the boundaries between atheism and theism. To this end, I examine the issue of transcendence in Taylor's work and the work of Benjamin and Bloch across the themes of religion, God, time and death. I show that despite the ultimate atheist/theistic split on the belief in God, we can explore the boundaries and crossovers around these themes that allow the tension that Geoghegan mentions to arise in Bloch's work, and also that of Benjamin's, which offer interesting comparisons with Taylor, and which he might have fruitfully utilised in his own theory.

Religion

Bloch's materialist attitude to religion is immensely positive because he sees it as an expression for the 'explosive hope' for a better world.[13] Moreover, against the traditional Marxist aspiration to transcend religion, Bloch does not think it would eventually disappear. On the contrary, because religion expresses some of our deepest longings and fundamental questions about the meaning of life its continued relevance was assured.[14] On this basis, Bloch, like Taylor, also tries to grasp the dichotomy of the struggle for human flourishing in the here and now and a 'venturing beyond' our current condition to a situation where we are at one with ourselves: 'homeland'.[15] Bloch, like Taylor, realises the negative aspects of religion throughout the ages in terms of oppression and a denial of human flourishing, but he also, again like Taylor, sees the positive aspects as well. For instance, Bloch notes how the Bible was rooted in the hopes and fears of ordinary people and how biblical imagery permeated the struggles of the poor and dispossessed.[16] Consequently, for Bloch, Christianity is a *'humane eschatological, explosively posited messianism'*.[17]

---

[13] Ernst Bloch, *The Principle of Hope*, 3 Volumes, Volume 3, Oxford, Basil Blackwell, 1986, p. 1193.
[14] Bloch, *The Principle of Hope*, Volume 3, pp. 1202–1203.
[15] Bloch, *The Principle of Hope*, Volume 3, p. 1376.
[16] Ernst Bloch, *Atheism in Christianity*, New York, Herder & Herder, 1972, pp. 21–22. Cf. Geoghegan, *Ernst Bloch*, p. 83.
[17] Bloch, *Principle of Hope*, Volume 3, p. 1193.

Benjamin's attitude to religion is reflected in the influence of the Kabbalist tradition, the sacred texts of Jewish mysticism[18], and his emphasis on religion as salvation from the disasters of the world.[19] Benjamin uses the notion of the '"Doctrine"', which is closely linked with the Judaic '"Torah"', and which itself means law and doctrine in Hebrew.[20] 'Torah', in Benjamin's hands, emphasises God's transcendence of all material existence as it existed before the world was created. Additionally, the 'Torah' is a doctrine of divine language in Hebrew that transcends profane language. The Kabbalist Judaic influence was therefore a major part of Benjamin's emphasis on transcendence and salvation. This is reflected in his understanding of history as being in eternal decline and decay but from which we can achieve salvation. Such an understanding of history through decay is reflected in the Kabbalistic understanding of the end of history, which preceded the advent of the Messianic era.[21] The horrors and atrocities that beset Jewish History, as in the expulsion from Spain in 1492, led the Kabbalists to give mythical significance to these events and saw them as the embryonic instances of an emerging Messianic age. Similarly, Benjamin offers a going beyond the decay to salvation and redemption. This is evident, for instance, in his ninth thesis of his 'Theses on the Philosophy of History' where he shows, through a discussion of Paul Klee's painting *Angelus Novus*, how the Messianic age is portended in the realm of the profane.[22] Referring to Klee's angel as the 'angel of history', Benjamin notes how the angel's face is 'turned towards the past' that piles 'wreckage upon wreckage'. The angel wants to stay to wake the dead, but the storm of progress is 'blowing from paradise' and 'propels him into the future' while the 'pile of debris ... grows skyward' behind him.

Benjamin's emphasis on religion as redemption through history offers a further interesting comparison with Taylor on this issue. For Taylor, 'redemption happens through Incarnation', which is the 'weaving of God's life into human lives',[23] but he notes how, historically, such an 'incarnational mode of life' has been confronted with a

---

[18] Robert Wolin, *Walter Benjamin. An Aesthetic of Redemption*, New York, Columbia University Press, 1982, p. 37.
[19] Julian Roberts, *Walter Benjamin*, London, Macmillan, 1982, p. 109.
[20] Roberts, *Walter Benjamin*, pp. 110–111.
[21] Wolin, *Walter Benjamin*, pp. 61–62.
[22] Walter Benjamin, 'Theses on the Philosophy of History' in Walter Benjamin, *Illuminations*, Hannah Arendt (ed.), London, Fontana, 1992, p. 249.
[23] Taylor, 'A Catholic Modernity?', p. 14.

'closing off to God' from secularism.[24] Ironically, such a rejection of religion has actually resulted in carrying some of its most positive aspects 'further than they ever were taken, or could have been taken, within Christendom'. For Taylor, this is evinced in the affirmation of universal human rights that is deeply embedded in liberal political culture, but this seeming intermingling of an incarnational mode of life and its secularist negation still means that the latter offers the rejection of transcendence and puts the former under threat.[25] This denial has had disastrous consequences historically as well as in the present. For example, looking at the history of the twentieth century, Taylor notes how it can be seen either progressively or horrifically.[26] The same century that produced the 'debris' of Auschwitz and Hiroshima also produced Amnesty International and Médecins sans Frontières. The former therefore represents the closing off to God that Taylor bemoans, and the latter a reflection of the weaving of God's life into the world offering us redemption through incarnation as we open the 'transcendent ... window, gaze, and then go beyond'.[27]

For Bloch, Benjamin and Taylor, then, religion is a positive force that allows thinking of the transcendent to take place. For Bloch, religion was not to be rejected or abandoned but was itself a vehicle for the hope of a better world. For Benjamin, religion was a form of salvation from the misery of the present and the past. Most importantly, though, for all these three thinkers, is that religion is construed as an ameliorating force. As we saw at the outset, this is what makes Benjamin and Bloch so special for Taylor, because they were writing against the grain of the orthodox Marxist tradition that rejected religion completely.

God

The issue of the idea of God raises further interesting comparisons between Bloch, Benjamin and Taylor. For Taylor, humans are 'made in the image of God' as we also stand with others in the 'unconditional' 'stream of love'.[28] Such love is only possible he suggests, if 'we open ourselves to God' and thereby go beyond the boundaries that have been constructed by exclusive humanisms. The 'weaving of

[24]   Taylor, 'A Catholic Modernity?', p. 16.
[25]   Taylor, 'A Catholic Modernity?', p. 26.
[26]   Taylor, 'A Catholic Modernity?', p. 37.
[27]   Taylor, 'A Catholic Modernity?', pp. 26–27.
[28]   Taylor, 'A Catholic Modernity?', p. 35.

God's life into human lives' gives redemption through incarnation, recognises the 'diversity in humanity that God created', and therefore posits 'complementarity and identity' to achieve 'our ultimate wholeness'.[29] In this way, we can have an incarnational mode of life.[30] Taylor, then, is recognising the presence of God in the world, which gives us glimpses of something beyond and allows us to have a 'transcendental outlook'.[31]

For Bloch and Benjamin, they materialistically appropriate the real human concerns that are expressed in the idea of God. Benjamin considers God's relation to the world through a discussion of language.[32] He argues that as God created the world in his word and in his naming of things, God therefore engages in creative acts. Other profane languages can therefore be nothing more than a semblance of God's word and are in no sense creative. What links the divine and the profane is that humans can also name things but this is a communicative rather than creative act. Even so, such naming offers a reflection of God's creative activity in the human world.[33] Humans, then, could communicate lower languages into higher languages in a process of translation that ultimately ends with the word of God.[34] The 'unity of this movement of languages' results therefore in the 'final clarity' of the 'word of god'. Such a hierarchy of language is used by Benjamin to apply to the arts where sculpture and painting were a form of language in that they offered a translation of things into artistic forms. Similarly, translating itself in the literary arts offers a higher spiritual level because the text is being rendered into 'pure' language as distinct from the communicative language of the author.[35] Indeed, Taylor also realises the importance of art as a vehicle for showing us something beyond. For instance, in the article in which he endorsed Benjamin's and Bloch's approach in 1989, he briefly mentions the poetry of Rilke as being part of the artistic process in 'which what we are struggling to express is not ourselves, but

[29] Taylor, 'A Catholic Modernity?', p. 14.
[30] Taylor, 'A Catholic Modernity?', p. 16.
[31] Taylor, 'A Catholic Modernity?', p. 19.
[32] Walter Benjamin, 'One Way Street', in Walter Benjamin, *One-Way Street and Other Writings*, London, Verso, 1997, pp. 115–116. Cf. Roberts, *Walter Benjamin*, pp. 112–113.
[33] Benjamin, 'One-Way Street', p. 116.
[34] Benjamin, 'One-Way Street', p. 123. Cf. Roberts, *Walter Benjamin*, p. 120.
[35] Walter Benjamin, 'The Task of the Translator', in Walter Benjamin, *Illuminations*, Hannah Arendt (ed.), London, Fontana, 1992.

something beyond ourselves'.[36] As we shall shortly see, art is important in offering us ways to think about the transcendent for Taylor and this is also reflected in Benjamin's own work.

Such an emphasis on transcendence in Benjamin's writings is explicitly approved of in Taylor's discussion of naming.[37] Taylor notes how, for Benjamin, things can only be named as 'constellations' or 'clusters of terms and images' if their particularity is not to be subsumed or hidden under the universal. Benjamin's constellation approach, Taylor argues, means that not achieving full reconciliation between universal and particular allows the particular to emerge. Instead, then, full reconciliation is not achieved but there is a pointing towards it so that it gives 'a kind of presence in our lives, and constitutes a sort of messianic premonition, in Benjamin's religious language'. Again, as Taylor recognises, the value in Benjamin's approach is in framing a space within which something that could be 'infinitely remote' is brought within our grasp. As Taylor is a writer who is trying to overcome the tendency to stifle sprit and instead emphasise liberation, the writings of Benjamin would seem to offer some help here, especially as art is one way to discuss the transcendent.[38]

Taylor's theistic weaving of God's life into our lives can be interestingly compared with Bloch's conception of the 'eternal now. Bloch, in attempting to expose the real human concerns that arise out of the idea of God, notes how the founders of religions have increasingly put the human into God.[39] He argues that the emphasis on the human brings religion back to the 'human wish' towards 'essence'.[40] Prevention of this essence is, in mythology, hell, whereas its non-prevention is 'apotheosis'. In this sense, God 'appears as the *hypostasised ideal of the human essence which has not yet become in reality'*. Such a fusion of the human and the divine means that God should not remain 'on high',[41] and Bloch gives the example of the Three Wise Men to illustrate this. Bloch argues that once the Three Wise Men, guided by the lone star, reach Jesus' birthplace, then 'God ceases'.[42] This cessation is not 'nothingness', but is a god-becoming-man process in the world. Alternatively, man can become 'dis-

---

[36] Taylor, 'Marxism and Socialist Humanism', p. 69.
[37] Taylor, *Sources of the Self*, pp. 478–479.
[38] Taylor, *Sources of the Self*, p. 520.
[39] Bloch, *Principle of Hope*, Volume 3, p. 1288.
[40] Bloch, *Principle of Hope*, Volume 3, p. 1289.
[41] Bloch, *Principle of Hope*, Volume 3, p. 1290.
[42] Bloch, *Principle of Hope*, Volume 3, p. 1298.

solved in God' as in the case of Christian mysticism.[43] Bloch argues that Christian mysticism results in a 'breaking into God' where the division between subject and object disappears and we enter the *'nunc aeternum'* (eternal now). So the idea of God is not an external or distant being but is instead part of our own essential being where our consciousness can glimpse moments of the not-yet.[44]

Both Bloch and Benjamin, therefore, have pertinent points to make in their discussion of the idea of God that links into Taylor's own religious vision. Taylor explicitly applauds Benjamin's emphasis on language as a mediation of God's creation in the world and the use of art to express notions of transcendence. Similarly, the presence of God in our own lives that Bloch discerns from the origins of religion is implicitly endorsed in Taylor's own emphasis on God's place in the world that allows us to achieve wholeness. Where a problem might arise in relation to Bloch is that Taylor is careful to avoid God's presence being a unitary, universal imposition. For example, Taylor argues that if God weaves himself into a Catholic vision this should not then be imposed universally on everyone. Whereas Bloch's emphasis on the dissolution of subject and object into the 'eternal now' may mean that just identity and not complementarity would occur. Let us not forget that Taylor, at the end of *Sources of the Self*, explicitly argued for the Judaeo-Christian tradition as the way forward for arguing for notions of transcendence. He was careful to say this is not the only way to do this, but this was his preferred way. Bloch himself offers the 'primacy of the Judaeo-Christian tradition' against any other religious vision, which might mean that difference would not be allowed.[45] This would be problematic for Taylor. For instance, Taylor discusses how other religions exist alongside his own religious vision and this he thinks is perfectly acceptable.[46] Through dialogue aspects of these differing visions may complement or identify with each other, but he will not allow them to be subsumed in each other. This does not seem to be the case for Bloch. As Geoghegan notes, for Bloch, Buddhism, for instance, offers a utopian message for which it should be praised, but he ultimately rejects it because of its abstract devotion to nirvana.[47] Despite this, the emphasis on using the Judaeo-Christian tradition for grasping God's presence in the world certainly finds resonance

[43]   Bloch, *Principle of Hope*, Volume 3, p. 1300.
[44]   Bloch, *Atheism in Christianity*, p. 213. Cf. Geoghegan, *Ernst Bloch*, pp. 93–94.
[45]   Geoghegan, 'Bloch: Postsecular Thoughts', p. 61.
[46]   Taylor, 'Charles Taylor Replies', pp. 226–230.
[47]   Geoghegan, 'Bloch: Postsecular Thoughts', pp. 61–62.

in Taylor's own religious vision, although for Bloch this is premised on the human concerns that arise from the idea of God rather than any belief in such a Being.

Time

The theme of time also plays an important part in Taylor's religious vision and emphasis on transcendence. Taylor makes a distinction between secular time and higher time.[48] Secular time relates to living an ordinary life in contrast to those who worship God and live within the time frame of eternity: higher time. Secular time is regular and linear in that events succeed each other. In contrast, higher time is ordered more by the significance of events rather than one day passing into the next. However, secular time and higher time are not completely independent because an event in secular time could take on a new meaning in higher time. Taylor then argues that contemporary society has only a single, linear, uniform conception of time which, following Benjamin, he calls 'homogenous empty time'.[49] Taylor relates this discussion of time to modernist writers and poets. He notes how modernist writers offered a critique of the spatialisation of time, which in one instance seemed to present history as being in decline, but in another instance seemed to contain an 'optimistic variant' that understands history as a spiral movement towards a 'reconciliation of reason and feeling'.[50] He explains this through a consideration of the use of history in the poetry of T.S. Eliot and Ezra Pound.[51] He argues that in one sense Eliot and Pound seem to long for a meaningful past from the emptiness of the present which is in decline. On closer inspection, Eliot's and Pound's work actually seems to be telling us that the past can be recaptured and made alive again in the here and now. For Taylor, Eliot and Pound are bringing 'the long-dead back to speech', which offers a 'unity across persons, or across time'. In this sense, these great poets are carrying out Taylor's own desire for 'retrieval', in 'an attempt to

---

[48] Charles Taylor, 'Modes of Secularism', in Rajeev Bhagarva (ed.), *Secularism and its Critics*, Delhi, Oxford University Press, 1998, pp. 31–32. Cf. Abbey, *Charles Taylor*, pp. 204–205.
[49] Taylor, *Sources of the Self*, p. 463. Taylor, 'Modes of Secularism', p. 43. Benjamin, 'Theses on the Philosophy of History', p. 252.
[50] Taylor, *Sources of the Self*, p. 464.
[51] Taylor, *Sources of the Self*, pp. 464–465.

uncover buried goods' with which to 'bring the air back again into the half-collapsed lungs of the spirit'.[52]

Now Benjamin's discussion of time can be employed to offer an interesting insight to Taylor's emphasis on time and retrieval. Benjamin contrasts 'homogenous empty time' with the 'presence of the now',[53] which involves 'transition' and 'blast[s] open the continuum of history'.[54] This '"time of the now"' is 'shot through with chips of Messianic time' where 'the strait gate through which the Messiah might enter' can appear.[55] For Benjamin, the Messiah entering in this way will introduce a new calendar, with many different holy days in stark contrast to the emptiness of uniform, linear clock-time. Moreover, Benjamin emphasises the importance of retrieving such 'visions of transcendence' through 'redemptive criticism' of which works of art should be the main object.[56] So both in the emphasis on higher time and in the possibility of art to offer redemptive qualities, Taylor and Benjamin share interesting similarities. Moreover, it is even more ironic that Taylor should use the poetry of Pound and Eliot as examples of this redemptive approach, because, as George Steiner has noted, Benjamin's own method is 'akin' to that of Pound and Eliot with its 'collage and montage-aesthetic'.[57]

Bloch also has a dual conception of time that he splits into 'natural time' and '*historical-cultural time* which corresponds respectively to pre-human and human history'.[58] Pre-human time leaps into human time as humanity '"crowns"' nature by succeeding it,[59] but Bloch finds this unilinear advance of history and time problematic, and instead puts forward a 'topology of times' that is meant to contain not only pre-human and human history but also the time of nature.[60] The future-oriented nature of his philosophy again manifests itself in that the onset of human time is not the final act. Instead, the humanisation of nature waits in a '*dawning morrow-to-come*' but is also manifest in some sense now as a moment in human or historical

[52]   Taylor, *Sources of the Self*, p. 520.
[53]   Benjamin, 'Theses on the Philosophy of History', pp. 252–253.
[54]   Benjamin, 'Theses on the Philosophy of History', p. 254.
[55]   Benjamin, 'Theses on the Philosophy of History', p. 255.
[56]   Wolin, *Walter Benjamin*, p. 48.
[57]   George Steiner, 'Introduction' to Walter Benjamin, *The Origin of German Tragic Drama*, London, Verso, 1998, pp. 21–22.
[58]   Ernst Bloch, *A Philosophy of the Future*, New York, Herder & Herder, 1970, p. 134. Cf. Geoghegan, *Ernst Bloch*, pp. 156–157
[59]   Bloch, *A Philosophy of the Future*, p. 135.
[60]   Bloch, *A Philosophy of the Future*, p. 136.

time.[61] Moreover, as Geoghegan notes, with his conception of 'non-contemporaneity', Bloch also fruitfully grasps how people living in one time would still in their consciousness hold a host of different times.[62] In this sense, religion itself is therefore an expression of the longings, hopes and fears of people in and across time.

The notion of time in the work of Bloch and Benjamin therefore makes for an interesting comparison with Taylor's own analysis. That Taylor explicitly endorses Benjamin here may indicate why he was so impressed with his philosophical outlook in the first place. Contrasting 'homogenous empty time' with higher time allows both Benjamin and Taylor to emphasise the transcendent. Moreover, Taylor's use of poetry to explain how we can retrieve past moments to aid us in our visions of the transcendent chimes nicely with Benjamin's use of art for the same purpose. As we shall shortly see, such an approach appears particularly in Benjamin's discussion of death in his analysis of German tragic drama. Additionally, Bloch is also emphasising the future-oriented nature of time within and ultimately beyond the present. Moreover, he is emphasising the need, as Taylor does, to link now time and past time as moments of retrieval in trying to offer a vision of something beyond.

Death

As we have seen, Taylor's main concern in his religious vision is to emphasise the importance of going beyond life.[63] He therefore bemoans the fact that in our culture death and suffering are given no human meaning other than as dangers to be avoided.[64] Instead, Taylor, emphasising the importance of transcendence, challenges us to reject this approach and realise 'that more than life matters'. In doing so, he does not want to diminish the need to help mankind in the present, but still wants to emphasise that accepting the transcendent means envisioning a point beyond the present.[65] Death therefore is not simply negation, but is an affirmation that there is somewhere 'that matters beyond life'. What, then, of Bloch's and Benjamin's discussion of the supposedly negative force of death?

Bloch argues that the resurrection of Jesus revealed the possibility for immortality and transcendence for people against nihilistic ten-

---

[61] Bloch, *A Philosophy of the Future*, p. 137.
[62] Geoghegan, 'Bloch: Postsecular Thoughts', p. 66.
[63] Taylor, 'A Catholic Modernity?', p. 20.
[64] Taylor, 'A Catholic Modernity?', p. 24.
[65] Taylor, 'A Catholic Modernity?', p. 20.

dencies.[66] Bloch therefore relates death to the issue of Christian transcendence and to eternal life that he captures with the term 'extra-territorial'.[67] He argues that death can be overcome because it cannot destroy something that is in the future. By facing the ultimate fear of life and death individuals are not what they are but what they will be.[68] For Bloch, then, true identity lies in the future. Repeating the words of God to Moses, Bloch states, 'I will be what I will be', and so emphasises the future possibility of overcoming our present circumstances to redefine ourselves.[69] In this way, our true selves wait 'extra-territorially, in the wings' as the imperfect nature of our current selves and the world forces us to struggle for a more perfect identity and a more perfect world.[70] Bloch's point is that humans are self-determining, pushing along their hopes towards an open and undetermined future to the not-yet. In one sense, this appears to represent the 'tacking back and forth' that Taylor himself desires in his attempt to overcome the tensions between the emphasis on human flourishing in the here and now and the longing for something beyond life. Moreover, Taylor's emphasis on transcendence as a change in identity is also clearly reflected in Bloch's arguments here. Overall, then, as Geoghegan has rightly noted, Bloch and Taylor are united in not seeing death as the end, and thereby recognising that in 'dying the awesome mystery of life and death can be as tangible to the atheist as it is to the believer'.[71] Again, though, this raises questions about demarcating Bloch as an atheist and Taylor as a theist. We have already seen that Geoghegan himself identifies this tension in Bloch's work.[72] So given both their emphases on transcending death, which are stated in similar ways, such a dichotomy may seem even less necessary. However, as I pointed out at the outset, we do come up against the fact that for Bloch these are materialist appropriations of religious insights and result in the tensions that Geoghegan has identified between the atheism/theism dichotomy. So whilst we can see similarities between Taylor and Bloch in that death is interpreted not simply as negative, we need to recognise that Bloch would not accept a notion of the afterlife on the basis of Taylor's theism, so it is here that the boundaries for a dialogue reach their limit.

---

[66] Geoghegan, *Ernst Bloch*, p. 89.
[67] Bloch, *Atheism in Christianity*, p. 253. Cf. Geoghegan, *Ernst Bloch*, pp. 97–98.
[68] Bloch, *Atheism in Christianity*, pp. 251–2.
[69] Geoghegan, *Ernst Bloch*, p. 85.
[70] Bloch, *Atheism in Christianity*, p. 261.
[71] Geoghegan, 'Bloch: Postsecular Thoughts', p. 65.
[72] Geoghegan, *Ernst Bloch*, p. 103.

As we saw in the quotation at the outset, what impressed Taylor about Benjamin was that his art and philosophy indicates 'something beyond'. This is particularly the case in *The Origin of German Tragic Drama*, where Benjamin mentions death in relation to tragedy. Benjamin argues that tragedy has its roots in legend and this is where any philosophical definition of tragedy has to begin.[73] He argues that tragedy is not simply legend in dramatic form because legend is impartial and is not aimed at helping a particular cause. Tragedy in the form of tragic poetry for instance, does offer a partial, 'tendentious re-shaping' of epic poetry as is evinced in the case of Oedipus. The purpose of this 're-shaping' of the legend by tragedy is to depict the hero's death as a sacrifice.[74] Benjamin argues that this sacrifice is unique in that it is both 'first' and 'final'. The finality lies in atonement to the gods who are upholding an ancient right. The 'first' aspect of the sacrifice lies in the fact that in the action of the hero, new aspects of the life of the nation begin to emerge. Tragic death, then, both rejects the ancient rights of the Olympians, and sacrifices the hero to an 'unknown god as the first fruits of a new harvest of humanity'.[75] Such a dual significance of tragic death also relates to tragic suffering as again depicted in Sophocles' *Oedipus* but also Aeschylus' *Oresteia*. The hero's death is replaced by a 'paroxysm', which is both a 'new conception', but also satisfies the old conception of the gods and sacrifice. For Benjamin, death therefore becomes 'salvation: the crisis of death'. He notes how the example of the sacrificial victim escaping from the altar with the knife of the priest allows the victim to use the altar as a place of refuge; makes the angry god merciful; and thereby become a prisoner and servant of god. For Benjamin, this represents the whole schema in the *Oresteia* with its focus on death, reliance on the community and the absence of any solution or salvation. He therefore argues that the suffering of the tragic hero is captured in his silence.[76] In his 'icy loneliness of the self', the tragic hero is disconnected from god and the world and elevates himself 'above the realm of personality'. Such 'tragic silence' and speechlessness of the hero mean that it is his actions and not his speech that reveal the content of his achievements. This leads Benjamin to argue that the tragic hero sacrifices 'only the dumb shadow of his being' to the ancient statutes, whereas his 'soul finds

---

[73]   Benjamin, *Origin*, p. 106.
[74]   Benjamin, *Origin*, pp. 106–107.
[75]   Benjamin, *Origin*, p. 107.
[76]   Benjamin, *Origin*, p. 108.

refuge in the word of a distant community'.[77] The death of the tragic hero is an 'act of atonement ... which grants the victory to man, but also to god' and 'thereby becomes salvation'.[78] Benjamin argues that the life of the tragic hero 'unfolds from death which is not its end but its form'.[79] Moreover, the tragic hero talks about the 'circumstances of his death as if they were circumstances of his life', and has a 'spiritual-cum-physical existence. As Wolin has noted, this emphasis on salvation through death is the 'cornerstone' of Benjamin's 'method of redemptive critique'[80], and is part of his allegorical understanding of the *Trauerspiel*. Benjamin argues that these Counter-Reformation dramas displayed the futility of mortal life and pointed towards the next life as a realm of salvation.[81] The playwrights of the *Trauerspiel* littered the stage with dead bodies and had the martyred heroes exaggerate their death agonies to show the mortality of all life. In this way, they could therefore show their religious beliefs, which would point to immortality and salvation. '*Redemption through death*' was therefore the allegorical leitmotif of the *Trauerspiel* and deeply informed Benjamin's own eschatological vision.[82] As Taylor himself notes, Benjamin preferred allegory over symbol precisely because allegory 'recognises the distance, the alterity, between sign and signified'.[83] It is this 'distance' that Benjamin is using in his analysis of drama to point to the beyond. Indeed, as we shall see in the next two Chapters, Taylor himself looks to art for its epiphanic qualities that can bring us into contact with what is beyond as a moral source.[84] For Taylor, the serious poet, then, is pointing us to God, which is presented to us 'refracted' through the poet's 'own sensibility'.[85] One poet Taylor focuses on here to express the importance of epiphanic art is Baudelaire[86] who, of course, Benjamin himself studied.[87] For Taylor, Baudelaire persistently affirms the spiritual against nature.[88] The spiritual world itself stands behind the fallen world of nature

---

[77]   Benjamin, *Origin*, p. 109.
[78]   Benjamin, *Origin*, pp. 109 & 106.
[79]   Benjamin, *Origin*, p. 114.
[80]   Wolin, *Walter Benjamin*, p. 52.
[81]   Benjamin, *Origin*, p. 62.
[82]   Wolin, *Walter Benjamin*, p. 62.
[83]   Taylor, *Sources of the Self*, p. 479.
[84]   Taylor, *Sources of the Self*, p. 425.
[85]   Taylor, *Sources of the Self*, p. 492.
[86]   Taylor, *Sources of the Self*, pp. 434–442.
[87]   Walter Benjamin, 'On Some Motifs in Baudelaire', in Walter Benjamin, *Illuminations*, Hannah Arendt (ed.), London, Fontana, 1992.
[88]   Taylor, *Sources of the Self*, p. 434.

and it is through art, which Baudelaire closely links with religion, that this can be brought to epiphany.[89] Benjamin is also acutely aware of the transcendent nature of Baudelaire's work. For instance, he notes how Baudelaire's 'restorative will ... transcends ... the limits of earthly existence' as is captured in the following lines of his poem 'Recueillment':

> See the dead departed Years in antiquated
> Dress leaning over heaven's balconies.[90]

For Benjamin, Baudelaire is here 'paying homage to times out of mind' as he assembles together 'days of remembrance into a spiritual year'. Remembrance, then, is an experience which attempts to transcend the given and so present itself as the 'beautiful' in which the 'value of art appears'.[91] For Benjamin, this was one of the key aspects of Baudelaire's writings.

The issue of death for grasping moments of transcendence is therefore interestingly explored in the work of Bloch and Benjamin. Bloch's emphasis on seeing death not as simply negative is reflected in Taylor's own desires on this issue. Even more pertinently, Bloch and Taylor both see death as offering a change in identity in the future where we can redefine ourselves, although for Taylor's theism this manifests itself in the afterlife, whereas for Bloch transcendence is present in the re-making of our humanity. Additionally, Benjamin's use of art and literature to explore the nature of death as depicting something beyond can certainly be interpreted as the reason why Taylor was praising Benjamin in the quotation at the outset, and is reflected in his own endorsement of epiphanic art.

Conclusion

Taylor was surely correct in 1989 to cite Benjamin and Bloch as exemplars for offering a transcendent philosophy, despite the limitations that must arise because of the atheism/theism dichotomy. Across the themes of religion, God, time and death both thinkers offer striking points of comparison and contrast with Taylor, but also indicate ways in which they might aid his own articulation for transcendence. From their positive response to the role of religion, to the importance of materialistically interpreting stories of God as indications for our common humanity, to the emphasis on a higher spiri-

[89]   Taylor, *Sources of the Self*, p. 436.
[90]   Quoted in Benjamin, 'On Some Motifs in Baudelaire', p. 179.
[91]   Benjamin, 'On Some Motifs in Baudelaire', p. 178.

tual time, and ultimately in seeing death not simply as a negative moment, Benjamin and Bloch forge a vision which Taylor was clearly aware of and supported but chose not to develop. This is despite the fact that, as we have seen, he has profound difficulties in trying to talk about the notion of transcendence except in general and evasive terms. Overall, perhaps the ultimate atheism of Bloch and Benjamin may have been one of the reasons he chose not to delve into their work. As we have seen, the tension identified by Geoghegan on the atheism/theism dichotomy has also raised problems at times in relating their theories to Taylor's own. This is of course inevitable and exposes just how far atheists and theists can go in having a dialogue with each other, irrespective of their appreciation of the positive aspects of religion. Nevertheless, there is still richness in this warm current of Marxism that might aid Taylor's religious vision, and is obviously why he was identifying the power of their philosophy in the first place. I now pursue this notion of transcendence further in the next Chapter through the aforementioned vehicle of epiphanic art.

Chapter Four

Epiphany

I am trying to give people some kind of intellectual pleasure or spiritual enjoyment by converting the bread of everyday life into something that has a permanent artistic life of its own for their mental, moral, and spiritual uplift. (James Joyce)[1]

For Taylor, the importance of art, by which he means literature and poetry in particular, lies in the fact that it is a crucial moral source, which involves a process of revelation that at the same time defines and completes what it makes manifest.[2] On that basis, he argues that art's importance is so deeply embedded within our culture, that people in general see the creative imagination of art as an 'indispensable locus of moral sources'.[3] Taylor contends that art is so powerful in this respect that it has to some extent replaced religion for many of us in the modern world.[4] Even more specifically, he further adds that what makes artworks so central to modern culture is that they issue from or realise an epiphany, the importance of which I briefly mentioned in the previous Chapter, and which I now examine more thoroughly in this. I begin by outlining Taylor's notion of an epiphany, which he says he inherits from James Joyce. I then explain the Joycean epiphany and suggest that given Taylor's theism, he is ultimately committed to a restrictive theistic or theophanic epiphany in contrast to the non-theistic epiphany proposed by Joyce. I then begin to outline the democratisation of the aesthetic that will be developed further in Chapter Seven on the aesthetic self, but is explored initially through a consideration of Joyce's *Ulysses*.

---

[1]   Quoted in Stanislaus Joyce, *My Brother's Keeper: James Joyce's Early Years*, New York, Viking Press, 1958, pp. 103–104.

[2]   Charles Taylor, *Sources of the Self, The Making of the Modern Identity*, Cambridge, Cambridge University Press, 1989, p. 419.

[3]   Taylor, *Sources of the Self*, p. 426

[4]   Taylor, *Sources of the Self*, p. 422.

Taylor's Epiphany

Taylor borrows the term epiphany from James Joyce but adds that he wants to use it in a 'somewhat wider sense than his'.[5] In doing so, Taylor defines a work of art as epiphanic when it is the:

> locus of a manifestation which brings us into the presence of something which is otherwise inaccessible, and which is of the highest moral or spiritual significance; a manifestation, moreover, which also defines or completes something, even as it reveals.[6]

Taylor argues that the term epiphany covers the aesthetic of the work of art, its spiritual significance and also says something about the nature and situation of the artist.[7] Moreover, realising an epiphany, he suggests, involves 'recovering contact with a moral source' that 'either fosters and/or itself constitutes a spiritually significant fulfilment or wholeness'. An epiphany, then, is a source of the good and it is a source that has developed from the Romantic era into the modern world.

Taylor demarcates different types of epiphany in relation to art. The first, which was prevalent in the Romantic era, portrays, for example, unsullied nature or human emotion, in order to make manifest a higher spiritual reality that resonates through it.[8] Taylor refers to such art as 'epiphanies of being' and cites Wordsworth's poetry and the paintings of Constable and Friedrich as exemplars of this form of art. What is so distinctive about this form of epiphanic art for Taylor, is that its meaning is intrinsic to itself because it 'exists in and for itself' and is, utilising a phrase from Yeats, '"self-begotten"'.[9] Consequently, this type of epiphanic art cannot be properly captured through explanation or paraphrase. Taylor is quick to point out that this form of epiphanic art is not mimetic even though it can contain a descriptive aspect. Rather, the aim of the work is one of transfiguration to 'render the object "translucent"'.[10] For Taylor, this epiphany of being materialises through the symbol of the work, which is not outside in some 'independently available object described or referent'.[11] Additionally, he continues, the epiphany of being must be understood separately from the intentions of the

[5] Taylor, *Sources of the Self*, p. 419.
[6] Taylor, *Sources of the Self*, p. 419.
[7] Taylor, *Sources of the Self*, p. 425.
[8] Taylor, *Sources of the Self*, p. 419.
[9] Taylor, *Sources of the Self*, p. 420.
[10] Taylor, *Sources of the Self*, p. 419.
[11] Taylor, *Sources of the Self*, p. 420.

author, because it is only in the work that such intentions are properly revealed. He endorses Oscar Wilde's view that '"when the work is finished it has, as it were, an independent life of its own, and may deliver a message far other than that which was put into its lips to say"'.

The second form of epiphanic art, which Taylor says dominates the twentieth century, is typified by the fact that the locus of the epiphany moves into the work itself, which results in it becoming unclear what the work is meant to say or even if it is actually saying anything at all.[12] For Taylor, much modernist poetry and non-representational visual art are examples of this form of epiphany. He refers to this type of epiphanic art in its extreme form as '"auto-telic"' in that it has a being or purpose only in itself. He notes that while this form of art attempts to retain its epiphanic aspect it also, paradoxically, tries to decouple itself from any relation to something beyond it. So the locus of revelation remains in the work, which is of the highest significance, but is also completely self-sufficient and self-contained. Taylor cites the Symbolist Mallarmé as a paradigm figure for this extreme form of epiphanic art.

Taylor therefore identifies two types of epiphany here, an epiphany of being which transfigures an object and makes it translucent, and a second type in which the epiphany is present within the work itself. However, the epiphany that Taylor sees as the most important, which develops in the twentieth century to replace the epiphany of being, is what he calls an 'epiphany of interspaces'[13] or an 'interspatial or framing epiphany' that he derives from the work of Joseph Frank.[14] Taylor argues that this form of epiphany 'makes something appear by juxtaposing images, or even harder to explain, by juxtaposing words.'[15] In this way, the 'epiphany comes from between the words or images, as it were, from the force field they set up between them, and not through a central referent which they describe while transmuting'.[16] For Taylor, this allows poetry to 'say the otherwise unsayable' by 'juxtaposing thoughts, fragments, images' and so 'reach somehow between them and thus beyond

---

[12] Taylor, *Sources of the Self*, p. 419.
[13] Taylor, *Sources of the Self*, p. 476.
[14] Taylor, *Sources of the Self*, pp. 478 & 588. n. 64. Joseph Frank, 'Spatial Form in Modern Literature' in *The Widening Gyre*, New Brunswick, N.J., Rutgers University Press, 1963.
[15] Taylor, *Sources of the Self*, p. 465.
[16] Taylor, *Sources of the Self*, pp. 465–466.

them'.[17] Consequently, 'the work of art as vortex is a cluster; it is a constellation of words or images which sets up a space which draws ideas and energy into it' and 'concentrates energies that are otherwise diffuse, and makes them available at one spot/moment'.[18] On this basis, Taylor claims that the epiphanic is therefore 'genuinely mysterious, and it possibly contains the key — or a key — to what it is to be human'.[19] He maintains that this form of 'interspatial' or 'framing epiphany' permeates throughout twentieth century culture'[20] and is present in the work of writers such as Eliot, Pound, Mann, Lawrence, Joyce, Proust and Rilke.[21]

The first point that needs to be made here is in relation to Taylor's own story about the development of the 'framing epiphany' from Frank's work. Taylor does not mention that Frank later changed his mind on this issue by arguing that 'the emergence of spatial form in twentieth-century narrative should no longer be regarded as a radical break with tradition'.[22] Instead, 'it represents only ... a shift in the internal hierarchy of the elements ["causal-chronological" versus "spatial"] composing a narrative structure'. Indeed, for Robert Langbaum, a sympathetic but critical reader of Frank, the origins of 'spatial form' are not distinctive to the twentieth century but begin in English literature with Wordsworth whom Taylor, of course, associates with epiphanies of being.[23] Moreover, Langbaum further criticises Frank's recognition of a shift rather than a break in the development of the 'spatial form', for still not recognising that such a shift 'derives from a changed world view that values experience over system, whether the system be causal-chronological, logical, theological, or ethical'. This again will not do for Taylor, because as we shall now see, simply emphasising experience results in subjectivism, which he virulently opposes.

Taylor argues that although 'the moral or spiritual order of things' that 'framing epiphanies' put us in contact with 'must come to us indexed to a personal vision', we must always be 'striving to avoid

[17]   Taylor, *Sources of the Self*, p. 473.
[18]   Taylor, *Sources of the Self*, p. 475.
[19]   Taylor, *Sources of the Self*, p. 481.
[20]   Taylor, *Sources of the Self*, p. 477.
[21]   Taylor, *Sources of the Self*, p. 491.
[22]   Joseph Frank, 'Spatial Form: Some Further Reflections', *Critical Inquiry*, V, Winter, 1978, p. 284. Cf. Robert Langbaum, 'The Epiphanic Mode in Wordsworth and Modern Literature', in Wim Tigges (ed.), *Moments of Moment. Aspects of the Literary Epiphany*, Amsterdam-Atlanta, GA, Rodopi, 1999, p. 47.
[23]   Langbaum, 'The Epiphanic Mode', p. 47.

the merely subjective'.[24] He defines subjectivism as a 'search for immediate unity, whether through a celebration of our own power or through a merging in the depths'.[25] He argues that whilst epiphanic art certainly produces inwardness and a greater understanding of personal experience, it must ultimately go beyond the subjective.[26] It follows then that on Taylor's view we must not comprehend the great works of modernist art simply in a subjective manner through how we feel or in the way we order our emotions.[27] Rather, he continues, modernist art in putting us in contact with moral sources involves empowerment rather than merely 'rearrang[ing] the furniture of the psyche'. In this sense, Taylor therefore rejects the psychological position of the literary critic I. A. Richards who sees poetry as a '"means of arranging the order of our internal lives by making a harmonious pattern of extremely complex attitudes, once thought to refer to an external order of metaphysics but now seen to be a symbolic ordering of our inner selves"'.[28] Remaining at the level of the subjective is, for Taylor, a lesser form of moral and spiritual experience than that which can be achieved by going beyond the subject to a source outside it. Subjectivism leads to a 'kind of shallowness' in that it only offers a 'celebration of our creative powers', which ultimately can 'make life thin and insubstantial'.[29] He therefore insists that overcoming subjectivism is 'a major task, both moral and aesthetic, of our time' and 'is in some ways the central issue of epiphanic art'.[30] Moreover, 'the poet, if he is serious, is pointing to something—God, the tradition which he believes to be there for all of us'.[31] Taylor argues that such a 'weaving of the subjective and transcendent' is 'best expressed' in the verse of Wallace Stevens' Opus Posthumus where he speaks of the world within us having little meaning without the world around us, and that whereas the idea of God has always been the main poetic idea, without God poetry is the source for the redemption of life.[32]

Now what is interesting here is that Taylor seems open in relation to the source the epiphany is pointing to. He stipulates above that it

---

[24] Taylor, *Sources of the Self*, pp. 428–429.
[25] Taylor, *Sources of the Self*, p. 472.
[26] Taylor, *Sources of the Self*, p. 481.
[27] Taylor, *Sources of the Self*, p. 490.
[28] Taylor, *Sources of the Self*, pp. 490–491.
[29] Taylor, *Sources of the Self*, pp. 507, 510 & 511.
[30] Taylor, *Sources of the Self*, p. 429.
[31] Taylor, *Sources of the Self*, p. 492.
[32] Taylor, *Sources of the Self*, p. 493

could be God, the tradition or even redemption, but such supposed openness must again come up against his restrictive theism that I identified in Chapter Two. To expose this further here I will now examine Joyce's epiphany and contrast it with Taylor's epiphany.

Joyce's Epiphany

What is initially strange about Taylor's outline of his version of an epiphany is that he does not inform us in what way he uses it in a 'wider sense' than James Joyce. Joyce's own definition of an epiphany occurs in *Stephen Hero*, the first draft of *Portrait of the Artist as a Young Man*, as follows:

> By an epiphany he meant a sudden spiritual manifestation, whether in the vulgarity of speech or of gesture or in a memorable phase of the mind. He believed that it was for the man of letters to record theses epiphanies with extreme care, seeing that they themselves are the most delicate and evanescent of moments.[33]

Joyce further explains how an epiphany occurs by utilising Aquinas' three things that are requisite for beauty: integrity or wholeness, symmetry and radiance. One famous example of a Joycean epiphany that displays this tripartite movement is in Chapter Four of *Portrait* when Stephen Dedalus experiences a revelatory moment as he observes a girl bathing in Dublin bay. Joyce argues that when the mind confronts an object as 'hypothetically beautiful' it splits the universe into the object itself and all that is not the object, the 'void'. Grasping the object in this way means that the mind differentiates it from something else, and in doing so it recognises the integrity or wholeness of the object and thereby the first quality of beauty. This first quality of beauty is encapsulated as the girl appears before Stephen 'midstream, alone and still, gazing out to sea' appearing 'like one whom magic had changed into the likeness of a strange and beautiful seabird'.[34]

The second quality of beauty emerges when the mind analyses the object as a whole and in part in relation to itself and other objects. The mind 'traverses every cranny of the structure' and realises that the object is now a '"thing" a definitely constituted entity' and so recog-

[33] James Joyce, *Stephen Hero*, Theodore Spencer, Rev. John J. Slocom and Herbert Cahoon, London, Cape, 1956, pp. 215–16.
[34] James Joyce, *A Portrait of the Artist as a Young Man*, London, Folio Society, 1965, p. 180.

nises its 'symmetry'.[35] So for this second quality of beauty, Stephen now begins to analyse the girl's body more carefully noticing her 'slender thin legs', her 'thighs, fuller and soft-hued as ivory', and the 'mortal beauty' of her face'.[36]

The third and final stage of beauty in which the object achieves its epiphany, occurs when the 'relation of the parts is exquisite' and 'adjusted to the special point'. The mind now recognises the object as that which it is and 'its soul, its whatness, leaps to us from the vestment of its appearance'. For Joyce, the 'soul of the commonest object, the structure of which is so adjusted, seems to us radiant' and so the 'object achieves its epiphany'. The girl suddenly realises that Stephen is watching her and 'feels the presence and worship of his eyes' which she reciprocates. After some time she eventually turns her attention to the stream where she stirs the water with her foot and breaks the silence between them. As 'a faint flame trembled on her cheek' the 'whatness' now leaps forward which causes Stephen to cry out 'Heavenly God!' in an 'outburst of profane joy' as the epiphany is realised. In this way Stephen's 'epiphany-producing mind'[37] leads him "to discover a mode of life or art whereby his spirit may express itself in unfettered freedom'.[38]

It is not therefore clear in what way Taylor widens the notion of epiphany from this definition and its general usage in Joyce's work. The revelatory nature of a spiritual moment and source of the good is an intrinsic part of the Joycean epiphany. Similarly, for Joyce, it also involves delineating the aesthetic aspect of a work of art and the role of the artist, all of which is explicit in the title of *Portrait*. So how does Taylor think he widens Joyce's epiphany? Given the discussion in Chapter Two, the answer appears to be by making the epiphany religious and theistic. I say appears because Taylor does not make an explicit contrast between his own epiphany and that of Joyce's, or even give an example of the latter's epiphanies, but it seems clear that it is this theistic portent that must constitute such a division, as we shall now see.

Joyce's own hostility to the restrictive nature of his Catholic upbringing is undoubted, and he renounced Catholicism at the age

[35] Joyce, *Stephen Hero*, pp. 215–216.
[36] Joyce, *Portrait*, p. 180.
[37] Mary T. Reynolds, *Joyce and Dante. The Shaping Imagination*, Princeton NJ, Princeton University Press, 1981, p. 183.
[38] Padraic Colum, 'Padraic Colum on Joyce and Dublin', in Robert H Deming (ed.), *James Joyce. The Critical Heritage*, Volume 1 – 1902–1927, London, Routledge, 1970, p. 165.

of ten after the premature death of his brother for whom he wrote an epiphany declaring: 'I cannot pray for him as others do'.[39] The cutting short of a life full of promise led Joyce to 'question all that the Church taught of God's goodness and love of His creation'.[40] His failure to carry out his Easter duty was the symbolic outcome of his break with Catholicism.[41] Additionally, the agonising death of his Mother added further to his disenchantment with the teachings of the Catholic Church and its promise of an afterlife.[42] He therefore 'rejected religious doctrines' whilst retaining 'some of the systematic bent of scholastic thought'.[43]

In relation to his epiphanies, Joyce did not see them as bringing us into contact with religion and God.[44] Indeed, his epiphanies were an attempt to 'create a literary substitute for the revelations of religion', which emanate out of his repudiation of the Catholic faith.[45] Joyce's epiphanies allowed him to move beyond religious authority and thereby 'create his own authority by the light of his senses'.[46] He was involved in 'hijacking the vocabulary of the old order for his own creatively blasphemous ends'.[47] Joyce was therefore following the general trend away from the religious interpretation of moments of new awareness[48] that had resulted in the displacement of the theophanic epiphany by the literary epiphany in the nineteenth century.[49] Theophanies were typified by the fact that that they 'record appearances of God' in contrast to literary epiphanies, which 'record the mind caught in the act of valuing particularly vivid images'. Instead of inspiration being tied to manifestations of divinity, non-theophanic inspiration means that the 'revelation is internal and the results of the revelation are unspecified' but still 'significant

[39]   Quoted in Peter Costello, *James Joyce. The Years of Growth*. 1882–1915, London, Kyle Cathie, 1992, p. 177.
[40]   Costello, *James Joyce*, p. 177.
[41]   Costello, *James Joyce*, p. 178.
[42]   Costello, *James Joyce*, p. 212.
[43]   Terry Eagleton, *The English Novel. An Introduction*, Oxford, Blackwell, 2005, p. 291.
[44]   Morris Beja, *Epiphany in the Modern Novel*, London, Peter Owen, 1971, pp. 74–75.
[45]   Harry Levin, *James Joyce: A Critical Introduction*, London, Faber & Faber, 1960, pp. 38 & 57.
[46]   Levin, *James Joyce*, p. 57.
[47]   Eagleton, The English Novel, p. 299.
[48]   Beja, *Epiphany in the Modern Novel*, p. 74.
[49]   Ashton Nichols, *The Poetics of Epiphany. Nineteenth-Century Origins of the Modern Literary Moment*, Tuscaloosa & London, University of Alabama Press, 1987, p. 29.

or life altering'.[50] To this extent, the secular use of epiphany as employed by Joyce pervades the twentieth century, and was used by the majority of modernist poets with the exception of T.S. Eliot who 'returns epiphany to a theological framework'.[51] For Eliot, the 'experiences that give rise to epiphany are associated ... with meaning that moves from partial insight toward a theophanic image of God made manifest through Christ'.[52] In this way, while the epiphany involves making the ordinary extraordinary, the theophanic epiphanies of Eliot 'attempt not simply to establish significance but to transcend mortality'.[53] So while Eliot is keen to emphasise the divine nature of the source of his inspirations, he also still emphasises the 'revelatory details of ordinary experience', which means that he is not only re-affirming the theophanic tradition, but also further promoting the secular epiphany in twentieth century art.[54] Taylor is therefore re-inserting theophany against the literary epiphany, which, as we have seen, replaced the former in the nineteenth century.[55]

So does this mean that Taylor therefore rejects a non-theistic, non-religious epiphany of the Joycean type? It might not be completely rejected because it is putting us into contact with a spiritual or moral source that is otherwise inaccessible, but it surely must be seen by Taylor to be inferior to his own theistic religious epiphany, given the discussion in Chapter Two.[56] This must be behind Taylor's desire to 'widen' Joyce's non-theistic epiphany. Joyce's epiphany is too narrow because it does not allow for any theistic import. However, it is Taylor himself who is narrowing the epiphany by making it theistic. He is closing the epiphany off because he is implying that the true epiphanic moment points towards God. It therefore follows from this discussion that Taylor should find the Joycean epiphany wanting in Joyce's writings. Taylor may be able to 'widen' the epiph-

[50]   Nichols, *The Poetics of Epiphany*, p. 30.
[51]   Nichols, *The Poetics of Epiphany*, p. 181.
[52]   Nichols, *The Poetics of Epiphany*, p. 196.
[53]   Nichols, *The Poetics of Epiphany*, p. 197.
[54]   Nichols, *The Poetics of Epiphany*, p. 198.
[55]   Nichols, *The Poetics of Epiphany*, p. 29.
[56]   Michael L. Morgan, 'Religion, History and Moral Discourse', in James Tully (ed.), *Philosophy in an Age of Pluralism: The Philosophy of Charles Taylor in Question*, Cambridge, Cambridge University Press, 1994, pp. 63–65, suggests there is an openness about Taylor's religious epiphany, but Taylor's circumspection in *Sources* is undermined by his comments elsewhere which, as I have shown, point to the restrictive nature of his theism and, by implication, his epiphanies.

any for his own theistic purposes, but he cannot therefore endorse its non-theistic form as explicated in Joyce's works. Indeed, quite the contrary is the case. As we have seen, Taylor mentions a number of modernist writers who engage in epiphanic art and James Joyce is approvingly included amongst them, but this does not sit comfortably with Taylor's desire for a theistic or theophanic epiphany, which plays no part in the Joycean epiphany.[57] Moreover, as we also saw earlier, we should not be surprised that Taylor is looking for moral sources outside the subject because he wants that moral source to be God and religion. Indeed, it is interesting that Taylor mentions the tradition alongside God as possible moral source, but that will not do at all given his restrictive theism. The tradition is not necessarily theistic or even religious as James Joyce as part of the modernist tradition amply proves. It follows then that these moral sources outside us that resonate within us need not be theistic, as Taylor would ultimately prefer. We can be called to something higher and greater through our common humanity, for example, rather than a calling from God, as the Joycean epiphany clearly shows us.

On this point it is interesting to note that Richard Rorty disagrees with Taylor's understanding and reading of the modernist writers he considers.[58] Rorty argues that a '"self-enclosed"' reading of modernist writers such as Eliot, Pound, Mann, Lawrence, Joyce, Proust or Rilke that Taylor opposes 'will do admirably' because these poets are 'edifying examples of how to be mere human self-fashioners, rather than as people who open us up to something other than themselves, and perhaps other than human'. In contrast, Taylor reads these writers as pointing to something such as God or the tradition, whereas Rorty reads them with the conviction that 'seriousness can, and should, swing free of any such universalistic belief'. Rorty is therefore endorsing I.A. Richards' view of poetry in opposition to Taylor. Against Rorty, I side with Taylor on the epiphanic route to transcendence that modernist writers offer.[59] In relation to Joyce, I

---

[57]   Taylor, *Sources of the Self*, p. 489

[58]   Richard Rorty, 'Taylor on Truth', in James Tully (ed.), *Philosophy in an Age of Pluralism: The Philosophy of Charles Taylor in Question*, Cambridge, Cambridge University Press, 1994, p. 20.

[59]   It is worth pointing out that Rorty's reading of Nabakov and Orwell, for example, does result in universals in that they are exemplars of Rorty's edict that 'cruelty is the worst thing we do'. See his *Contingency, Irony and Solidarity*, Cambridge, Cambridge University Press, 1989, p. xv. Cf. J.M. Bernstein, *The Fate of Art. Aesthetic Alienation from Kant to Derrida and Adorno*,

will show shortly that he was pointing to utopia rather than God, and that he offers what I call a democratisation of the aesthetic that links into my discussion of the aesthetic self in Chapter Seven. This importance arises because, as Nicholas H. Smith has noted, there is a perceived elitism in Taylor's emphasis on epiphanic art, and by implication this could also be levelled at my own notion of the aesthetic self.[60] As Smith indicates in relation to Taylor, such an emphasis on experiencing transcendent epiphanic moments through the great modernist writers is, sadly, the preserve of the few rather than the many. Despite this, Smith defends Taylor by arguing that his project could be expanded to encompass wider epiphanic sources in different mediums such as, for example, popular culture. Indeed, Taylor himself has intimated this possibility in an exchange with Mette Hjort, where he states that his 'discussion of certain nine-teenth- and twentieth-century works didn't involve a depreciation of today's popular art'.[61] Moreover, he further adds that his feelings about popular art are 'complex and many sided' and something he would need to reflect on further. So the apparent elitism present in Taylor's discussion is therefore open to question.

My concern, on the other hand, is to emphasise the importance of the democratisation of the aesthetic in so-called 'high art', which I want to explore through a consideration of Joyce's *Ulysses*. For Joyce, it is the mission of the artist, such as himself, to record epiphanies, but it is also the case that anyone can experience them.[62] The irony is not lost here in that Joyce is the supreme intellectual writer, and that *Ulysses* is not as accessible to all, albeit perhaps more so than the 'un-readable' *Finnegans Wake*.[63] However, my point is that Joyce is important because he points to the everyday ordinariness of life out of which arise epiphanic moments of utopia that are there for every-one to experience and share. Indeed, as Henri Lefebvre, who placed the everyday at the core of his Marxism notes, Joyce understood that the 'report of a day in the life of an ordinary man had to be predomi-

Cambridge, Polity, 1992, p. 286. n. .8, on the futility of Rorty's aversion to the universal in preference to remaining in the private realm.

[60] Nicholas H. Smith, *Charles Taylor. Meaning, Morals and Modernity*, Cambridge, Polity, 2002, p. 225.

[61] Taylor, 'Charles Taylor Replies', p. 243, in response to Mette Hjort, 'Literature: Romantic Expression or Strategic Interaction', both in James Tully (ed.), *Philosophy in an Age of Pluralism: The Philosophy of Charles Taylor in Question*, Cambridge, Cambridge University Press, 1994.

[62] Levin, *James Joyce*, p. 37.

[63] Seamus Deane, 'Introduction' to James Joyce, *Finnegans Wake*, London, Penguin, 1992, p. vii.

nantly in the epic mode'.[64] The epic and the everyday therefore go
hand in hand. Moreover, whilst I am utilising Joyce to develop a
notion of the democratisation of the aesthetic, Lefebvre's emphasis
on the everyday is important for the type of humanist Marxism I am
re-affirming in my discussion.[65] Lefebvre, himself, encapsulates my
point here when he states that:

> Should we admit for one moment that ... the plebeian substance
> of day-to-day living and the higher moments of life are forever
> separated, and that the two cannot be grasped as a unity and
> made to become part of life—then it will be the human that we
> are condemning.[66]

The everyday is dialectically linked with the extraordinary. To
suggest otherwise is to negate what makes us human, and forces us
to be complicit in our own alienation. As Joyce illustrates with the
character of Leopold Bloom in *Ulysses*, the ordinary man is anything
but ordinary. There is no such thing as trivial day, because we are all
caught up in a web of social relations that have huge consequences
for our own existence and that of others. Alienation is the ongoing
condition of this everyday life that must be exposed to critique for
the possibility of alienation being overcome. As Lefebvre correctly
points out, critique will reveal the 'human reality beneath this general unreality' in which the 'human "world" ... takes shape within
us and around us: in what we see, what we do, in humble objects and
(apparently) humble and profound feelings'.[67] Out of the supposed
ordinariness of everyday life we need to 'extract what is living, new,
positive—the worthwhile needs and fulfilments—from the negative
elements: the alienations', and contribute to the '*art of living*'.[68] On
that basis, I now turn to an exploration of the everyday in Joyce's
Ulysses.

---

[64]   Henri Lefebvre, *Critique of Everyday Life*, Volume 1, London and New York,
       Verso, 1991, p. 27.
[65]   Lefebvre states that the origins of a call to focus on the everyday emanated
       from Lenin's interpretation of Marx's analysis of capitalism. Lefebvre,
       Critique of Everyday Life, p. 3. V.I. Lenin, 'What the Friends of the People Are',
       in *Collected Works*, Volume 1, Moscow, Progress Publishers, 1963, p. 141,
       where Lenin says that 'the reason *Capital* has enjoyed such tremendous
       success is that the book by a "German economist" showed the whole
       capitalist social formation to the reader as a living thing—with its everyday
       aspects'. Lefebvre suggests that Lenin's error was in not linking the critique
       of everyday life to the concept of alienation.
[66]   Lefebvre, *Critique of Everyday Life*, p. 200.
[67]   Lefebvre, *Critique of Everyday Life*, p. 168.
[68]   Lefebvre, *Critique of Everyday Life*, pp. 42 & 199.

Utopian Epiphanies of Everyday Life

As I have said, Joyce believed that epiphanic moments were possible for all of us if we tried to discern them. Indeed, the incredibly democratic nature of Joyce's epiphanies is evinced in his almost 'prurient obsession with ordinariness' that particularly permeates *Ulysses*, which itself was 'one of the very first novels in English to portray what we would now call mass culture'.[69] Additionally, the work also captures the 'traditional culture of the people, from song and anecdote to jokes, pub talk, gossip, satirical invective and political wrangling'.[70] It is out of these surroundings that the now older Stephen Dedalus could declare: 'signatures of all things I am here to read'.[71] Everything is therefore open to interpretation and experience.

Taylor himself praises Joyce as one example of the trend in the rise of the modern novel in the twentieth century in its 'portrayal of the particular'.[72] He argues that these novels are typified by the fact that they departed from traditional plots and archetypical stories whilst placing less emphasis on universals. Instead, the universal now 'emerges out of the description of particular, situated people in their peculiarity, people with first names and surnames' such as Joyce's 'un-Irish-sounding "Daedelus"' (sic). Taylor praises Joyce here for having shown in our time how the great archetypical myths of the tradition can be reintegrated into the novel through this emphasis on the particular. In other words, Joyce epitomises the need to analyse the particular to arrive at the general. So nothing should be ruled out of the remit in identifying and experiencing epiphanies, especially the epiphanies of everyday life as Joyce encapsulates in his definition above where even 'vulgarity of speech' is seen as an epiphanic source. What, though, is Joyce pointing us towards through his epiphanies?

There is a utopian vision at the heart of Joyce's epiphanies that points to a different order of things,[73] and typifies the situation of Ireland at Joyce's time in that it seemed to combine the everyday and the esoteric.[74] Ireland was a land of scholasticism and spirituality, but it was also a land ravaged by war, famine and imperial occupation. The way out from this was to 'escape into idle fantasy or uto-

---

[69]　Eagleton, *The English Novel*, p. 283.
[70]　Eagleton, *The English Novel*, p. 283.
[71]　James Joyce, *Ulysses*, London, Penguin, 1992, p. 45.
[72]　Taylor, *Sources of the Self*, p. 287.
[73]　Eagleton, *The English Novel*, p. 297. Declan Kiberd, 'Introduction' to James Joyce, *Ulysses*, London, Penguin, 1992, pp. lxxix–lxxx.
[74]　Eagleton, *The English Novel*, p. 285.

pian idealism' and 'momentarily transcend' the 'meagreness of
everyday life', but only in 'jokes, art or anecdotes'.[75] However, language, whilst indicating impotence, also offers the possibility of
hope in that its sundering from existing impoverished conditions
can then be seen as 'prefiguring a reality that has yet to come to
birth'. Joyce's use of language offered a history of the Irish nation,
which in its 'playfulness and plurality' and 'multiple identities' 'pre-
figures an Ireland which is yet to come into being'. In *Ulysses*, for
example, Dublin is depicted as 'seedy and inert', but it is described in
a language that is so incredible it seems to be a portent for the future
where 'freedom and plurality, sexual emancipation and shifting
identities' are the norm.[76] In the writing of Joyce therefore is the presence of the 'transitory Now', to use Bloch's pertinent phrase.[77]

In the character of Leopold Bloom Joyce offers a multiple rather
than a single self in that he is, among other things, a Hungarian, Irish
Jew. Indeed, in the Cyclops Chapter the locals are so perplexed
about his fluid identity that one asks: 'is he a jew or a gentile or a holy
Roman or a swaddler or what the hell is he … Or who is he?'[78] In this
way, Joyce uses the character of Bloom to offer his own critique of
Irish national identity. The crude Irish nationalism that was typical
of the character of the citizen who is hostile to Bloom, is countered by
the latter's rejection of that form of nationalism which resulted in
persecution and in 'perpetuating national hatred among nations'.[79]
Indeed, Bloom further contends, that 'force hatred, history, all that.
That's not life for men and women, insult and hatred. And everybody knows that it's the very opposite of that that is really life' which
is 'love … the opposite of hatred'.[80] Against the crude nationalist
desire for one identity, Bloom shows that there is rather a 'field force
subject to constant re-negotiations; and no Irish mind, but Irish
minds shaped by a predicament which produces some common
characteristics in those caught up in it'.[81] Against the machismo culture of Ireland, Bloom is a 'new womanly man' challenging the

[75] Eagleton, *The English Novel*, p. 286.
[76] Eagleton, *The English Novel*, p. 297. Taylor makes a similar point in relation
      to *Finnegans Wake*, which he says, 'explores a level of experience in which
      the boundaries of personality become fluid'. Taylor, *Sources of the Self*,
      p. 463.
[77] Ernst Bloch, *The Principle of Hope*, Volume 1, Oxford, Basil Blackwell, 1986,
      p. 101.
[78] Joyce, *Ulysses*, p. 438.
[79] Joyce, *Ulysses*, p. 430.
[80] Joyce, *Ulysses*, p. 430.
[81] Kiberd, 'Introduction', p. lxxvii.

boundaries between male and female sexuality.[82] Bloom undermines accepted gender roles by making breakfast for his wife Molly,
taking it to her in bed, and obediently carrying out her orders.[83]
Moreover, his empathy with the female sex is what attracted Molly
to him in the first place as she herself says: 'I liked him because I saw
he understood or felt what a woman is'.[84] Bloom is the 'androgynous
man of the future' whose many-sided identity is 'tenuous and provi-
sional, everything and nothing'.[85] His 'sheer versatility seems like a
liberation' that is pointing to a different state of affairs.[86] Indeed, for
Joyce himself as exemplified in Bloom, the authentic being is therefore one who realises that the issue is not being true to one's self, 'but
the finding of the many selves that one might be true to'.[87] It follows
that a 'person or a nation has a plurality of identities, constantly
remaking themselves as a result of perpetual renewals'. Bloom is
therefore the 'humble vessel elected to bear and transmit
unimpeached the best qualities of the mind'.[88]

There is also a sense of the immortal and a pointing beyond that
pervades the book, and this is overtly discussed when Molly asks
Bloom what metempsychosis means.[89] Bloom unsuccessfully
attempts to explain it to Molly as the 'transmigration of souls', and
then remembering the term more simply as 'reincarnation', explains
to her that 'some people believe ... that we go on living in another
body after death, that we lived before'.[90] This is particularly encapsulated at the end of the *Circe* Chapter when Stephen realises that
Bloom is his surrogate Father and Bloom realises that Stephen is his
surrogate son.[91] This epiphanic moment for Bloom becomes manifest through the apparition of his dead son Rudy, who 'appears
slowly, a fairy boy of eleven, a changeling ... holding a book in his
hand', who 'gazes unseeing into Bloom's eyes and goes on reading,
kissing, smiling' and which leaves Bloom 'wonderstruck'. For Joyce,
'nothing is irreplaceable' as 'life passes into death and out of it

[82] Joyce, *Ulysses*, p. 614.
[83] Joyce, *Ulysses*, pp. 76–77.
[84] Joyce, *Ulysses*, p. 932.
[85] Kiberd, 'Introduction', p. l.
[86] Kiberd, 'Introduction', p. lxxviii.
[87] Kiberd, 'Introduction', p. lxxvii.
[88] Richard Ellman, *James Joyce*, Oxford, New York, Toronto, Melbourne,
      Oxford University Press, 1983, p. 5.
[89] Joyce, *Ulysses*, p. 77.
[90] Joyce, *Ulysses*, p. 78.
[91] Joyce, *Ulysses*, pp. 702–703.

again'.[92] On that basis, *Ulysses* itself 'is an endlessly open book of utopian epiphanies' that reflected the realities of colonial Dublin of 16 June 1904, whilst also offering 'redemptive glimpses of a future world which might be made over in terms of those utopian moments'.[93]

Conclusion

Taylor's attempt to widen the Joycean epiphany seems, on examination, only to have led to a restrictive theistic epiphany given his religious leanings. The richness of the Joycean epiphany pointing beyond to a utopia of a different order of things as evinced in *Ulysses*, is an indication of the democratisation of the aesthetic of everyday life that I want to develop further in Chapter Seven, and link in with the notion of a politicised aesthetic that is present in movements opposed to capitalism. Next, I want to further examine Taylor's understanding of art where we will find the haunting spectre of Marxism in the form of Theodor Adorno.

[92] Terry Eagleton, *Sweet Violence. The Idea of the Tragic*, Oxford, Blackwell, 2003, p. 199.
[93] Kiberd, 'Introduction', p. lxxx.

Chapter Five

Art: The Presence of Adorno

Art can conceive reconciliation, which is its idea, only as the reconciliation of what has been estranged.[1]

Art plays a fundamental role in Charles Taylor's account of the making of the modern identity, as we have just seen in the previous Chapter.[2] One interesting figure that Taylor sees as crucial in relation to art is Theodor Adorno, but the presence of Adorno in Taylor's thought has gone largely unnoticed by commentators on the latter.[3] In one sense this is not surprising given Taylor's brief discussion of Adorno and art in *Sources of the Self*. However, on closer inspection Taylor's account raises a number of important issues both in relation to his own thought and in his reading, or at times misreading, of Adorno. To this end, I therefore seek to examine and contrast the positions of both writers, and ultimately expose similarities and differences whilst also trying to defend Adorno against Taylor. Taylor praises Adorno for his attack on instrumentalism and for his emphasis on epiphanic art as a source of the good. He also supports Adorno's pessimism, but he ultimately rejects Adorno for his anthropocentrism, subjectivism and lack of theism. I therefore examine Adorno's understanding of the subject-object relation in aesthetic theory, and, whilst agreeing with Taylor that Adorno

---

[1] Theodor Adorno, 'Trying to Understand *Endgame'*, in *Notes to Literature* Vol. 1, New York, Columbia University Press, 1991, p. 250.

[2] Charles Taylor, *Sources of the Self. The Making of the Modern Identity*, Cambridge, Cambridge University Press, 1989, p. 419.

[3] The brief exceptions that I comment on later are Nicholas. H. Smith, *Charles Taylor. Meaning, Morals and Modernity*, Cambridge, Polity, 2002, pp. 202 & 220 and J.M. Bernstein, *The Fate of Art. Aesthetic Alienation from Kant to Derrida and Adorno*, Cambridge, Polity, 1992, p. 8.

rejects theism, this should be seen as positive rather than negative. Indeed, Taylor's dismissal of Adorno on this issue further exposes the restrictive and superior air to Taylor's own theism, as he also fails to see the rich religious dimension to Adorno's thought. Finally, I respond to Habermas' critique of both Taylor and Adorno on epiphanies and the relation between aesthetics and philosophy. In doing so, I show that Taylor's views on art are far closer to Adorno's than he is prepared to admit, and that together their work presents a strong case for the emancipatory potential of art.

Taylor on Adorno: For and Against

Taylor argues that there are two aspects to Adorno's approach to art.[4] On the one hand, he sees Adorno as a Romantic who believes that reason and sensibility can be fully reconciled. On the other hand, he also sees him endorsing the modernist rupture of previous art forms because they resulted in an opening up of human experience. For Adorno, modernist art broke through the reification of society, and in doing so offered a deeply critical perspective on reality that revealed possible moments of redemption. Even so, Taylor argues that because Adorno witnessed the 'traumatic period of disappointment of the Marxist hope', he did not think that total fulfilment was possible and this accounts for the pessimistic nature of his thought. However, it is precisely this pessimism that Taylor has great sympathy with because it offers an 'undistorted recognition of conflict between goods'.[5] So Taylor shares with Adorno the view that there is a pessimism that makes us question that total spiritual fulfilment can be achieved, but the moment of optimism is that it is through art that we can see aspects of this possible fulfilment, which makes liberation possible and offers us the prospect of redemption.

The second aspect of Adorno's approach to art that Taylor fully endorses is the presence of epiphanies. As I pointed out in the previous Chapter, for Taylor, a work of art is epiphanic when it brings us into contact with something that is not readily accessible, and is of the highest moral or spiritual significance. He prefers the framing or interspatial epiphany because of the way it allows the spiritual or moral realisation to emerge from a work of art, which acts as a vortex or constellation of words or images. When he considers those who have advocated epiphanic art, he notes how they have generally been hostile towards the development of commercial-indus-

[4] Taylor, *Sources of the Self*, pp. 477–478
[5] Taylor, *Sources of the Self*, p. 506.

trial-capitalist society, and he cites thinkers such as Schiller, Marx, Marcuse, Adorno, Blake, Baudelaire, Pound and Eliot, in this regard.[6] For Taylor, these writers have contrasted the epiphanic with our ordinary experiences of the world as 'out of joint, dead or forsaken'. The link between them is that they are all opposed to seeing and experiencing the world in a mechanistic and instrumental manner. In relation to Adorno, Taylor singles him out as 'an interesting case in point' as a twentieth century writer in whose works the interspatial or framing epiphany is present.[7] For Taylor, its presence is part of Adorno's idea of 'constellation', which the latter appropriated from Walter Benjamin.[8] Taylor argues that for Adorno reconciliation or fulfilment is only possible by articulating concepts as universals. In this way, we would be able to 'name' things, a term Adorno borrows from the Kabbalist tradition, but as Taylor points out, because the universal hides aspects of the particular such reconciliation and naming is not possible. Taylor maintains therefore that even though naming things is not possible we can 'frame them in "constellations", such as clusters of terms and images whose mutual affinity creates a space in which the particular can emerge'. The Adorno constellation approach, continues Taylor, aims towards full reconciliation and also gives it a degree of presence in our lives. So on two fronts then, a pessimistic optimism and the presence of interspatial or framing epiphanies, Taylor and Adorno are at one, but Taylor decides he must ultimately reject Adorno's approach for three reasons. First, because it is 'entirely anthropocentric'. Second, because it is subjectivist, and third because it is closed to any theistic perspective. I now want to examine these criticisms in turn.

Anthropocentrism

Taylor argues that Adorno's approach must be rejected because it is still 'entirely anthropocentric, and treats all goods which are not anchored in human powers or fulfilments as illusions from a bygone age'.[9] As such, this means that it cannot have a place for the kind of non-anthropocentric exploration of sources that has been, according to Taylor, an important part of modernist art, in writers such as Rilke, Proust, Mann, Eliot or Kafka. However, Taylor's use of the word 'entirely' is far too strong in relation to Adorno on the issue of

---

[6]   Taylor, *Sources of the Self*, p. 422.
[7]   Taylor, *Sources of the Self*, p. 477.
[8]   Taylor, *Sources of the Self*, p. 478.
[9]   Taylor, *Sources of the Self*, p. 506.

anthropocentrism. Both Adorno and Horkheimer in *Dialectic of Enlightenment* were very critical of the anthropocentric nature of Enlightenment thought that allowed nature and nonhuman animals to be treated instrumentally.[10] Indeed, they linked the latter to the incessant atomisation of human beings that resulted in a repressive totalitarianism,[11] and was therefore a just punishment by nature in response to the merciless plundering it had suffered for many generations.[12] Adorno and Horkheimer therefore rejected a positive anthropology[13], and Adorno himself liked to be called an antihumanist precisely because he feared that anthropocentricity would imply the denigration of the natural world.[14] On this basis, it is therefore difficult to see how Taylor can describe Adorno as being 'entirely anthropocentric'.

Subjectivism

Taylor's second criticism against Adorno's position is that it is tied to subjectivism, and thereby offers a reductive account of the explorations of modernist artists, which is only concerned with the expressive fulfilment of the subject.[15] For Taylor, as we saw in the last Chapter, it is the overcoming of such subjectivity that is the most important aspect of epiphanic art.[16] He argues therefore that the anti-subjectivism of modernist works, particularly of the authors mentioned previously, is the reason why they profoundly influence us and also why they have lasted. By implication, then, the subjectivism of Adorno misses these important aspects of the works of these modernist writers, according to Taylor. But what Taylor ignores here is that Adorno's aesthetic theory is an attempt to articulate the 'primacy of the object in art', and to criticise subjectivist theories of aesthetics that he perceived were present in Kant and even Hegel.[17] Adorno therefore puts forward a 'dialectical aesthetics' that criticises subjectivism because it centres on individual taste, and

---

[10] Theodor Adorno & Max Horkheimer, *Dialectic of Enlightenment*, London, Verso, 1992, pp. 245–246. Cf. Martin Jay, *The Dialectical Imagination. A History of the Frankfurt School and the Institute of Social Research 1923–1950*, London, Heinemann, 1973, pp. 256–257.

[11] Jay, *The Dialectical Imagination*, p. 261.

[12] Jay, *The Dialectical Imagination*, pp. 256–257.

[13] Jay, *The Dialectical Imagination*, p. 266.

[14] Jay, *The Dialectical Imagination*, pp. 348–349. n. 45.

[15] Taylor, *Sources of the Self*, p. 506.

[16] Taylor, *Sources of the Self*, p. 429.

[17] Theodor Adorno, *Aesthetic Theory*, London, Athlone, 1997, p. 109. Cf. Simon Jarvis, *Adorno. A Critical Introduction*, Cambridge, Polity, 1998, p. 99.

criticises objectivism because it ignores how the subject is mediated by the objectivity of art.[18] It follows that Adorno's 'dialectical aesthetics' understands the subject-object relation in artworks as a delicate balance that both inform each other. The observer of an artwork engages in a dialectical process whereby the more he or she adds to this process, the greater becomes the energy to penetrate it and gain a sense of objectivity from within.[19] Adorno realises, similarly to Taylor, that there is a subjective aspect to this process but also emphasises, again as Taylor does, how 'the subjective detour may totally miss the mark, but without the detour no objectivity becomes evident'. For Adorno, the one-sided slide into subjectivism must be rejected because it can only result in philistinism. Artworks therefore need to be understood by the subject as a dialectical process of becoming between its whole and its parts in which the parts are 'centres of energy that strain toward the whole' in a 'vortex' that 'ultimately consumes the concept of meaning'.[20] The epiphanic moment here for Adorno lies with the fact that in every work of art there is a spiritual aspect, which is in a process of development and formation and 'integrated into an overarching process of spiritualization: that of the progress of consciousness'.[21] Adorno's 'dialectical aesthetics' does not therefore remain tied to subjectivism and instead puts us in contact with an objective source, with spirit, which in turn through our interaction with it leads to our own spiritual development and growth.

This pointing to something outside the subject, which Taylor sees as essential, is further evinced in Adorno's contention that artworks say 'more' than what they are.[22] This 'more' appears in the form of a 'crackling noise' that is an 'other', which is mediated through a nexus of elements from which it is also divided.[23] For Adorno, artworks are paradoxical because what they posit they are actually not permitted to posit, which is what constitutes their substantiality. The substantiality of artworks is where the moment of transcendence emerges, and there is a movement beyond the appearance of what they are to something higher.[24] If art cannot achieve this transcendence then Adorno suggests it can no longer be considered to be

[18]   Adorno, *Aesthetic Theory*, p. 166.
[19]   Adorno, *Aesthetic Theory*, p. 175.
[20]   Adorno, *Aesthetic Theory*, p. 178.
[21]   Adorno, *Aesthetic Theory*, pp. 91–92.
[22]   Adorno, *Aesthetic Theory*, p. 78.
[23]   Adorno, *Aesthetic Theory*, p. 79.
[24]   Adorno, *Aesthetic Theory*, p. 78.

art. Indeed, Adorno continues, artworks can only be truly spiritual when they achieve transcendence, and although such transcendence is mediated subjectively it manifests itself objectively. Artworks offer the 'remembered shudder' through which they become 'qualitatively transformed epiphanies', which as *'apparition'* or the 'heavenly vision ... rises above human beings and is carried beyond their intentions and the world of things'.[25] Taylor is therefore mistaken in depicting Adorno as being tied to subjectivism. For both Adorno and Taylor, aesthetic experience is a matter of transcendence through our contact with works of art. The 'more' in art for Adorno is encapsulated in Taylor's contention, as I mentioned in the previous Chapter, that art can 'say the otherwise unsayable' and therefore realise an epiphany. Consequently, it is therefore difficult to see how J.M. Bernstein can argue that what divides Adorno from Taylor is that for the former 'access to sources of meaning beyond the self are therefore blocked' whereas for the latter they are not.[26]

Such a pointing to something beyond is further captured by Adorno's notion of utopia, which Taylor also fails to mention. Ironically, Taylor's point, as we noted earlier about the instrumentalisation of society and those who have opposed it, shines through in Adorno's comment that 'in the midst of a world dominated by utility, art indeed has a utopic aspect as the other of this world, as exempt from the mechanism of the social process of production and reproduction'.[27] For Adorno, capitalism reduces everything to commodification, and only art offers the possibility of breaking through such commodification. As he explains further, 'every artwork must ask itself if and how it can exist as utopia: always only through the constellation of its elements'. So artworks are bringing us into contact with something beyond ourselves because 'the constellation of the existing and nonexisting is the utopic figure of art'.[28] We are therefore groping towards the 'nonexisting' in and through the 'existing' and although art 'is compelled toward absolute negativity, it is precisely by virtue of this negativity that it is not absolutely negative'.[29] Adorno offers therefore what has been referred to as a

---

[25]   Adorno, *Aesthetic Theory*, p. 80. Cf. Shierry Weber Nicholsen, *Exact Imagination, Late Work on Adorno's Aesthetics*, Cambridge, Mass, & London, MIT Press, 1997, pp. 23–24.
[26]   See Bernstein, *The Fate of Art*, p. 8.
[27]   Adorno, *Aesthetic Theory*, p. 311.
[28]   Adorno, *Aesthetic Theory*, p. 312.
[29]   Adorno, *Aesthetic Theory*, p. 233.

'utopian negativity',[30] and as we have seen, Taylor is attracted to Adorno because of this pessimistic optimism that he thinks art displays. Adorno is keeping us alert to the fact that we must be constantly searching for utopia rather than think we have achieved it, which is why for him 'the new is the longing for the new, not the new itself'.[31] Indeed, for Adorno, 'art is the ever broken promise of happiness', but it is the searching for this happiness in an instrumental world that is important for our spiritual fulfilment.[32] In this sense, aesthetic experience 'is possibility promised by its impossibility' because 'art holds fast to the promise of reconciliation in the midst of the unreconciled'.[33] For Adorno, then, hope in the form of redemption lies not in politics or in some social movement, but in art where, as Jay puts it, the 'faint heartbeat of utopia' can be heard 'amidst the deafening cacophony of contemporary culture'.[34] This chimes nicely with Taylor's concern for the possibility of redemption and a critical and sceptical air towards existing reality, and, as we have seen, this is exactly what is attracting Taylor to Adorno in the first place.

Theism

The final criticism Taylor makes against Adorno is that the latter's approach 'is closed to any theistic perspective'[35] even though Taylor is prepared to leave the 'issue of theism aside'.[36] Given that theism plays such an important role in Taylor's thought as a crucial moral source that cannot be wished away or ignored this is a major concession, but Taylor only does so because he thinks he can undermine Adorno on the issue of subjectivism. I have defended Adorno on the issue of subjectivism earlier. The point I want to make here is that in dismissing Adorno for his lack of theism, Taylor ignores the positive role non-theistic religion plays in Adorno's thought. Taylor's own restrictive theism seems to hamper an open engagement with a thinker that, as we have seen, he shares some important arguments with. To this end, I here explore the role of religion in Adorno's thought and show that there are interesting comparisons that can be made with Taylor's position, albeit from a non-theistic perspective.

[30] Jarvis, *Adorno*, p. 222.
[31] Adorno, *Aesthetic Theory*, p. 32.
[32] Adorno, *Aesthetic Theory*, p. 136.
[33] Adorno, *Aesthetic Theory*, p. 33.
[34] Martin Jay, *Adorno*, Cambridge, Mass, Harvard University Press, 1984, p. 109.
[35] Taylor, *Sources of the Self*, p. 506
[36] Taylor, *Sources of the Self*, p. 429.

The role of religion in Adorno's though has not gone unnoticed amongst commentators. For instance, some have noted 'Adorno's interest in Jewish theological motifs' and have even gone as far to say that 'theology is always moving right under the surface of all of Adorno's writings'.[37] Indeed, Martin Jay contends that a 'Jewish impulse'[38] forms one of the five constellations that typify Adorno's thought.[39] Jay points out that Adorno, half-Jewish by birth, and who had indeed played with idea of adopting his Mother's Catholicism, began to appreciate the implications of his Jewish heritage whilst in exile and particularly after Auschwitz.[40] Whilst the Holocaust certainly brought about pessimism and despair for Adorno, it is also the case that his Jewishness played a more positive role in his thought. For example, he declared that philosophy practised 'in the face of despair' must 'attempt to contemplate all things as they would present themselves from the standpoint of redemption'.[41] 'Perspectives must be fashioned', Adorno urges, 'that displace and estrange the world, reveal it to be, with its rifts and crevices, as indigent and distorted as it will appear one day in messianic light'. Adorno holds to what Jay calls a 'reverse messianism' in that evil events such as Auschwitz or Hiroshima act as ruptures in the course of history which are the obverse of messianic interventions.[42] To talk of 'after Auschwitz', therefore, holds the same significance for Adorno as AD does for a Christian. On the other hand, Adorno also realised that messianic interventions could be benign as is evinced by his emphasis on the importance of redemption as mentioned above. What he was careful to avoid was an unbridled optimism in historical development as demonstrated in his comment that 'no universal history leads from savagery to humanitarianism, but there is one leading from the slingshot to the atomic bomb'.[43] It follows then that the 'hope for better circumstances — if it is not a mere illusion — is not so much based on the assurance that these circumstances would be

---

[37] Anson Rabinbach, '"Why were the Jews Sacrificed?" The Place of Antisemitism in Adorno and Horkheimer's *Dialectic of Enlightenment*', in Nigel Gibson and Andrew Rubin (eds.), *Adorno: A Critical Reader*, Oxford, Blackwell, 2002, pp. 137–138.

[38] Martin Jay, *Adorno*, Cambridge, Mass, Harvard University Press, 1984, p. 19.

[39] Jay, *Adorno*, p. 15.

[40] Jay, *Adorno*, p. 19.

[41] Theodor Adorno, *Minima Moralia. Reflections from Damaged Life*, London, Verso, 1978, p. 247.

[42] Jay, *Adorno*, p. 108.

[43] Theodor Adorno, *Negative Dialectics*, London, Routledge, 1990, p. 320.

guaranteed, durable and final, but on the lack of respect for all that is so firmly rooted in the general suffering'.[44] This is why 'Christianity, idealism, and materialism' although containing 'truth, are therefore also responsible for the barbaric acts perpetrated in their name'.[45]

There are some interesting parallels that can be drawn between Taylor and Adorno here. As we have seen, the distorted view of the world that Adorno has is what attracts Taylor to his work. Taylor, like Adorno, is wary of thinking that full redemption is possible. Rather he looks to art in particular to point towards moments of full redemption. Similarly, Taylor is not myopic when looking at the effects of Christianity throughout history. Indeed, he states explicitly that 'it is very evident that we have reason to fear the Christian faith' because 'we have reason to fear any belief which holds out hope of major transformation in human life', but he is adamant that by putting our faith in something that does give us fear is the only way to continue to have hope for humanity as a whole.[46] So just as Christianity can contain moments of truth, as Adorno recognises, it can also contain moments of barbarism, as Adorno also recognises. So too does Taylor. Taylor is fully aware of the disastrous consequences Christianity can usher in, not least historically with the Inquisition.[47] As we have seen in previous Chapters, he also recognises that the age that produced the barbarism of Hiroshima and Auschwitz, has also produced Amnesty International and Médecins sans Frontières, the Christian roots of which run deep. This is why Taylor's hope for a better world is in the Judaeo-Christian theistic tradition, despite some of its barbaric consequences.

The religious dimension to Adorno's thought takes a further interesting twist when writing with Horkheimer in *Dialectic of Enlightenment* where they offer a far more positive view of Judaism rather than Christianity. Adorno and Horkheimer note that as enunciating the name of God is not allowed in Jewish religion, the link between name and being is therefore still recognised.[48] This results in the 'destruction of myth' because the 'disenchanted world of Judaism conciliates magic by negating it in the idea of God'. In this way, the 'Jews succeeded where Christianity failed: they diffused magic by its own

[44]   Adorno & Horkheimer, *Dialectic of Enlightenment*, pp. 224–225.
[45]   Adorno & Horkheimer, *Dialectic of Enlightenment*, p. 224.
[46]   Charles Taylor, 'Charles Taylor Replies', in James Tully, (ed.), *Philosophy in an Age of Pluralism*, Cambridge, Cambridge University Press, 1994, p. 225.
[47]   Taylor, 'A Catholic Modernity?', p. 18.
[48]   Adorno & Horkheimer, *Dialectic of Enlightenment*, p. 23.

power—turned against itself as ritual service of God'.[49] In contrast, Christianity humanised God in the form of Christ, which led to idolatry and the intellectualisation of magic. Indeed, Judaism offers further advantages for Adorno and Horkheimer in their response to the Olympian myth. They argue that whereas the Olympian myth is self-contained within a natural cycle of retribution and fate, the Jewish God, whilst representing this natural cycle, can also free us from it and, through the 'concept of grace', offer the 'messianic promise'.[50] In this way, Adorno and Horkheimer could assert that 'reconciliation is the highest notion of Judaism, and expectation is its whole meaning',[51] which implies that for them Judaism offers the 'possibility of a radically different world'.[52] For Adorno, then, Judaism is preferable to Christianity whereas for Taylor, as we have just seen, both Judaism and Christianity can act as sources of the good. However, the notion of grace mentioned above also figures in Taylor's own Catholicism when he says we must open ourselves to God's grace, which means affirming human flourishing and is encapsulated in the notion of agape, as we saw in Chapter Two. So the 'messianic promise' mediated through grace in Adorno's work is reflected in Taylor's endorsement of agape.

Adorno also offers a pertinent examination of the relation between art and religion. On the one hand, he argues that the unity between art and religion that had existed historically was now lost, even though there is still a desire for that unity because there is a need to understand a culture endangered by collective alienation and a lack of meaning.[53] For Adorno, the aim of uniting art and religion is precisely a 'romantic projection into the past of the desire for organic, nonalienated relations between men'.[54] On the other hand, he insists that the separation between art and religion that has occurred historically, should not let us forget the fruitful unity that they had with each other, and which contributed so much to the productive imagination.[55] Adorno argues that all artworks display a moment of their magical origin, and if they did not it would signal

---

[49] Adorno & Horkheimer, *Dialectic of Enlightenment*, p. 186.
[50] Adorno & Horkheimer, *Dialectic of Enlightenment*, p. 177. Cf. Lambert Zuidervaart, *Adorno's Aesthetic Theory. The Redemption of Illusion*, Cambridge, Mass & London, MIT Press, p. 163.
[51] Adorno & Horkheimer, *Dialectic of Enlightenment*, p. 199.
[52] Jarvis, *Adorno*, p. 64. Cf. Zuidervaart, *Adorno's Aesthetic Theory*, p. 163.
[53] Theodor Adorno, 'Theses upon Art and Religion', in *Notes to Literature* Vol. 2, New York, Columbia University Press, 1992, p. 292.
[54] Adorno, 'Theses upon Art and Religion', p. 293.
[55] Adorno, 'Theses upon Art and Religion', p. 296.

the decline of art. This magic is to be found in 'traits such as the spell cast by any true work of art, the halo of its uniqueness, its inherent claim to represent something absolute'. Consequently, Adorno admits that whilst the dichotomy between art and religion is 'irreversible', he also maintains that it 'cannot be naively regarded as something final and ultimate'.[56] In other words, a religious moment can reside in great epiphanic works of art for Adorno just as it can do for Taylor. To see how this is the case it is interesting to consider a writer whom both Taylor and Adorno deeply admire, namely, Marcel Proust.

For Taylor, Proust's epiphany in the final volume of *Remembrance of Things Past* disrupts normal narrativity, because it links epiphanic moments together at different points in time that can only be understood through memory.[57] It is through, what Taylor calls, the Proustian framing or "intertemporal" epiphany that this recovery and unity occurs.[58] Taylor points out that the Proustian epiphany is linked to an experience, such as the madeleine or the uneven pavement, which is realised not at the time of the experience, but later through a recurrence or something that 'triggers off the memory'. He argues that for Proust, the epiphany is initially hindered by the original experience so it is 'only when we recall it in memory can we see behind it to what was revealed through it'. It follows then that the 'epiphany can't be seen *in* an object but has to be framed *between* an event and its recurrence, through memory', according to Taylor's interpretation of Proust. Taylor therefore understands Proust's "temps perdu" as referring to 'time which is both wasted and irretrievably lost, beyond recall, in which we pass as if we had never been',[59] whilst also realising that recovering these moments from the past, which appear "wasted" time, can be brought into a unity with immortality or the 'life yet to live'.[60]

The emphasis on memory and immortality is also central to Adorno's reading of Proust. Adorno argues that a reader of a passage from Proust 'feels addressed by it as by an inherited memory, an image that suddenly flashes out, perhaps in a foreign city, an image that one's parents must have seen long before one's own

[56] Adorno, 'Theses upon Art and Religion', p. 297.
[57] Taylor, *Sources of the Self*, p. 464.
[58] Taylor, *Sources of the Self*, p. 479.
[59] Taylor, *Sources of the Self*, p. 43.
[60] Taylor, *Sources of the Self*, p. 51.

birth'.[61] In this sense, Adorno interprets Proust as using memory to overcome ageing and death aesthetically.[62] For example, Proust's 'obsession with the concrete and the unique, with the taste of a madeleine or the colour of the shoes of a lady worn at a certain party', materialises a 'truly theological idea, that of immortality'.[63] For Adorno, Proust's 'concentration upon opaque and quasi-blind details through which [he] achieves that "remembrance of things past"' means he 'undertook to brave death by breaking the power of oblivion engulfing every individual life'. In a 'non-religious world' Proust 'took the phrase of immortality literally and tried to salvage life, as an image, from the throes of death ... by concentrating on the utterly mortal'. There is, then, a spiritual dimension to Proust's writings that both Adorno and Taylor recognise. For Taylor, contact with a Proustian epiphany results in a 'great moral and spiritual significance', which offers us a kind of 'depth, or fullness, or seriousness, or intensity of life, or to a certain wholeness' and brings about a change in identity.[64] For Adorno, reeling from the instrumentalisation of society, art is the only refuge from where these qualities could be inculcated on the path to a transcendent immortality.

It also has to be pointed out here that whilst Taylor and Adorno both recognise the religious moment in epiphanic art, Taylor ultimately goes one step further. As we saw earlier, Taylor puts a tremendous emphasis on religion and ultimately God as a source of the good that can be accessed through epiphanic art, and is why he eventually puts forward a religious theistic epiphany that gives people access to the divine. Taylor therefore seems to be operating with a more restrictive theistic epiphany than Adorno would allow for, but it is Adorno that is closer to Proust than Taylor. For example, in a discussion of Ruskin, Proust recognised the 'religious fervour' that 'guided his aesthetic feelings'.[65] However, Proust decided to 'retain the divine without religion' from Ruskin's work, and although he inherited Ruskin's love for Christian art he did so 'without the faith'.[66] There is therefore a spiritual dimension to Proust's writings that both Adorno and Taylor recognise, but it is not pointing just to

[61] Theodor Adorno, 'On Proust', in *Notes to Literature* Vol. 2, New York, Columbia University Press, 1992, p. 315.
[62] Adorno, 'On Proust', p. 317.
[63] Adorno, 'Theses upon Art and Religion', pp. 297–298.
[64] Taylor, *Sources of the Self*, p. 422.
[65] Jean-Eves Tadié, *Marcel Proust. A Life*, Harmondsworth, Viking, 2000, p. 360.
[66] Tadié, *Marcel Proust*, p. 361.

God, as Taylor would like us to believe, and which again exposes his restrictive theism.

Habermas' Critique

Standing in the way of my attempt to elide the epiphanic aspects of Taylor and Adorno on art is Jürgen Habermas. In total contradiction to my argument, Habermas cites Adorno, and also Derrida it should be added, as authorities for the argument that modern art can no longer be deemed to be epiphanic.[67] For Habermas, 'modern art can no longer be tapped as a source of the moral' because, following Schlegel, the 'aesthetic' tears itself loose from the good and the true'.[68] Indeed, Habermas pushes his argument further here, and suggests that even if we could accept an ethical basis to modernist aesthetics the implications for philosophy would be 'of a *renunciatory* nature'. This is because, according to Habermas, philosophy would become itself aesthetic or be reduced to aesthetic criticism, and would therefore 'have to abandon any pretension to convince on the basis of its *own* arguments'. Habermas suggests that Adorno also faced this problem and developed a negative dialectics in response to it, but asserts that such a response is not open to Taylor because the latter's 'philosophical goal' is to bring a 'modern ethics of the good to bear *within* the discourse of experts'.[69]

If we take the epiphanic point first, it is fairly clear from the preceding discussion that Adorno is emphasising the epiphanic in relation to art. He sees art as a source of the good that is pointing beyond the world of things to a transcendent 'heavenly vision' and the object of utopia. His constellation approach, which Taylor endorses, is the groping towards this epiphanic moment of *possible* fulfilment. Moreover, the utopian moment in Adorno's discussion of art is its redemptive character, which Habermas completely ignores in Adorno's thought and in so doing puts a false dichotomy between

---

[67]   Jürgen Habermas, *Justification and Application*, Cambridge, Polity, 1993, p. 74, who draws on Christoph Menke, *The Sovereignty of Art. Aesthetic Negativity in Adorno and Derrida*, Cambridge, Mass & London, MIT Press, 1998. Cf. Smith, *Charles Taylor*, pp. 226–7.

[68]   Habermas, *Justification and Application*, p. 74.

[69]   Habermas, *Justification and Application*, p. 75.

the latter and Taylor.[70] As we have seen, Taylor explicitly endorses Adorno's emphasis on redemption.

What, though, can Habermas mean when he says that Adorno, unlike Taylor, has recourse to negative dialectics when faced with the relation between philosophy and aesthetics? Habermas leaves this stated rather than explained, so we have to go to his *Philosophical Discourse of Modernity* to discover his meaning here. Habermas describes negative dialectics as 'identity thinking turned against itself', which 'becomes pressed into continual self-denial and allows the wounds it inflicts on itself and its objects to be seen'.[71] Negative dialectics therefore offers a 'groundless reflection turned against itself that preserves our connection with the utopia of a long since lost, uncoerced and intuitive knowledge belonging to the primal past'. For Habermas, Adorno's negative dialectics results in an 'aesthetically certified, residual faith in a de-ranged reason that has been expelled from the domains of philosophy and become, literally, utopian [having no place]'. Consequently, Habermas sees Adorno as retreating from philosophy into aesthetics through his negative dialectics and thereby abandoning the importance of reason.[72] For Habermas' procedural ethics, of course, reason is crucially placed as 'part of a more encompassing *communicative rationality*'.[73]

To agree with Habermas first, he is correct to say that Adorno's negative dialectics involves 'identity thinking turned against itself' but what exactly does that mean? Adorno argues that to 'define identity as the correspondence of the thing-in-itself to its concept is *hubris*; but the ideal of identity must not simply be discarded'.[74] This is because definition 'approaches that which the object itself is as nonidentical' and the latter is the 'secret *telos* of identification'. So the act of identification must be an act that involves nonidentification, otherwise identification becomes ideological because it is mistakenly assumed that a thing or object is identical with its concept. It follows therefore that 'identity is the primal form of ideology' because

[70] See Peter Uwe Hohendahl, *Prismatic Thought. Theodor W. Adorno*, Lincoln & London, University of Nebraska Press, 1995, p. 251 for this criticism of Habermas in relation to redemption.

[71] Jürgen Habermas, *The Philosophical Discourse of Modernity*, Cambridge, Polity, 1992, p. 186.

[72] Jürgen Habermas, *The Theory of Communicative Action Vol. 1. Reason and the Rationalisation of Society*, Cambridge, Polity, 1984, pp. 385 & 390.

[73] Habermas, *Theory of Communicative Action*, p. 390.

[74] Adorno, *Negative Dialectics*, p. 149.

it conceals contradictions rather than exposing them.[75] Now as we saw earlier, Adorno emphasises a 'constellation' approach that highlights the difficulty of naming things and instead understands things as clusters of terms or images, but it is this approach that Taylor explicitly endorses as part of his interspatial or framing epiphany, and which he also pinpoints in Adorno's work. It is a way in which a space can open that allows a particular to emerge and point towards the universal. For instance, when Adorno considers the relationship between a work of art to the universal he suggests that such a relationship is indirect.[76] He argues that the work of art can be compared to Leibniz's 'monad' which '"represents" the universe, but it has no windows' because it 'represents the universal within its own walls'. The work of art or 'monad' therefore relates to the universal by not immediately relating to it. Instead, the work of art needs to emphasise the particular and in this way 'truly become the bearer of the universal'. As we have seen, this is precisely the type of approach to art that Taylor is agreeing with, but Habermas suggests this recourse to negative dialectics is not open to Taylor because his 'philosophical goal' is to bring a modern ethics of the good to bear *within* the discourse of experts'. However, Taylor explicitly rejects this demarcation between philosophy and aesthetics and in doing so criticises Habermas.[77] Taylor argues that 'we delude ourselves if we think that philosophical or critical language ... is somehow more hard-edged and more free from personal index than that of poets or novelists'. For Taylor, we need to explore moral sources in art with language rooted in 'personal resonance' or 'not at all'. On that basis, he criticises Habermas' own proceduralist ethics, which abandons an exploration of these moral sources via this route as being far too narrow. Taylor maintains that it is only through 'exploring the human predicament, the way we are set in nature and among others, as a locus of moral sources' that we begin to clarify some of the most pressing issues of our existence. Indeed, in a response to Habermas on behalf of Taylor, Nicholas H. Smith argues that the moral sources Taylor points to are not some kind of philosophical proofs or judgements that can be assessed by science or common sense.[78] Instead, argues Smith, contact with these moral sources is rather an 'achievement of the spirit'. The purpose of epiphanic artworks for Taylor is

---

[75]   Adorno, *Negative Dialectics*, p. 148.
[76]   Adorno, 'Theses upon Art and Religion', p. 297.
[77]   Taylor, *Sources of the Self*, p. 512.
[78]   Smith, *Charles Taylor*, p. 226.

that they are 'bringing about or constituting a certain quality of experience, and beyond that, a way of seeing that orients a form of life'. This may not do for a hard-nosed rationalist such as Habermas but it will certainly do for Taylor and Adorno.

Conclusion

My justification for examining the presence of Adorno in Taylor's discussion of art should now be clear. I have shown how Taylor positively identifies with the pessimistic hopefulness of Adorno's approach which, undetected by Taylor, is captured in the notion of negative utopia, in that as we question whether we can attain spiritual fulfilment, we ultimately hope we can do so. I have also exposed how Taylor relies on Adorno's constellation approach as part of his interspatial or framing epiphany. I have then defended Adorno against Taylor's charges of anthropocentrism, subjectivism and lack of theism to show how Taylor either misreads Adorno here or does not give due account to the richness of his thought, which further exposes the restrictive nature of Taylor's own theism. Finally, against Habermas I have shown how both Taylor and Adorno are at one on the importance of epiphanic art as an emancipatory source of the good that can point us towards redemption. So rather than ultimately rejecting Adorno's aesthetics, Taylor should perhaps instead be looking to them as a crucial aid in his task of realising the epiphanies of the past and the present to expose us to sources of the good.

Chapter Six

Social Imaginaries

The reform of consciousness consists solely in letting the world perceive its own consciousness by awakening it from dreaming about itself.[1]

History, Stephen said, is a nightmare from which I am trying to awake.[2]

Modern Social Imaginaries, published in 2004, is Taylor's most recent statement on his examination of the modern identity, which builds and expands on some of the themes that have been considered in the previous Chapters. On that basis, I offer an extensive explication and assessment of this work in which he attempts to identify the shared self-understandings or social imaginaries of Western modernity.[3] By social imaginary, Taylor says that it is not a set of ideas but is instead 'what enables, through making sense of, the practices of society'.[4] Explaining this notion further, he sees a social imaginary not as objective intellectual theorising about society, but the ways in which ordinary people imagine their social existence, how they link these imaginings with other people, and how their expectations are met on the basis of normative notions and images.[5] Consequently, Taylor draws a distinction between social theory and a social imaginary in three ways. First, his focus is on ordinary people and how they construct their social imaginings, which is not always expressed theoretically but through legends and stories. Second, large groups and

[1]   Karl Marx, Letter to Arnold Ruge, 1843, in David McLellan (ed.), *Karl Marx. Selected Writings*, Oxford, Oxford University Press, 2000, p. 45.

[2]   James Joyce, *Ulysses*, London, Penguin, 1992, p. 42.

[3]   Charles Taylor, *Modern Social Imaginaries*, Durham & London, Duke University Press, 2004, p. 2. Taylor emphasises at the outset that he is drawing 'heavily' on the 'pioneering' work of Benedict Anderson in his *Imagined Communities*, London and New York, Verso, 1991.

[4]   Taylor, *Modern Social Imaginaries*, p. 2.

[5]   Taylor, *Modern Social Imaginaries*, p. 23.

even whole societies mainly share a social imaginary, whereas theory is often the preserve of the few. Third, a social imaginary offers the possibility of common understandings and practices and a widely shared sense of legitimacy. Taylor emphasises that this is not to say that theories held by elites cannot become part of a social imaginary, but its complex nature means it resists being turned into an explicit doctrine.[6]

As one example of a social imaginary, Taylor gives the incidence of organising a demonstration.[7] He argues that there is a shared common understanding amongst the demonstrators in terms of what is required, such as how to assemble, make banners and go on a march. The background understanding of what is involved here is more complex, but Taylor suggests that it involves the demonstrators in a form of dialogue or speech act with those whom they are trying to influence such as fellow citizens or the government. This dialogue is not simply of the present, but is part of a becoming and a future and past with all those who, alive and dead, have stood in relation to others and to power. The social imaginary is therefore both factual and normative in that we understand how collective practices are meant to take place and also how they ought to take place.[8] Indeed, the social imaginary takes us beyond our immediate experience of, say, demanding from the government the ending of cuts, and links us to a wider understanding of our predicament in relation to others.[9] Taylor contends that the demonstration in Tiananmen Square, China, in 1989, for instance, was linked back to the French Revolution and, in the American case, the citation of the Statue of Liberty. For Taylor, these moments are part of the important aspect of background to the social imaginary, which relates us to others throughout time, space and history.

A crucial part of this wider background is, what Taylor calls, a moral order that involves not only an understanding of the norms involved in social practices, but also the possible realisation of those norms. The demonstrators in Tiananmen Square were marching in the hope of bringing about a more democratic society, and such a hope is premised on the fact that humans can sustain a democracy together. That this is possible is brought to us through images of a moral order, which allows us to make sense of history and human

---

[6]   Taylor, *Modern Social Imaginaries*, pp. 24–25.
[7]   Taylor, *Modern Social Imaginaries*, pp. 26–28.
[8]   Taylor, *Modern Social Imaginaries*, p. 24.
[9]   Taylor, *Modern Social Imaginaries*, pp. 27–28.

life. Taylor argues that the starting point for the modern moral order of Western modernity that this emanates from is the Natural Law theories of Grotius and Locke in the seventeenth century that were developed in response to the turmoil of the wars of religion.[10] Out of the works of Grotius and Locke emerge notions of natural rights and the recognition that people have moral obligations to each other. Taylor notes that for Grotius, the grounding of political legitimacy in consent in existing regimes was to ward off rebellion and to act as basis for the rules of war and peace.[11] For Locke, in contrast, consent, through the continuing agreement to taxation, was the basis for limited government and the possibility of revolution. Taylor argues, therefore, that from the seventeenth century right up to the present, this understanding of society as being part of a mutual benefit for people and their rights has grown in importance and resulted in the doctrine of popular sovereignty.[12] The moral order that is in the background of this view of society extends over time to include more and more people, and in its intensity it makes greater and greater demands as the order progresses through a series of '"redactions"'.[13] For example, this double expansion of extension and intensity is reflected in the development of natural law from a discourse amongst an elite group of legal theorists and philosophers about legitimacy of government and rules concerning war and peace, into other areas such as the descriptions of God's providence and the order he has established among humans and the cosmos. Over time, natural law theory, once the preserve of an elite few, permeates into society and becomes part of a social imaginary.[14] Taylor argues, therefore, that there is a three-axis expansion that involves the movement from a specialist group to the many, from theory to social imaginary, and finally the demands the moral order makes on us. He suggests that a moral order can be ultimate in the sense that it provides something to strive for, but not necessarily everyone will achieve it. As an example, he offers the Christian Gospel with its idea of a community of saints inspired by the love of God, which in the Middle Ages only a few saints aspired to but over time might be more prevalent. As a further analogous example, Taylor proffers the

[10]   Taylor, *Modern Social Imaginaries*, p. 3.
[11]   Taylor, *Modern Social Imaginaries*, p. 4.
[12]   Taylor, *Modern Social Imaginaries*, pp. 4–5.
[13]   Taylor, *Modern Social Imaginaries*, p. 5.
[14]   Taylor, *Modern Social Imaginaries*, p. 6.

notion of utopia, which again offers us something to strive for, but which can or will be realised in some distant future.[15]

For Taylor, a moral order can also be one where the demand is to be realised in the present and this can take two forms: hermeneutic or prescriptive.[16] The hermeneutic implies that the order is actually realised, is part of the normal state of affairs, and offers us a way to understand reality. The prescriptive, on the other hand, demands that the moral order be carried out and realised eventually. Historically, then, Taylor argues that the modern idea of order pertains to the here and now of the present in contrast to the medieval Christian ideal. Through Grotius and Locke there was a 'hermeneutic of legitimation', which under Locke translated into a justification of revolution and also legitimised property.[17] Further redactions take place with even more revolutionary changes being demanded in relations of property as reflected in the ideas of Rousseau and Marx in particular.[18] Overall, then, the modern idea of order moves from an elite niche group to the many, from social theory to social imaginary, and creates discourses from the hermeneutic to the prescriptive. In doing so, it links in with many ethical concepts that make use of this understanding of the political and moral order that has emerged out of modern natural law theory.

Taylor admits that his account of the moral order of Western modernity, which began with theory and then was later involved in forming social imaginaries, could be guilty of idealism because it seems to present ideas as being an independent force in history.[19] Indeed, he recognises that a counter-argument could be that a more materialist explanation is viable, which sees the modern moral order as a reflection of the rise of merchants, nascent capitalist agriculture, and the development of the market. However, he thinks that such a causal opposition between idealist and materialist explanations is mistaken because human practices throughout history are both simultaneously. So social imaginaries are created through self–understandings in the process of human practices. Nevertheless, Taylor realises that a materialist explanation is possible, and he cites the historical materialist approach of G.A. Cohen for giving primacy to the economic base of society determining the legal and political

[15]   Taylor, *Modern Social Imaginaries*, pp. 6–7.
[16]   Taylor, *Modern Social Imaginaries*, p. 7.
[17]   Taylor, *Modern Social Imaginaries*, pp. 7–8.
[18]   Taylor, *Modern Social Imaginaries*, p. 8.
[19]   Taylor, *Modern Social Imaginaries*, p. 31.

superstructure.[20] Taylor rejects this account as teleological rather than causal because he sees it as 'implausible' in explaining historical development merely in economic terms.[21] For example, he suggests that any attempt to explain the spread of the doctrine of salvation by faith that typified the Reformation economistically is untenable.[22] He argues that there is no one rule that can be the driving force behind ideas because the latter are always a part of human practices. So any attempt to operate with oppositional causes such as the economic versus the political, or idealism versus materialism, is invalid for explaining human history.

Taylor's critique of Cohen's technological determinism is to be commended here, but he does not seem to realise that the force of his own critique emanates from Marx and the humanist Marxist tradition. As we saw in Chapter One, Taylor made a similar move by focusing on the structuralism of Althusser and Balibar in relation to this issue, rather than the enlightened anti-structuralist Marxism of E.P. Thompson. This was despite the fact the latter was also mentioned by Taylor. Cohen's emphasis on the determinist Marx of the 1859 'Preface' to *A Contribution to the Critique of Political Economy* is trotted out again here, to undermine a more enlightened reading of Marx on historical development.[23] The place of the 1859 'Preface' within the history of Marxism is certainly *one* way to interpret Marx, but as I argued in Chapter One, E.P. Thompson, following Marx, and implicitly recognised by Taylor, emphasises the unfolding of history as one of an open, non-determinist class struggle. This is a dynamic process with its emphasis on the social relations people enter into in order to produce that is a far cry from the economic determinism of the base/superstructure model. Throughout history and still in the present day, these relations have taken antagonistic forms, from master/slave, to lord/serf, to worker/capitalist, which are the materialist bases to production that drive historical development. Now to say this does not mean that the realm of ideas is somehow separated from this process as secondary. These moments are dialectically interlinked in a situation of struggle with the possibility of the development of class-consciousness for either side, whether it is lord or serf or capitalist or worker, for example. Both can, and do, as Taylor correctly realises, inform each other. As I pointed out in Chapter One

[20]   Taylor, *Modern Social Imaginaries*, p. 32.
[21]   Taylor, *Modern Social Imaginaries*, pp. 32–33.
[22]   Taylor, *Modern Social Imaginaries*, p. 33.
[23]   Karl Marx, 'Preface' to *A Contribution to the Critique of Political Economy*, Moscow, Progress Publishers, 1977.

in the discussion of the self and method in the *Grundrisse*, Marx's commitment to dialectics means he cannot hold phenomena in a static relation to one another despite what he says in the 1859 'Preface'. Marx does not divorce theory from practice but grasps their dialectical interaction so that we don't *just* interpret the world in different ways but change it as well, as Marx says in the eleventh thesis on Feuerbach.[24] Similarly, in the eighth thesis he states that 'all mysteries which lead theory to mysticism find their rational solution in human practice and in the comprehension of this practice'.[25] For Marx, mysteries are solved by understanding the way things are in practice, so theory and practice are therefore in a contradictory unity. Taylor himself, writing in *Hegel* in 1975, realised this when in a comparison of Hegel with Marx, he suggested that Marx spoke incorrectly 'at times as though he [Hegel] was somehow concerned with "abstract thought" alone, and not also the protagonist of another kind of praxis'.[26] It follows, then, that under a dialectical class struggle understanding of Marxism, Taylor's point about the falsity of explaining the expansion of the doctrine of salvation by faith that typified the Reformation only economistically, must be directed at those commentators who hold to such a deterministic base/superstructure model such as Cohen. It is part of a Marxist tradition that mistakenly separates the economic base from the political superstructure, rather than seeing both the economic and political spheres as a set of social relations engendering exploitation and, by implication, class struggle, as has been ably pointed out by Ellen Meiksins Wood.[27] Understanding historical development in this way is intrinsically political as relations of production are theoretically grasped in their practical contestation to 'illuminate the terrain of struggle by viewing modes of production not as abstract structures, but as they actually confront people who must *act* in relation to them'.[28] Consequently, ideas emanate from these human interactions as Taylor himself realises.

---

[24] Karl Marx, *Theses on Feuerbach*, in Karl Marx & Frederick Engels, *Collected Works*, Volume 5, London, Lawrence & Wishart, 1976 p. 5.

[25] Marx, *Theses on Feuerbach*, p. 5.

[26] Charles Taylor, *Hegel*, Cambridge, Cambridge University Press, 1975, p. 551.

[27] Ellen Meiksins Wood, 'The Separation of the Economic and the Political in Capitalism', *New Left Review*, 127, 1981, pp. 68 & 77.

[28] Wood, 'Separation of the Economic and the Political', p. 77.

Taylor then contrasts the modern moral order with the pre-modern moral order.[29] He argues that the pre-modern moral order was typified by two ideas.[30] One was the Law of a people that was prevalent amongst Indo-European tribes in Europe, and also in the seventeenth century in the form of the Ancient Constitution that manifested itself in the right of rebellion against the king. For Taylor, the latter is evidence that these ideas are therefore not intrinsically conservative and he adds to them the important idea of the '"moral economy"', borrowed, ironically, from E.P. Thompson, which typified the rights of peasant communities throughout history in their resistance against exploitation and exclusion from the land. Again, Taylor's use of the argument of Thompson is obviously of interest here, because it is an implicit recognition of the important notion of class struggle and its crucial role in historical development.

This becomes slightly more overt when he considers how, in the North Atlantic liberal democracies, in contrast to the United States, the forms of the modern imaginary, economy, public sphere, and self-governing polity, emerged and developed through a 'crystallisation of a class imaginary of subordinate groups, particularly workers'.[31] Taylor mentions the class imaginaries of the British Labour movement or the French and German trade unions who negated the independent interests, and instead emphasised a shared community and thereby a common identity, such as the mining villages of the UK or the volonte generale or those who shared the same fate of being exploited.[32] In some instances, he continues, these imaginaries belonged to a culture that was shaped by the Rousseauean redaction of the modern moral order, which he sees as alien to the development in the U.S. Taylor points out that modern social imaginaries have been refracted in different ways in the divergent media of the respective national histories of the West, and this should warn us about expecting a mere repetition of Western forms of these social imaginaries when they are adopted or imposed in different civilisations.[33] Our concern here is Taylor's brief use of 'class imaginary' as a reflection of the social imaginary, because, following Marx and Thompson, it is through class-consciousness premised on class struggle that historical change and development occurs. Why does Taylor feel the need to use the term 'class imaginary' rather

[29] Taylor, *Modern Social Imaginaries*, pp. 8–14.
[30] Taylor, *Modern Social Imaginaries*, p. 9.
[31] Taylor, *Modern Social Imaginaries*, pp. 152–153.
[32] Taylor, *Modern Social Imaginaries*, p. 153.
[33] Taylor, *Modern Social Imaginaries*, pp.153–154.

than the standard Marxist term of class-consciousness? It is not clear what the advantage is in Taylor's use of the concept in that way, except to hide its Marxist origin.

Taylor suggests that another type of pre-moral order is society as hierarchical, which is reflected in the order of the cosmos and theorised in the Platonic-Aristotelian notion of Form. Similarly, Taylor suggests this type of hierarchy is also reflected in theories of correspondence with the king in his kingdom, which is equivalent to a lion among animals and so on.[34] One example Taylor offers of this is from Macbeth and the strange events that occur on the night of Duncan's murder, such as the day remaining dark and strange screams piercing the night air. On this basis, Taylor argues that the moral order is not simply a set of norms, but contains what he calls an '"ontic"' component that identifies features of the world that can realise these norms. In the pre-modern order this ontic component was related to God or the cosmos, but in the modern order it is now related to humans.[35] He argues that pre-modern social imaginaries were typified by positions of hierarchical complementarity, which were reflected in the established orders of society.[36] In the idealisations of natural law theory of the modern moral order, there is now no place for such hierarchies as people now relate to each other through the mutual benefit of satisfying each other's needs, and society is seen and used instrumentally in achieving these ends.[37] The modern moral order is therefore one of mutual respect and reciprocation in securing the 'life, liberty, sustenance of self and family' and engaging in economic exchange to achieve prosperity.[38] Taylor argues that this ideal order was thought to be created by God and acts as a norm to judge by how much we have deviated or followed it in our human affairs.[39] He cites Locke here in seeing humans as being endowed with reason that can tell us God's purposes. Through reason given to us by God, we engage in the preservation of ourselves and mankind by being industrious and partaking in profitable exchange.[40]

To try to avoid the accusation of idealism that he raised earlier, Taylor attempts to explain how the new idea of moral order devel-

[34]   Taylor, *Modern Social Imaginaries*, p. 10.
[35]   Taylor, *Modern Social Imaginaries*, pp. 10–11.
[36]   Taylor, *Modern Social Imaginaries*, p. 11.
[37]   Taylor, *Modern Social Imaginaries*, pp. 11–12.
[38]   Taylor, *Modern Social Imaginaries*, pp. 13–14.
[39]   Taylor, *Modern Social Imaginaries*, p. 14.
[40]   Taylor, *Modern Social Imaginaries*, pp. 14–15.

oped the power to forge the social imaginaries of modernity.[41] He reiterates his earlier explanation of the response of theorists to the wars of religion in trying to offer stability and legitimacy, but now wants to put this in a broader context of the 'taming or domestication of the feudal nobility' that occurred between the end of the fourteenth century and into the sixteenth. He argues that during this period there was a transformation of a noble class of warriors who in theory gave their allegiance to the king, but in reality where semi-independent and carried out military actions not ordained by the Crown. Additionally, there emerged a nobility of servants who only engaged in military action when the Crown endorsed it. For Taylor, this transformation from warrior to courtier changed the self-understanding or social imaginary of noble and gentry elites rather than society as whole.[42] He depicts this change as the development of the new gentleman being offered a humanist training in sociability and conversation and how to behave at court.[43] Indeed, the word courtesy itself indicated just where these qualities where to be acted out.[44] Taylor notes how courtesy did exist in the past but in its new meaning it becomes associated with the term civility. He dates the notion of civility back to the Renaissance where it was understood as civilisation, and denoted refinement against savagery and life in the city against life in the forest.[45] Furthermore, civility was also related to government, which was meant to operate with a code of law through rulers and magistrates.[46] For Taylor, this process took place in England after the Wars of the Roses and under the rule of the Tudors.[47] The life of the nobility changed dramatically under the Tudors with the movement from fighting to domestic peace and an emphasis on the importance of commerce.[48] He realises that these changes did not occur in a benign manner and, indeed, were associated with resistances from nobles, vagabonds and peasants making the onset of civility a 'fighting creed'. So again, there is an implicit understanding of the role of class struggle, but it seems to be an 'add on' for Taylor, rather than a dialectical dynamic. Indeed, the historical picture he paints seems a top-down one, with elites

[41] Taylor, *Modern Social Imaginaries*, p. 33.
[42] Taylor, *Modern Social Imaginaries*, p. 34.
[43] Taylor, *Modern Social Imaginaries*, pp. 34–35.
[44] Taylor, *Modern Social Imaginaries*, p. 35.
[45] Taylor, *Modern Social Imaginaries*, pp. 35–36.
[46] Taylor, *Modern Social Imaginaries*, p. 36.
[47] Taylor, *Modern Social Imaginaries*, p. 34.
[48] Taylor, *Modern Social Imaginaries*, p. 37.

developing theory that gets passed on and down hierarchically to the masses, which is the opposite of what he contends a social imaginary is meant to signify.

Civility itself brought about ordered government, developments in the arts and sciences, which Taylor says we would refer to today as technology, rational moral self-control, education and political manners.[49] So civility is a process of developing and remaking selves, and, in particular, it involves distinguishing between culture and the savagery of nature. Civility and courtesy meant a taming of the aristocratic elite and brought about order and stability, internally at least.[50] Moreover, this civilising mission was also meant to permeate all classes of society, and not just the aristocracy through economic, military, religious, and moral forms of discipline, which Taylor sees as a notable feature developing from the seventeenth century.[51] He argues that the motive forces behind this transformation were the Protestant and Catholic desire for a more completely religious reform, combined with states craving for extra military power and, concomitantly, a more productive economy. Indeed, it is against this background of order that Puritanism emphasised hard work, discipline and trade against the idleness of both the rich and the poor and the desire of a well-ordered society.[52] Similar to the Calvinist Reformation that began in Geneva, the emphasis was on bringing the ungodly and the unruly under the auspices of Christian obedience.[53] To this end, Taylor detects two movements that oppose but also overlap with each other. On the one hand, late medieval elites emphasised the importance of church reform and more intense devotion, whereas on the other, some members of these elites were stressing the significance of civility and a more stable social order.[54] This civilising mission, he continues, was also an attempt to stop the vice and debauchery that typified carnivals, festivals and general sexual misconduct, such as the acceptance of prostitution during the Middle Ages.[55] There is, then, a sea change in values that manifest themselves in four types of programmes.

The first programme Taylor identifies is the enactment of new poor laws in the fifteenth century that attempted to demarcate the

---

[49]   Taylor, *Modern Social Imaginaries*, p. 38.
[50]   Taylor, *Modern Social Imaginaries*, pp. 38–39.
[51]   Taylor, *Modern Social Imaginaries*, p. 39.
[52]   Taylor, *Modern Social Imaginaries*, pp. 39–40.
[53]   Taylor, *Modern Social Imaginaries*, p. 40.
[54]   Taylor, *Modern Social Imaginaries*, pp. 40–41.
[55]   Taylor, *Modern Social Imaginaries*, p. 41.

poor who could work from the poor who could not.[56] For the poor who could work their fate was expulsion or forced labour on low pay under strict control. Those unable to work were given relief but again only under strict conditions, and often in institutions that were little more than prisons. As Taylor indicates, this was in stark contrast from attitudes to the poor that prevailed prior to the fifteenth century. Then, following Matthew's gospel to help those in need and thereby help Christ, the rich felt it incumbent to show some recompense to the poor in the hope of sanctification. As I pointed out in Chapter One, this development emanated from the onset of a brutal primitive accumulation of the peasantry from the land in a process of class struggle that Taylor does not pay enough attention to.

The second programme that Taylor discerns from this period is a crackdown by government and church authorities on certain aspects of popular culture such as carnivals, dancing and feasts.[57] Whilst these activities had certainly been criticised by the church for a number of centuries, Taylor suggests that the attack now becomes ever greater because there were concerns about the place of the sacred, and the development of civility made a breach between the elites and these debased activities.[58]

Taylor sees these two programmes becoming subsumed under a third that was attempted by the absolutist states in France and central Europe to civilise their subjects, particularly through the development of schooling and an emphasis on the work ethic. He realises that part of this was due to the need for ready-made soldiers when required, but he also suggests that it was an end in itself, especially as the ideas of the Enlightenment began to permeate legislation in the twentieth century, which also emphasises the importance of the above values for the benefit of mankind.[59]

The fourth and final programme that Taylor sees emerging from this era is related to the last in that there is a proliferation of these modes of discipline both individually and socially.[60] Endorsing Foucault here, Taylor emphasises how these forms of discipline enter military training but also permeate schools, hospitals and later factories. Indeed, Taylor continues, in terms of the transformation of the self, Loyola's mediation in order to achieve spiritual change was

[56] Taylor, *Modern Social Imaginaries*, pp. 42–43.
[57] Taylor, *Modern Social Imaginaries*, p. 43.
[58] Taylor, *Modern Social Imaginaries*, p. 44.
[59] Taylor, *Modern Social Imaginaries*, pp. 44–45.
[60] Taylor, *Modern Social Imaginaries*, p. 45.

the most prominent at the time, but also appears later in Descartes who was educated by the Jesuits.

For Taylor, then, these two developments of civility joined with elite sociability, and the extension of civility into society, have links with the modern notion of moral order.[61] He suggests that the development of the latter into the polite society of the eighteenth-century resulted into a new form of self-consciousness, which was new historically in that it was aware of its importance of its economic basis, but understood its own place in history as belonging to a commercial society.[62] Citing Adam Ferguson, Taylor then contends that the eighteenth century generated stages theories of history, from the hunter-gatherer to the agricultural, which had resulted in the contemporary commercial society. He argues, therefore, that this allowed people to see this whole period, which he has called the taming of the nobility and the pacification of societies, in a new way, making modernity an epoch without precedent.[63]

The Disembedded Self

Taylor then turns to another context within which the modern idea of order has developed, namely, the 'disembedding' of individuals.[64] He begins this discussion by noting that disenchantment, in terms of the decline of superstition and magic, was a central feature of Western modernity. He argues that this was typified in the Protestant Reformation on the back of the reform movement in Latin Christendom, which also transformed the Catholic Church. The emphasis was on individual religion, obedience and devotion rather than some collective or cosmos-related worship.[65] This led to the development of a new way of self-understanding of special existence that gave a new primacy to the individual. For Taylor, this new self-understanding is linked with his notion of the social imaginary in which we collectively imagine, even prior to theory, our social life in the contemporary Western world.

Taylor suggests that in early small-scale paleolithic and neolithic tribal societies an agent was embedded in three crucial ways.[66] The first was social in that religious life and social life were inextricably

[61]   Taylor, *Modern Social Imaginaries*, pp. 45–46.
[62]   Taylor, *Modern Social Imaginaries*, p. 47.
[63]   Taylor, *Modern Social Imaginaries*, p. 48.
[64]   Taylor, *Modern Social Imaginaries*, p. 49.
[65]   Taylor, *Modern Social Imaginaries*, p. 50.
[66]   Taylor, *Modern Social Imaginaries*, pp. 50–51.

entwined.[67] The second, and another way in which early religion was social which is relevant to the '"Great Disembedding"', was that people primarily related to God as a society through collective rituals and ceremonies.[68] These societies were hierarchical through the sacrosanct roles of priests and chiefs, for example, but Taylor argues that such inequalities also reveal what we would call today the identity of the human beings involved.[69] The individuals themselves in their various roles were totally connected to the social group of the clan or the tribe, and it was impossible for them to see themselves outside this social relationship. Social embeddedness was therefore a form of identity that made it unthinkable for individuals to see themselves outside such a grouping.[70] It was also understood as a social reality where people collectively imagine their social existence, and where the most important actions of the society as a whole are, which are then organised in some way in order to be implemented. For Taylor, the presence and our experience of such a social imaginary means that it sets limits on our sense of self.

Taylor's third form of embedding in social reality in early religion emphasises ordinary human flourishing with an emphasis on long life, fertility and prosperity, and, in contrast to later '"higher"' religions, there is no real desire to go beyond these earthly wishes.[71] On this basis, Taylor suggests that early religion is similar to exclusive humanism with its emphasis on the here and now and its rejection of anything higher beyond the subject.[72] Indeed, he contends that early religion was part of an '"axial"' age which accepted the order of the world through these three forms of embeddedness.[73] Out of this era emerged the '"axial"' religions figure-headed by the likes of Confucius, Gautama, Socrates and the Hebrew prophets that began to question this embeddedness. In Buddhism, for example, the order of the world is questioned because of the emphasis on rebirth, and, in a similar fashion, for Christianity the world is seen as disordered and therefore must be made anew.[74] Overall, Taylor thinks the most important new development of these postaxial religions is that they

[67]   Taylor, *Modern Social Imaginaries*, p. 51.
[68]   Taylor, *Modern Social Imaginaries*, pp. 52–53.
[69]   Taylor, *Modern Social Imaginaries*, p. 54.
[70]   Taylor, *Modern Social Imaginaries*, p. 55.
[71]   Taylor, *Modern Social Imaginaries*, p. 56.
[72]   Taylor, *Modern Social Imaginaries*, p. 57. As we have seen in Chapter Two, Taylor discussed his criticisms of exclusive humanism earlier in 'A Catholic Modernity?'
[73]   Taylor, *Modern Social Imaginaries*, pp. 57–58.
[74]   Taylor, *Modern Social Imaginaries*, p. 58.

do question the restrictive emphasis on human flourishing, and thereby the structure of society and features of the cosmos through which this flourishing was meant to be fulfilled. The importance of the axial period lies in the fact that it allowed new ways for disembedding religion and relating oneself to the divine or a higher being, which undermines and transcends ordinary notions of human flourishing, and can be carried out individually and free from the established sacred order.[75] So a sort of break takes place where the new axial spiritualities develop, but are not allowed to fully disembed because of the power of the dominant old religion of society.[76] What was yet to happen was a transformation of this state of affairs where society is re-made as part of a new Christian order, and which begins to dispel any connections with an enchanted cosmos.[77] Taylor sees this transformation as 'thoroughly disembedding' because it involves removing behavioural and social forms through instrumentalism. In the Christian context, as specified in the New Testament, it encouraged people to leave their clan or family and come into the Kingdom, and in certain forms of Protestantism it asked people to answer the call of God rather than accept the call through family birth.[78] Society, therefore, could now be seen as being founded on a covenant by free individuals, and Taylor's thesis is that whilst the latter is fairly obvious, he suggests that the Christian attempt to bring in the notion of the modern individual in the world was pervasive, and began the first moral and then social imaginary towards modern individualism. He sees this development as being behind the natural law theory of the seventeenth century.

Taylor argues that it is possible to see the buffered identity and the project of reform as contributing to this disembedding. This is because embeddedness is both a mater of identity in terms of the contextual limits to the imagination of the self, and of the social imaginary that indicates the way we think about or imagine the whole of society.[79] However, he suggests that the new buffered identity with its emphasis on personal devotion and discipline resulted in disidentification with the older forms of collective ritual and,

[75]   Taylor, *Modern Social Imaginaries*, p. 59.
[76]   Taylor, *Modern Social Imaginaries*, pp. 60–61.
[77]   Taylor, *Modern Social Imaginaries*, p. 61.
[78]   Taylor, *Modern Social Imaginaries*, p. 62.
[79]   Taylor, *Modern Social Imaginaries*, pp. 62–63.

indeed, imagined their abolition.[80] He sees this process driven by elites who in their own sense of self and in their project for society conceived the social world as being made by individuals.

It is at this point that Taylor realises that there is a problem with the overarching historical account he has just given, which he says has already been identified in Weber's account of the Protestant ethic, and which is close to his own position. Taylor realises that one of the main criticisms levelled at Weber's argument is that it is difficult to substantiate, given the problems in showing connections between spiritual outlooks and capitalist development. Taylor says such a relation must be 'diffuse and indirect' rather than clear and straightforward. As he argued in his discussion of Cohen earlier, he suggests that the vulgar Marxist tendency to give primacy to the economic to explain the spiritual is too simplistic. However, I have countered this argument by emphasising a Marxism with a dialectical understanding of social relations previously so I will not repeat it here. He then goes on again to suggest that such changes involve an interaction between ideas and practices rather than one conditioning the other, because certain moral self-understandings are embedded in such practices. His aim, therefore, is to plot the modern conception of the primacy of the individual, which is a crucial feature of the modern moral order, back to understanding how our present self-understandings grew through early radical attempts to transform society along the principles of axial spirituality.[81]

Taylor's distancing himself from Weber here again exposes some of his affinities with Marx that I outlined in Chapter One. Taylor argues that he wants to avoid the mistaken assumption that the modern individual is the taken for granted starting point, whereas in reality the starting point of our first self-understanding of our identity was as a tribe member, or Father or son. It is only later in history that we came to view ourselves as individuals first, and this identity-shift involved a major change in our moral world.[82] On this basis, Taylor distinguishes between a formal mode of social embedding where we learn our identities dialogically through language, and a material mode of embedding where we learn to have opinions, work out our relation to God, and have our own conversation experience.[83] For Taylor then, an individual is not a Robinson Crusoe fig-

[80] Taylor, *Modern Social Imaginaries*, p. 63.
[81] Taylor, *Modern Social Imaginaries*, p. 64.
[82] Taylor, *Modern Social Imaginaries*, pp. 64–65.
[83] Taylor, *Modern Social Imaginaries*, p. 65.

ure because individuals can only be understood in relation to other human beings. The 'Great Disembedding' is therefore a revolution in our understanding of moral-social order that is accompanied by ideas of a moral order. Again, this replicates Marx's criticism of the Robinsonades such as Smith and Ricardo, for mistakenly positing the atomised individual of bourgeois society as existing throughout history, as I pointed out in Chapter One.

The consequence of this process, according to Taylor, is that we become disembedded from the cosmos and a new relation to God as designer develops. The new relation is itself capable of being overcome because the moral order is powered by human flourishing. He argues that the transcendent moment of the axial revolution is reversed, but only partly because flourishing remains and is revised within the modern moral view and becomes part of the postaxial condition. He suggests that the final phase of the Great Disembedding was powered by Christianity but also by its corruption, because the Gospel itself is part of this disembedding in its attempt to break way from communal and familial solidarities.[84] Christianity ushers in new forms of solidarity in the form of agape, but the corruption also enters in through the form of a disciplined society.[85] Even so, Taylor continues, it was with the Christian aim of making over the world that we get this new disembedding in the new moral order of society. He then turns to how the Great Disembedding has worked in our modern social imaginary and argues that the economy, the public sphere and democratic self-rule are the three forms of social self-understanding, all emanating from the Grotian-Lockean theory of moral order, that are essential for modernity.[86] I will now examine Taylor's discussion of these forms in turn beginning with the economy.

The Economy

Taylor argues that in the eighteenth century the economy becomes to be typified by mutual benefit that is encapsulated in the 'invisible hand' of Adam Smith, where the self-interest of individuals has the design of satisfying the welfare of the whole of society.[87] The economy itself, therefore, involves humans engaging in the exchange of

---

[84] Taylor, *Modern Social Imaginaries*, pp. 65–66.
[85] Taylor, *Modern Social Imaginaries*, p. 66.
[86] Taylor, *Modern Social Imaginaries*, p. 69.
[87] Taylor, *Modern Social Imaginaries*, p. 70.

services.[88] Taylor then emphasises the importance of state power in giving dominance to the economic in that, given the experience of Holland and England, states began to see the need for direct action through political and military power in terms of economic development.[89] Indeed, he sees this rise in state power as not only supplementing the 'old Marxist' thesis on the rise of the business, merchant and manufacturing class, but also perhaps being an even greater factor in this process. However, he qualifies this by arguing that even the foregoing factors need to be supplemented by others such as the political and the spiritual, and on this he again endorses Weber.[90]

On the political aspect, Taylor detects the influence of Puritanism at work here in that it emphasised the importance of taking up a trade and developing a disciplined and ordered life and society. On the spiritual side of this demand, which Taylor says Weber realised, was the need to locate this emphasis on work and order in the everyday notion of the ordinary life of production, family relationships and so on. As we saw in Chapter One, and as Taylor reiterates here, this is his notion of the affirmation of ordinary life which he sees as having an important influence on the development of Western civilisation and which he also linked with Marxism.[91] He sees it as a crucial form of ant-elitism over and against the power of the established Catholic Church, and it fires the important notion of equality in social and political life. Moreover, he suggests that the more society turns to commerce, the more civilised it becomes as it throws off the previous aristocratic search for military glory. For Taylor, then, all these factors contributed to the importance of the economic to its core role in eighteenth century society. He argues that this prominent position of the economy in the eighteenth century as an interlocking system of production, consumption and exchange with its own laws and dynamics, is a crucial part of our social imaginary that continues right down to today.[92]

I have refuted the economic reductionist charge against Marxism earlier, but it is worth asking again how is it that Taylor can make such a charge when he has read the works of Marxists such as Thompson? As we saw in Chapter One, Thompson rejects forms of economic reductionism outright in Marxist and non-Marxist theory for 'obliterating the complexities of motive, behaviour, and function'

[88]   Taylor, *Modern Social Imaginaries*, p. 71.
[89]   Taylor, *Modern Social Imaginaries*, pp. 72–73.
[90]   Taylor, *Modern Social Imaginaries*, p. 73.
[91]   Taylor, *Modern Social Imaginaries*, p. 74.
[92]   Taylor, *Modern Social Imaginaries*, p. 76.

and offering 'an abbreviated view of economic man'.[93] As I have been arguing, a Marxism that emphasises understanding individuals in social relations of struggle cannot be accused of saying that the economy determines everything. It is also ironic that Taylor aligns himself with Weber, given that the latter, as the 'grand old man of bourgeois social science', understood capitalism solely in economic terms without reference to any social factors such as the exploitation of labour.[94] Moreover, Taylor's brief account of the development of Puritanism does seem to ignore this social aspect. For example, Christopher Hill argues that the protestant Puritan emphasis on inner discipline was 'unthinkable without the experience of masterlessness' that occurred through the onset of primitive accumulation.[95] For Hill, Puritanism was the search for a 'new master in themselves' through rigid self-control in order to develop a new personality in the unsettled conditions of the time.[96] This was to be achieved through 'conversion, sainthood, repression [and] collective discipline', but the reason for this was precisely the outcome of the expulsion of producers from the land through primitive accumulation. Taylor's attempt to explain Puritanism without recourse to primitive accumulation or class struggle suggests these desires appear as if by magic or simple preference. On the contrary, by focusing on the social relations pertaining to society at the time, and not seeing the economic separate from the political, the rationale for Puritan edicts begin to be explained. In addition, Taylor's account of the arrival of modernity, which he seems to elide with capitalism, appears almost as an inevitable process at times precisely because he under-emphasises class struggle. As Christopher Hill indicates, there were two revolutions in mid-seventeenth-century England. One that triumphed and ushered in property rights, gave power to the propertied and spread the ideology of the protestant ethic.[97] The other one was the threatened but unrealised revolution which might have 'established communal property, a far wider democracy in political and legal institutions, disestablished the state church and

---

[93] E.P. Thompson, *Customs in Common*, London, Merlin, 1991, p. 187.

[94] Wood, 'Separation of the Economic and the Political', p. 77.

[95] Christopher Hill, *The World Turned Upside Down*, London, Penguin, 1991, pp. 47–48. Hill is endorsing the arguments of Michael Walzer, *The Revolution of the Saints*, Harvard, Harvard University Press, 1965, pp. 308–316. Taylor also refers to Walzer's text but does not note how the 'masterlessness' produced by primitive accumulation led to Puritanism.

[96] Hill, *The World Turned Upside Down*, p. 48.

[97] Hill, *The World Turned Upside Down*, p. 15.

rejected the protestant ethic', but Taylor pays little or no real attention to this as he is swept along on his great arch of history.

Before discussing the other two forms of the modern social imaginary, the public sphere and democratic self-rule, Taylor first wants to contrast them with the economy. He argues that whereas the public sphere and democratic self-rule are based on collective agency, the economy is based on individualism that results in certain laws which can be unearthed by political economy, as in the case of William Petty's analysis of Ireland.[98] For Taylor, there is a 'bifocal' approach to understanding this development in terms of the way human agency imposes itself on reality behind the backs of individuals, and in terms of how the latter is analysed through the objectifying science of political economy. Taylor asserts that this objectifying account, derived from the modern moral order, is just as much a part of the modern understanding as the new ways of imagining social agency. He realises that this emphasis on the modern bifocal certainly has tensions.[99] In relation to freedom in particular, he notes how it is overdetermined in the modern moral order in that humans consent to it, and it is part of how humans construct their world. The tension can arise here where reality is treated as given rather than as something which we can change, and it is with Rousseau, Fichte, Hegel and Marx that Taylor associates the latter viewpoint. As Taylor notes, the Hegelian-Marxist desire to move from *an sich* to *fur sich* is ever recurring.[100] Indeed, he sees part of this process as emphasising the importance of civic humanism and self-rule against the dangers of commercial society, which he associates with both Marx and Rousseau.[101] Moreover, he sees the latter as trying to save civic virtue or freedom or nonalienated self-rule. Conversely, Taylor continues, there were those such as Smith and De Tocqueville who also noticed the danger in this new order, but wanted to find some preventative measure to stop it descending into degeneracy.

What is missing from Taylor's discussion here is an explicit mention of the importance of fetishism and class. As Peter Linebaugh correctly argues, Petty, the so-called '"father of political economy"', was crucial in using his process of quantification, measurement and abstraction to make profit from the labour of the poor, and his emphasis on measurement led to fetishism as 'social relations

---

[98]   Taylor, *Modern Social Imaginaries*, p. 77.
[99]   Taylor, *Modern Social Imaginaries*, p. 80.
[100] Taylor, *Modern Social Imaginaries*, p. 81.
[101] Taylor, *Modern Social Imaginaries*, p. 82.

among people would appear as reified relations between things'.[102] Petty did not see humans in moral terms but as mere numbers, weights and measures. Indeed, by using the phrase 'behind the backs', which Marx uses persistently in *Capital*, Taylor realises the presence of fetishism here again without using the term, but it is through the impersonal market mechanism and the alienation of individuals in capitalism that such reification comes about. Additionally, in relation to Taylor's use of the formulation of *an sich* and *fur sich*, he does so without any reference to class. The point for Marx in making this formulation was to emphasise how the working class had to move from a class in itself (*an sich*) to a class for itself (*fur sich*) for capitalism to be overthrown.[103]

There is also an important point to make when considering Taylor's brief account of the development of the market economy. As E.P. Thompson points out in a discussion of the market, it can be the case that 'intellectual history, like economic history before it, becomes imperialist and seeks to over-run all social life'.[104] It is therefore important to note that the way people thought their times, may not be how those times actually were. Concomitantly, the thought of the market does not prove that market took place in actuality. Just because Smith offered a clear analytical demonstration of how markets work does not mean that this was how markets worked in empirical reality.[105] As Thompson argues, Smith's emphasis on the free market impresses 'less as an essay in empirical enquiry than as a superb, self-validating essay in logic'.[106] So the dangers inherent in Taylor's approach should be clear, despite his concern to understand ideas being interrelated with practices.

Public Sphere

Taylor argues that the economy was the first aspect of civil society to gain independence from the polity but the public sphere followed soon after.[107] He defines the public sphere, which he sees as a central feature of modern society, as a common space where members of society meet and exchange ideas through various forms of media

[102] Peter Linebaugh, *The London Hanged. Crime and Civil Society in the Eighteenth Century*, Harmondsworth, Penguin, 1991, pp. 48–49.
[103] Karl Marx, *The Eighteenth Brumaire of Louis Bonaparte*, in Karl Marx, *Surveys from Exile*, Harmondsworth, Penguin, 1973, pp. 238–239.
[104] Thompson, *Customs in Common*, p. 273.
[105] Thompson, *Customs in Common*, pp. 273–274.
[106] Thompson, *Customs in Common*, p. 203.
[107] Taylor, *Modern Social Imaginaries*, p. 83.

such as print, electronic and face-to-face discussions. Drawing on the work of Habermas and Michael Warner, Taylor suggests that in Western Europe in the eighteenth century a new notion of public opinion developed out of the spread of publications and the development of small group discussions into major issues of debate.[108] People therefore became linked in a common space through media, despite the fact they may never have met. These people were the 'educated elite' communicating through books and newspapers and the ideas that emanated from them. Discussions took place in drawing rooms, coffee houses and, of course, Parliament. For Taylor, the general view that emerged from this was what he refers to as public opinion.

It is at this point that Taylor suggests that a public sphere exists only if it can be imagined as one all-encompassing exchange.[109] Taylor notes that while, as Benedict Anderson contends, print capitalism is important in this process, it should not disguise the fact that this needed to be situated in the right cultural context where a common understanding could emerge and be shared. For Taylor, then, the public sphere was a mutation of the social imaginary which was essential to the development of modern society and an important step on the long march.

In explaining the public sphere further, he distinguishes it from common space where people come together for a common act such as play or some major event. The public sphere, in contrast, transcends the 'topical common place', as Taylor now calls it, and is instead 'metatopical' in that it brings together a plurality of spaces without an identified form of assembly.[110] However, Taylor contends that the metatopical is not new because the church and the state already exist in metatopical spaces, but he sees the public sphere as a step in the long march as the mutation in the social imaginary that was inspired by the modern idea of order. Two features emerge from this: its independent identity from the political, and its force as a benchmark of legitimacy. This importance, Taylor continues, is grasped by reconsidering the Grotius-Locke formulation, which imagined social life independently of the political, that is, the

[108] Taylor, *Modern Social Imaginaries*, p. 84. Jürgen Habermas, *The Structural Transformation of the Public Sphere*, Cambridge, Polity, 1992, first published in German in 1962. Michael Warner, *The Letters of the Republic*, Cambridge, Mass, Harvard University Press, 1990.
[109] Taylor, *Modern Social Imaginaries*, p. 85.
[110] Taylor, *Modern Social Imaginaries*, p. 86.

economy and the public sphere. [111]Additionally, freedom relates to
the rights' society and government by consent, which must be an
on-going process to ensure legitimacy.[112]

Taylor then explains what the public sphere does, what is done in
it, and what it is. As regards to what it does, he interprets it as a 'locus
of discussion potentially engaging everyone ... in which the society
can come to a common mind about important matters'. He recognises this was only possible for an enlightened minority in the eighteenth century, but suggests that such a common mind emerges
from critical debate and is not just a sum of the views of the population at any particular time.[113] The public sphere therefore has a normative element in that the government ought to listen to it because
firstly, the opinion is likely to be enlightened and so government
would be wise in following it, and secondly, the people themselves
are sovereign.[114] Taylor sees the public sphere as an arena within
which rational views are aired and thereby meant to guide government.[115] The public sphere is therefore 'extra political' in that it is
outside the formal processes of Parliament.[116] Indeed, the public
sphere allows society to come to a common mind unmediated by the
political sphere, in a discourse of reason outside power but which is
normative for power.[117]

Taylor uncritically appropriates Habermas' account of the historical rise of the public sphere with the obvious danger that he inherits
any weaknesses that have been exposed in Habermas' story. For
example, James Holstun points out that the eighteenth century bourgeois public sphere emerged, according to Habermas, by its separation from the state and civil society.[118] Whilst this then appeared to
open the public realm to all adult men and offer them a degree of
freedom, the reality was that the private sphere of civil society
restricted entry on class grounds in terms of free time, education and
bourgeois acquaintances. Additionally, civil society absorbed any
form of dissent from the private sphere and left it as a 'relatively
untouched realm of necessity', allowing the bourgeoisie to consoli-

[111] Taylor, *Modern Social Imaginaries*, pp. 86–87.
[112] Taylor, *Modern Social Imaginaries*, p. 87.
[113] Taylor, *Modern Social Imaginaries*, pp. 87–88.
[114] Taylor, *Modern Social Imaginaries*, p. 88.
[115] Taylor, *Modern Social Imaginaries*, p. 89.
[116] Taylor, *Modern Social Imaginaries*, pp. 89–90.
[117] Taylor, *Modern Social Imaginaries*, p. 91.
[118] James Holstun, *Ehud's Dagger. Class Struggle in the English Revolution*,
London & New York, Verso, 2000, p. 194.

date its rule through the divisions of state, family, public sphere and private sphere. Holstun argues that in these types of situations emancipation for the labouring class emerges not within the bourgeois sphere, but from without through organising its own public sphere and by winning over the main sections of the army. Consequently, in the case of the New Model Army of the 1640s, just as in the case of the proletarian public spheres of England, France and the United States, the public sphere appeared alongside or even before the bourgeois public sphere rather than after it. Therefore, radical liberals such as Habermas 'chronically underestimate the role of force in history', and by implication so too does Taylor, as I have tried to point out. Consequently, Holstun correctly argues that most public sphere theorists, such as Habermas, and by following his argument Taylor also, need to re-focus their attention away from the classical republicanism of the university-educated aristocrats and gentry.[119] They ignore the 'far larger group of writers and actors who also believed in fundamental popular sovereignty, and tried to create new forms of popular government, new institutions of democratic discourse, and a social revolution that would prevent the emergence of a new oligarchy'. Holstun suggests examples such as the 'tumultuous days of 1640-42', which should be seen not as a uniform bourgeois public sphere, but as a diverse collection of pamphlets and petitions from wage-labourers, small producers and women, in an empowered public sphere that Parliament took very seriously. Indeed, a case in point here in relation to Taylor is that he does not consider writers before Locke who emphasised legitimating property communally rather than privately. For example, Taylor does not mention Gerard Winstanley's arguments for the defence of the common lands for all and with it the rejection of the enclosure movement that Locke would later vociferously defend.[120] The resistance to the emerging bourgeois society is but a bit player on Taylor's grand narrative of history. Moreover, for Habermas, and by implication Taylor, there is the missing dimension of class that permeated the discussions in the bourgeois public sphere, which itself was entwined with, and not separate from, the private sphere.[121]

---

[119] Holstun, *Ehud's Dagger*, p. 112.

[120] For a useful comparison between Winstanley and Locke see Laura Brace, *The Politics of Property: Labour Freedom and Belonging*, Edinburgh, Edinburgh University Press, 2004, Ch. 2.

[121] Holstun, *Ehud's Dagger*, p. 110. Cf. John Michael Roberts & Nick Crossley, 'Introduction' to their edited collection *After Habermas. New Perspectives on the Public Sphere*, Oxford, Blackwell, 2004, pp. 10–11.

Another weakness in Habermas' discussion that Taylor inherits, is in ignoring the existence of plural public spheres rather than the singular public sphere, and so endorsing the 'classically ideological implication that the ruling classes existed (or, at least, thought and talked) before the labouring classes'.[122] In Habermas' case, he claims that the plebeian public sphere that emanated from the French Revolution, the Chartists and the February revolt on the Continent, was not really a public sphere at all but an '"arena of competing interests fought out in forms of coarser forms of violent conflict"'.[123] So whilst Habermas certainly offers a cogent critique of modern reification, he fails to link this with a close interest in proletarian cultural institutions and commits the same sins as his teacher, Adorno.[124] Similar points can certainly be made in relation to Taylor's preoccupation with non-elite discussions and his lack of attention to class struggle.

Having outlined what the public sphere does, Taylor now considers what it has to be. He focuses on the novelty of its 'extra political' aspect where all members of a political society are seen as also forming a society outside the state, and which seemed to extend to all of civilised Europe.[125] Additionally, Taylor emphasises another novelty of the public sphere, which is its radical secularity.[126] He notes how secularity has a common meaning in terms of the absence of God, religion or the spiritual from the public sphere. He also suggests that its radical basis contrasts with any divine foundation for, and, also any transcendent understanding of, society. Secularity, he continues, is also to be contrasted with the perception of society as constituted by law that has existed since time immemorial.[127] The public sphere, therefore, is radically secular in that it makes no appeal to any framework or any transcendent criteria, but rather constitutes itself through self-sufficient common actions and exchanges.[128] Taylor realises that these actions and exchanges take place within structures and institutions such as the media, for example, which may suggest they are ongoing and transcend time. However, he suggests that these structures can be modified and indeed even abolished, although they can be made anew again through

---

[122] Holstun, *Ehud's Dagger*, p.111.
[123] Habermas, *Structural Transformation*, pp. 122–129. Holstun, *Ehud's Dagger*, p. 111.
[124] Holstun, *Ehud's Dagger*, p. 111.
[125] Taylor, *Modern Social Imaginaries*, p. 92.
[126] Taylor, *Modern Social Imaginaries*, p. 93.
[127] Taylor, *Modern Social Imaginaries*, pp. 93–94.
[128] Taylor, *Modern Social Imaginaries*, p. 94.

common action in the public sphere.[129] So in a purely secular association, common agency emanates out of common action.[130] Taylor argues that this form of secularity is modern because in the past people always related to something transcendent that manifested itself in society, but always pointed beyond to God or a Great Chain of Being. In the eighteenth century, the public sphere brings forth a 'metatopical' common space and common agency rooted in its own actions and without reference to the transcendent. Moreover, he links modern secularity with an emphasis on profane time compared to the higher time of spirituality.[131] Following Benedict Anderson, who utilises Benjamin's notion of time that I discussed in relation to transcendence in Chapter Three, Taylor sees this emphasis on profane time as vertical slices holding together different events and occurrences as part of the modern mode of social imagination. The public sphere, on this account, was a new metatopical space where ideas were exchanged between members of society and developed into common agreement.[132] Furthermore, this took place in profane time and independently of the political constitution of society. In short, the public sphere was and is an 'extra political', secular, metatopical space, which was part of a development that transformed our whole understanding of time and society, according to Taylor.

Considering the notion of the public sphere further, Taylor argues that the market economy, which he discussed earlier, and society as a people that pre-existed and founded politically organised society, are the other two extra political secular spaces that have played a crucial role in the development of society in the modern West.[133] He sees these three areas as interlocking and developing a private space within which human life attains greater significance beyond the auspices of church and state. Taylor relates this back to his notion of the 'affirmation of ordinary life' that emphasises the importance of the family and production, and which emanated out of the Protestant Reformation.[134] Indeed, as he rightly notes, the Reformation meant a turning away from established Catholic religion and the sanctity and authority of the church, to a more personalised God with whom people could have direct contact and serve in their daily lives. The

[129] Taylor, *Modern Social Imaginaries*, p. 95.
[130] Taylor, *Modern Social Imaginaries*, p. 96.
[131] Taylor, *Modern Social Imaginaries*, p. 98.
[132] Taylor, *Modern Social Imaginaries*, p. 99.
[133] Taylor, *Modern Social Imaginaries*, p. 101.
[134] Taylor, *Modern Social Imaginaries*, p. 102.

good life to pursue was therefore now situated in ordinary life and profane time. As Taylor indicates, this change was encapsulated in Marx's Promethean notion of humans as producers transforming the world through their labour.[135] The private world of production is therefore given a form of dignity and importance that it was not in previous times, but the consequence of this was the development of an individualism that operated within market exchange as a self-regulating system, and which was encapsulated particularly in the work of Adam Smith. This economic sphere is extra political and secular although not public, Taylor contends, because its exchanges are not a matter of common decision by a public authority.[136] Rather, it is the outcome of individual decision-making and action.

I mentioned previously how at times Taylor seems to read the great texts of intellectual history as though they are an accurate account of the times they are recording, and this view of the supposed operations of the market is a case in point. However, to his credit here he notes how uprisings could occur in towns, for example, when wheat prices increased dramatically and local merchants were suspected of secret hoarding to make a substantial profit. The severity of these instances often resulted in the gruesome death of the merchants, which would bring a response from the royal government in terms of more killings and the restoration of order.[137] Despite this, Taylor notes how the authorities would endeavour to accede to the initial demands by dropping grain prices, putting a cap on any increases and bringing in imports.[138] He suggests that this was a 'bloody process between the base and the summit' and that power resided in the latter rather than the former. Indeed, he argues that there was no claim to popular sovereignty here, with the people preferring to believe that his advisors had somehow misled the king. Moreover, he suggests the period was typified by trying to reinterpret old practices in a new way. In relation to the food riots, for instance, he argues, again following E.P. Thompson, that they were based on the '"moral economy"' of the crowd that had its own conception of a just price. Any movement away from normal prices was blamed on the ill will of merchants and agents of the state, both of whom were often seen as being in collaboration with each other.[139] This meant that the people had no conception of the economy deter-

---

[135] Taylor, *Modern Social Imaginaries*, p. 103.
[136] Taylor, *Modern Social Imaginaries*, pp. 103–104.
[137] Taylor, *Modern Social Imaginaries*, pp. 126–127.
[138] Taylor, *Modern Social Imaginaries*, p. 127.
[139] Taylor, *Modern Social Imaginaries*, pp. 129–130.

mining prices in terms of market demand and supply, and instead they held their rulers responsible for not meeting shortages through importation for instance, as Taylor mentioned above.[140] Additionally, the people also assumed that someone was to blame if things went wrong, and that the person responsible was an evil-doer or criminal who should be severely and ceremoniously punished.[141]

However, Taylor seems to have slightly misread Thompson here in suggesting that there was no notion of popular sovereignty present. Thompson argues that the food riots in eighteenth century England were certainly triggered by the type of malpractices Taylor mentions above, 'but these grievances operated within a popular consensus as to what were legitimate and what were illegitimate practices', which 'in its turn was grounded upon a consistent traditional view of social norms and obligations, of the proper economic functions of several parties within the community'.[142] All these aspects taken together are what Thompson refers to as the 'moral economy of the poor'.[143] Moreover, Taylor's suggestion that power lay with the ruling elite rather than the masses misses Thompson's point that in their defence of these customs and rights they were 'on occasion' given licence to do so by the authorities, but 'more commonly, the consensus was so strong that it overrode motives of fear or deference'.[144] To assume power lies simply with the ruling elite as Taylor does is to underestimate the strength of the masses in a process of class struggle, and again offer an air of inevitability to the emerging capitalist system.

Taylor notes a further development of ordinary life in the eighteenth century in that the demands for privacy result in an intimate sphere of the family that is sheltered from the outside world.[145] Taylor argues that this is linked with a new emphasis on subjectivity, inwardness and sentiment, which manifests itself in literature in the paradigm example of Rousseau's *Julie*.[146] If literature allowed a new understanding of intimate relations, then this was also the case in terms of art and music that prompted from people aesthetic reflection and enjoyment. The public sphere itself emerges out of this development as these private concerns develop into public ones

[140] Taylor, *Modern Social Imaginaries*, p. 130.
[141] Taylor, *Modern Social Imaginaries*, pp. 130–131.
[142] Thompson, *Customs in Common*, p. 188.
[143] Thompson, *Customs in Common*, p. 188
[144] Thompson, *Customs in Common*, p. 188.
[145] Taylor, *Modern Social Imaginaries*, pp. 104–105.
[146] Taylor, *Modern Social Imaginaries*, p. 105.

through discussion and criticism. On this basis, Taylor argues that a new definition of human identity is possible but only through its definition and affirmation in public space.

Taylor also posits Calvinism as a third way in which the Reformation helped to create the conditions of metatopical agency in secular time.[147] Far more radical than Lutheranism, Calvinism demanded a re-organising of the church, which led to the generation of free churches and voluntary associations, and ultimately took the form of Methodism and the Great Awakening. As Taylor points out, there is still a reference to God here, but there is less reference to any notion of higher time and a greater emphasis on profane time. Indeed, he observes how modern forms of common agency developed out of these new churches and sects, which demanded strong commitment and attachment beyond normal familial and communal relations.[148] Being part of a religious community took precedence over private relations and prepared the way for what Taylor calls '"horizontal"' or direct-access societies, where membership is not through any particular group and where new forms of association begin to emerge. He concludes, then, that the rise of the public sphere in Europe can only be understood in relation to this economic, ecclesial and intimate-sentimental background, which he understands as part of a network of extra political and secular constitutions of society. One aspect is its relation to the economy, and another is its relation to popular sovereignty, which often resulted in 'new and sometimes frightening forms of political action in the eighteenth century'. It is this emphasis on popular sovereignty that Taylor considers next.

Sovereignty of the People

Taylor posits popular sovereignty, which also begins as a theory, as the third mutation in the social imaginary that has forged modern society.[149] He suggests that it emerges from two origins although in reality they often overlap. One refers to the development of new activities with new practices that are adopted by certain groups and become their imaginary. He offers the example of the early Puritan churches with their emphasis on conversion that bestowed full citizenship in their communities. Another change in the social imaginary refers to a re-interpretation of a practice that existed before,

[147] Taylor, *Modern Social Imaginaries*, p. 106
[148] Taylor, *Modern Social Imaginaries*, p. 107.
[149] Taylor, *Modern Social Imaginaries*, p. 109.

such as forms of legitimacy in the cases of Britain and America, which manifested into the English Civil War and the rebellion of the colonies.[150] For Taylor, the appeal was to an ancient constitution that had existed since time immemorial, and which emphasised Parliament's rightful place beside the king.[151] Indeed, this idea enters the American Revolution where popular sovereignty is enshrined in the U.S. constitution in the terms '"We, the people"', which resulted in elected assemblies, consent to taxation, and eventually the role of elections as the source of legitimate power. So to transform society in this way the actors needed to have a way of internalising and actualising this theory of legitimacy, and agree collectively on what right courses of action to take.[152] Taylor evokes Kant here in arguing that theories needed to be '"schematised"' for concrete interpretation to take place in order for them to occur in history.[153] Taylor argues that in the case of the Russian Revolution in 1917, for example, this schematisation was not present because the peasantry could not grasp all the Russian people as a sovereign agent replacing despotic power, so their social imaginary was only local.[154] In the case of the French Revolution, by contrast, Taylor argues that there were different ways to realise popular sovereignty with the unrepresentative Estates General on one side, and a variety of theories that were influenced by Rousseau on the other.[155] One theory that Taylor denotes here is Rousseau's general will, which he sees as a new and more radical redaction of the modern idea of order.[156] Taylor interprets Rousseau as trying to overcome the motivational dualism between our own self-interest against the interest of others, and also the fact that we can, due to certain factors such as a fear of God or impersonal benevolence, act for the general good. He argues that Rousseau's solution was to avoid this dualism by joining the love of one's self with the desire to fulfil the goals of others and achieve true harmony.[157] Taylor suggests, utilising Rousseau's language, that self-love (*amour de soi*) and sympathy (*pitié*) intertwine in a rational and virtuous person who loves the common good and which asserts itself politically as

[150] Taylor, *Modern Social Imaginaries*, pp. 109–110.
[151] Taylor, *Modern Social Imaginaries*, p. 110.
[152] Taylor, *Modern Social Imaginaries*, p. 115.
[153] Taylor, *Modern Social Imaginaries*, pp. 115–116.
[154] Taylor, *Modern Social Imaginaries*, p. 116.
[155] Taylor, *Modern Social Imaginaries*, pp. 116–117.
[156] Taylor, *Modern Social Imaginaries*, p. 117.
[157] Taylor, *Modern Social Imaginaries*, pp. 117–118.

the general will.[158] For Rousseau, the self-love and the love of others
are at one in the perfectly virtuous man, but Taylor points out that
this still produces a new dualism because we also have egoistic ten-
dencies that militate against our love of humanity. For Rousseau,
this problem emanates from the motive of pride (*amour propre*), and
concern for your self can lead to two forms that oppose each other as
good opposes evil. Rousseau's goal, according to Taylor, is to har-
monise individual wills and in the process create a new identity of a
moi commun, whilst at the same time rescuing the individual liberty
of all, and enshrining the law we love with our self-love to achieve a
higher stage of morality and a more 'authentic self'.[159] According to
Taylor, Rousseau therefore offers a moral psychology that returns to
a will with two potential qualities of good and evil, and presents a
new way of relating reason and the good will that goes beyond
Lockean and Enlightenment notions of disengaged reason.[160] For
Rousseau, the latter simply leads to strategic thinking and power
calculations that results in an isolated, 'strategic self', which seeks
the approval of others and negates our 'true self'. On this interpretation of Rousseau, Taylor emphasises how it is through the
reengagement with our inner self, rather than any notion of disen-
gagement, that we can achieve what Rousseau refers to as our '"conscience"'. Taylor argues that Rousseau's theory here resulted in a
new kind of politics that was enacted in the aftermath of the French
Revolution between 1792-94, where there was an emphasis on virtue
through self-love and love of one's country.[161] Additionally, it leads
to Manichaeanism where self-interest is seen as a sign of corruption,
and the egoist identified as a traitor with the discourse of politics
itself becoming quasi-religious with the evocation of the sacred. Taylor suggests that one of the most fateful outcomes here was the complex notion of representation.[162] With Rousseau this is linked to his
emphasis on transparency rather than representation, and it is the
general will that ensures this transparency in an open process where
all wills eventually form into one. Taylor indicates that transparency
needs a certain form of discourse where the common will is publicly
and repeatedly defined.[163] So the struggles and revolutionary discourse between 1792-94 also involved festivals in order to make the

---

[158] Taylor, *Modern Social Imaginaries*, p. 118.
[159] Taylor, *Modern Social Imaginaries*, pp. 118–120.
[160] Taylor, *Modern Social Imaginaries*, p. 120.
[161] Taylor, *Modern Social Imaginaries*, p. 121.
[162] Taylor, *Modern Social Imaginaries*, p. 122.
[163] Taylor, *Modern Social Imaginaries*, p. 123.

republic manifest to the people. He notes how this emphasis on vir-
tuousness and the importance of a general will amongst the few
rather than the many can lead to an elitist, vanguardist form of politics that he sees as a form of representation through '"incarnation"'.[164] In this way, the minority take on the general will and
demarcate themselves from the representatives, but their role is one
of revolutionary transition rather than any theory of government.[165]
Taylor suggests this outcome has been typical of movements from
the Jacobinism of 1792-94, up to the main examples of the twentieth
century in Bolshevism and Leninist communism. I will respond to
the supposed anti-democratic nature of Marxism in the final Chapter, but suffice to say that there is a robust radical democratic aspect
to Marx's thought that cannot simply be reduced to Leninist
substitutionism in the way Taylor wants to.

Nationalism

Taylor argues that inventing the people as a new collective agency is
the third of the great mutations after the economy and public sphere
and it develops into the notions of patriotism and nationalism.[166]
Before the end of the eighteenth century, continues Taylor, the social
imaginaries of leading Western societies contained moments of people's relation to civil society through the economy, the public sphere
and independent associations, but he suggests that there is still a
great distance on his long march to society today. Indeed, he notes
how such a distance means that these forms of social imaginary were
the preserve of elites and activist groups with the larger population
remaining within the older forms. Additionally, he suggests, the distance can also be understood by the fact that the modern moral order
had shaped some forms of life, such as politics, the economy and the
public sphere, but not others.[167] Taylor cites the family as one example that was hierarchical, patriarchal and typified the wider depend-
ence and hierarchical complementarity that pervaded society itself,
and that was also part of the social imaginary of the time.[168] These
problems are challenged as the new social imaginary develops
down from the elites, and into the people in general as they begin to
break with previous hierarchical forms and instead emphasise the

---

[164] Taylor, *Modern Social Imaginaries*, p. 124.
[165] Taylor, *Modern Social Imaginaries*, pp. 124–125.
[166] Taylor, *Modern Social Imaginaries*, p. 143.
[167] Taylor, *Modern Social Imaginaries*, p. 144.
[168] Taylor, *Modern Social Imaginaries*, p. 146.

notion of equality.[169] In the revolution of the United States, this development meant that independence as a value now becomes something to be sought and enjoyed by all people equally. The elected leaders were certainly 'gentlemen' and constituted a republican elite, but they were also meant to be virtuous and devoted to the public good.[170] Taylor argues that this period saw an emphasis on personal independence that along with economic growth, the expansion of the internal market, the increase in manufactures and the opening up of the frontier, allowed both men and women to strike out on their own and leave their families and communities.[171] He contends that this new independence was not simply a break with old solidarities and moral ties, but had its own moral ideals that were particularly linked with the development of new religious groupings beyond the established church. Methodists and Baptists, for example, emphasised a personal relation to God and warned against the evils of idleness and drink.[172] For Taylor, personal independence also related individuals to society as the new 'disciplined, honest, imaginative, entrepreneurial people' were now the cornerstone of the new society in which order and progress were linked. Taylor depicts the entrepreneur as a hard working benefactor that was part of what was making America 'great, free and equal', and developed into a model of American patriotism that is still as powerful today.[173] The entrepreneur, then, is an inspiration to others in terms of going from rags to riches, and contributing to public well-being through benevolent acts with the wealth created. For Taylor, this shows that independence was therefore not just a personal ideal, but also a social one in that it contributed to national well-being and was admired and honoured in return. Entrepreneurs themselves looked for appreciation and offered leadership that bonded them to the wider society.[174] So independence did not imply isolated individualism, but rather its opposite, and this sense of community was furthered through the growth in newspapers and periodicals resulting in an 'impersonal equality'.[175] Taylor recognises that this was not true for all people. Indeed, he admits that the new principle did not reach into the family or those still enslaved on

[169] Taylor, *Modern Social Imaginaries*, pp. 147–148.
[170] Taylor, *Modern Social Imaginaries*, pp. 148–149.
[171] Taylor, *Modern Social Imaginaries*, p. 149.
[172] Taylor, *Modern Social Imaginaries*, p. 150.
[173] Taylor, *Modern Social Imaginaries*, p. 151.
[174] Taylor, *Modern Social Imaginaries*, pp. 151–152.
[175] Taylor, *Modern Social Imaginaries*, p. 152.

plantations or those suffering the 'oppressive dependency' of work in the emerging factories. Moreover, he points out that these marginalised groups did not have any cultural space to offer an alternative vision of the republic, as the United States never really had a serious socialist opposition, except briefly with Eugene Debbs.

However, Taylor's contention here that there was no cultural space for these groups does need questioning a little. As Howard Zinn points out in his excellent, *A People's History of the United States*, writers such as Upton Sinclair, Jack London, Theodore Dreiser and Frank Norris were not 'obscure pamphleteers', but were among the most famous of American literary figures who argued for socialism, criticised capitalism and 'whose books were read by millions'.[176] We also need to remember that groups such as the International Workers of the World, who may have had a membership of only a hundred thousand at any one period, still had the power to mobilise thousands of people in any place at any time indicating an influence way beyond that of their formal members.[177] Indeed, they communicated their message for socialism through word and song and had the full power of the state to contend with for doing so. Add to these labour struggles the struggles of blacks and women and American history takes on a different dimension. That these were minority forces against the juggernaut of the social imaginary of American capital, does not mean they should be glossed over as easily and as quickly as Taylor does leaving them almost hidden from history. His eulogising of the role of entrepreneurs as custodians of the American dream, and his emphasis on the formal political sphere, is even further evidence of his myopia in relation to the class anger that permeates American history in many different forms.

Taylor then turns his attention to the issue of nations and nationalism as part of the social imaginary. He argues that it was not until the late eighteenth century that there was a looking backwards to the rights that were propagated in social contract theory.[178] He sees the American Revolution as a watershed in this process because the colonists were asserting their rights as Englishmen through the colonial legislatures associated with Congress. It is out of this development that Taylor sees the emergence of the 'crucial fiction of '"we the people"' who articulate the new constitution and also a '"nation"'. Tay-

---

[176] Howard Zinn, *A People's History of the United States. 1492–Present*, Essex, Pearson, 2003, p. 322.
[177] Zinn, *A People's History of the United States*, pp. 331–332.
[178] Taylor, *Modern Social Imaginaries*, p. 156.

lor argues that the nation exists prior to and independently of its own constitution through its own action in secular time. On this basis, he suggests that a new way of conceiving things emerges as nations and/or a people have a personality that can operate outside any initial political ordering. He suggests that this implies that the right for people to make their own constitution is present, and is one of the key premises of modern nationalism, because without it the demand for self-determination would make no sense.[179]

Taylor then returns to Benedict Anderson to illustrate how the collective agency of the '"nation"' or '"people"' develops into a new understanding of time.[180] For Anderson, the sense of belonging to a nation implied a way of grasping society under the notion of simultaneity in that all the different events of society were grasped by its members at one moment and in homogenous, secular time in which society is understood horizontally and without reference to higher time. There were no mediations by any agencies such as kings or priests, and this therefore implies a 'direct access society' where everybody is immediately linked to the whole. Whilst Taylor sees Anderson correctly relating to this new understanding through the development of print capitalism, he notes how Anderson does not see this as *the* explanation for the transformations of the social imaginary. Transformations also involve the way we figure ourselves as societies, and by having a decentred, horizontal, lateral view of society that an objective observer might have.[181] He contends that any vertical notion of society depending on higher time is missing in the modern moral order which is now, as stated above, a 'direct access society' based on impersonal egalitarianism and direct citizenship, rather than a hierarchical order of personalised links.[182] Taylor suggests, then, that we relate to the state directly as an 'object of our common allegiance' in conjunction with our fellow citizens, and this creates a feeling of belonging.[183] So for Taylor, modernity has resulted in a revolution in our social imaginary that has marginalized forms of mediacy, and enhanced images of direct access through the social forms of the public sphere, market economies and the modern citizenship state.[184] Additionally, Taylor notes other ways in which direct access grips people's imagination such as

---

[179] Taylor, *Modern Social Imaginaries*, pp. 156–157.
[180] Taylor, *Modern Social Imaginaries*, p. 157.
[181] Taylor, *Modern Social Imaginaries*, pp. 157–158.
[182] Taylor, *Modern Social Imaginaries*, pp. 158–159.
[183] Taylor, *Modern Social Imaginaries*, p. 159.
[184] Taylor, *Modern Social Imaginaries*, pp. 159–160.

fashion and seeing ourselves as part of a worldwide audience of media stars.[185] He observes how there is still a form of hierarchy in these examples as they centre on 'quasi-legendary figures'. Indeed, this is replicated to some extent in the social, political, and religious movements that are an important feature of modern life, which link people together into a collective agency that is translocal and international.

For Taylor, these different forms of imagined direct access are linked to aspects of modern equality and individualism. Direct access leads to the overcoming of the heterogeneity of hierarchical belonging and develops into uniformity and the possibility of equality. Taylor sees individuals becoming aware of their developing self-consciousness, and growing more and more free from the mediations that link us to the whole. He is quick to add that modern individualism as a moral idea does not imply that people do not belong at all, as that would result in anomie and breakdown. Rather, he continues, it involves people imagining themselves as being part of wider, impersonal entities such as the 'state, the movement, the community of mankind', which involves a shift from '"network"' or '"relational"' identities to '"categorical"' ones.[186] He points out further that while direct access societies are more homogenous than premodern societies there are still differences in culture and lifestyle.[187] However, he also notes how the social imaginaries of different classes have become similar as the limitations of hierarchy and locality that typified the premodern era now begin to be overcome.[188] He suggests, therefore, that there were wide differences between the theory of the social imaginary of the elites and that of the less educated masses that lasted until very recently for many countries, but had to be breached for the development of the new modern moral order.

Taylor then turns his attention to the issue of collective agency that emerges through common action when we imagine ourselves in this new horizontal and secular world, whilst also recognising society objectively and unrelated to any form of agency which can be acted

[185] Taylor, *Modern Social Imaginaries*, p. 160.
[186] Taylor mentions that he adopts this terminology from Craig Calhoun, 'Nationalism and Ethnicity', *American Review of Sociology*, 9, 1993, p. 230, and points out his debt to Calhoun's work in his discussion here. See *Modern Social Imaginaries*, pp. 212–213. n. 3.
[187] Taylor, *Modern Social Imaginaries*, pp. 160–161.
[188] Taylor, *Modern Social Imaginaries*, p. 161.

upon by 'enlightened administrators'.[189] He refers to this as the 'double focus of modern consciousness of society" that he previously mentioned in his discussion of the economy. For Taylor, the first independent understanding of society was when it was grasped as an economy, rather than as an extended household under the domain of a ruler, with its own laws operating 'behind the backs' of individuals as an 'invisible hand'. Whilst he realises that these two positions of collective agency and objectification have often been seen in opposition, he contends that they should be seen as 'coeval' because they are part of the same imaginings that emerge from the modern moral order.[190] A crucial component to this idea, Taylor contends, is that the modern social imaginary allows us to see society in extra political forms and not just through the science of political economy but also through what we now call sociology.[191] For Taylor, the modern imaginary therefore includes not only categories that allow common action, but also categories of process and classification that, again, operate 'behind the backs of the agents'.[192] The modern social imaginary is therefore both active and contemplative, and exists in a number of forms as 'people grasp themselves and great numbers of others as existing and acting simultaneously' in the economy, public sphere and as the sovereign people.[193] Taylor then adds a fourth structure of simultaneity, fashion, which is similar to the economy in that it has a number of individual actions operating 'behind the backs' of people, but differs in that actions also relate to each other in a common space of mutuality in which dress of a certain kind sends signs and meanings between people.[194] Taylor sees these common spaces as being particularly important in modern urban societies in the notion of the crowd and public gatherings that oscillated between loneliness and communication, and that were particularly captured by Baudelaire with his interest in the roles of the flâneur and dandy.[195] Taylor notes how these common spaces were topical in the nineteenth century, but become metatopical in the twentieth century due to the expansion in media and communications.[196] He argues that these moments, which veer between soli-

---

[189] Taylor, *Modern Social Imaginaries*, pp. 163–164.
[190] Taylor, *Modern Social Imaginaries*, p. 164.
[191] Taylor, *Modern Social Imaginaries*, pp. 164–165.
[192] Taylor, *Modern Social Imaginaries*, p. 165.
[193] Taylor, *Modern Social Imaginaries*, p. 167.
[194] Taylor, *Modern Social Imaginaries*, pp. 167–168.
[195] Taylor, *Modern Social Imaginaries*, pp. 168–169.
[196] Taylor, *Modern Social Imaginaries*, p. 169.

tude and togetherness, can lead to common action and shared feelings and emotions, and he gives examples of spectator sports, rock festivals and even the funeral of Princess Diana in this regard, which can achieve a sort of quasi-religiosity.[197] Additionally, he notes how they can take a more long-lasting form through the struggles of particular groups such as the unemployed or welfare recipients against the state for example.[198] Taylor's main point is that the modern social imaginary contains a whole host of forms in potential mutual transition and complex interaction.[199] But if this is the case what use is an all-embracing term of disparate moments such as a social imaginary? How can, using Taylor's example, the experience of the unemployed fall under the same social imaginary inhabited by someone as powerful and wealthy as the current incumbent of the White House, George W. Bush? The conflict of interests here are stark and it seems nonsensical or even meaningless to suggest that they are part of one social imaginary. Bush has done everything he can to increase the wealth of the rich, whilst at the same time decreasing the already little or non-existent wealth of the poor and unemployed. The social imaginary understood in these terms just seems to be a catch-all concept that can hide the real divisions that operate in society. One way Taylor might respond to this is through Anderson's own point that 'regardless of the actual inequality and exploitation that may prevail' within an imagined community, its 'fraternity makes it possible, over the past two centuries, for so many millions of people, not so much to kill, as willingly to die for such limited imaginings'.[200] For Anderson, the answer to this lies in the cultural roots of nationalism, and Taylor to some extent, seems to concur with this given his emphasis on the importance of nationalistic writers such as Herder.[201] However, what depictions of nationalism such as this fail to account for is that the imagined community is also illusory in the sense that it includes the alienated activities that produce and reproduce it.[202] The imagined community is where a

[197] Taylor, *Modern Social Imaginaries*, pp. 169–170.

[198] Taylor, *Modern Social Imaginaries*, p. 170.

[199] Taylor, *Modern Social Imaginaries*, pp. 170–171.

[200] Anderson, *Imagined Communities*, p. 7.

[201] Charles Taylor, 'The Importance of Herder' in his *Philosophical Arguments*, Cambridge, Mass, & London, Harvard University Press, 1997.

[202] Bertell Ollman, 'Toward a Marxist Theory of American Patriotism: How "They" Murder Us, and What We Can Do About It', available at http://nyu.edu/projects/ollman/docs/patriotism_content.php, pp. 5 & 1.

capitalist class uses its economic and political power to pursue its own class interests under the guise of the national interest.

Taylor argues that understanding society as having many facets and not just as a polity, has also meant that action in the political sphere must take account of the integrity of other forms and goals people seek in them.[203] He suggests that the onset of popular sovereignty gave politics a new importance particularly in reasserting the ancient republican rights of citizens. Any attempt to override the other spheres and have control over all aspects of life in the name of some utopian future, Taylor again contends, can only result in the totalitarian nightmare typified by the Jacobin Terror, Soviet communism and fascism. Indeed, Taylor, following Benjamin Constant, sees the modern age as offering a crucial place to the non-political and thereby showing that the error of Jacobinism, and Rousseau for that matter, was to privilege only political participation whilst ignoring economic prosperity and the satisfactions of private life.[204] I will return to this in the final Chapter by showing the radical democratic credentials in Marx's own thought that need not lead to tyranny.

To try and give a more complete picture of contemporary notions of the moral order, Taylor posits a fourth form of social existence in the modern imaginary and that is the importance of rights which, as we have seen, emanate from Grotius and Locke, and have become part of the modern normative order. Through the American Declaration of Independence and its various amendments, on to the developments after the Second World War, rights are therefore seen as prior to the political, and which the political itself must now respect.[205] Taylor links this movement into a horizontal, direct access world, based in secular time with a new understanding of history and modes of narration.[206] He argues that a new collective subject, people or nation emerges that needs new ways to tell its story and seeks to find its own state. Taylor suggests that this can happen accidentally where people overcome an autocratic ruler as with the French in 1789, or it can occur where a people is formed out of a political choice for self rule as in the case of the American revolution.[207] He contends that much of what we call nationalism is not a matter of historical contingency or political choice, but is rather based on the

[203] Taylor, *Modern Social Imaginaries*, p. 171.
[204] Taylor, *Modern Social Imaginaries*, p. 172.
[205] Taylor, *Modern Social Imaginaries*, p. 173.
[206] Taylor, *Modern Social Imaginaries*, p. 175.
[207] Taylor, *Modern Social Imaginaries*, pp. 176–177.

people having a sense of belonging in terms of 'common language, common culture, common religion or history of common action'.[208] Taylor admits this rendering of a common past is fictive, as Modernisation theorists such as Gellner and Hobsbawm have pointed out, but he argues that it has also been a particularly 'politically effective invention' that has been 'interiorised and become part of the social imaginary of the people concerned'. However, Hobsbawm at least goes further than this by not only exposing the fictive nature of nations and nationalism, but also suggesting that given the increasingly global nature of society they will be in decline.[209] Indeed, Hobsbawm cites support for his view from John Breuilly who also attacks Gellner and Anderson, whom Taylor supports, for assuming that the self-evident success of nationalism implies that it has a strong presence in people's thoughts and behaviour.[210] Hobsbawm sees this decline as a process in the making rather than an end result, which presages a time when people will identify themselves in various ways and not simply by a singular nationality. Indeed, as Leslie Sklair also points out, the advent of an increased globalised capitalist system has exposed the previous totems of national interest and national economy for the manipulative ideological tools that they were.[211] Ironically, and however imperfectly, as Sklair observes, it was the proletariat in the Internationals and the transnational capitalist class of the major globalising corporations that could see through the fiction of political and economic nationalisms. The fact that globalisation is now at its height means that this fiction is being exposed even further.

Taylor then emphasises three modes of narrativity in this process: progress, revolution and nation all of which combine with each other, and allow people to come together in different forms of commonality as a sovereign people. He suggests that this common belonging needed to be awoken and a common destiny realised through a growth in consciousness that moves from *an sich* to *fur sich*. As I pointed out earlier, this is the terminology used by Marx in terms of the development of the class-consciousness of the working class, but Taylor is wrapping it up in nationalist terms, which is far

[208] Taylor, *Modern Social Imaginaries*, p. 177.
[209] Eric J. Hobsbawm, *Nations and Nationalism Since 1780*, Cambridge, Cambridge University Press, 1993, p. 192.
[210] John Breuilly, 'Reflections on Nationalism', *Philosophy and Social Science*, 15, 1, 1985, p. 73.
[211] Leslie Sklair, *The Transnational Capitalist Class*, Oxford, Blackwell, 2001, p. 31.

too general and clearly ignores class differences. Moreover, even the awakening notion itself could be the result of the manipulation of elites and the 'rhetoric of nationhood' that they engage in, to use Michael Billig's pertinent phrase.[212]

Taylor also argues that whilst the nation state is the locus for the three main forms of social imaginary, they also have a supranational loci in that the economy can be seen as international, the public sphere can be seen as extending beyond national borders, and the state itself is depicted as always existing in a system of states that attained uniformity based on rules with the peace of Westphalia in 1648.[213] For Taylor, this sense of unity has been further developed through the civilising mission of '"Europe"' into a world system, which has been expanded to 'include all the (properly behaved) members of the global community', and the eventual advent of a more 'pacific, productive and egalitarian' modern society.[214] These developments were not without their difficulties in terms of the action of reactionary regimes and the possibility, a worry of de Tocqueville, that democracy would bring with it a decline in freedom.[215] Taylor notes that one response to this problem was to aim for a more 'heroic and full-bodied search for equality of self-rule', which was proposed by Rousseau and taken up by the 'Jacobins, and then with Marx and communism' in the 'attempt to establish a new kind of republic of virtue, or a community of equal sharers'.[216] The other path Taylor mentions is the Nietzschean one of heroism, domination and the will, and a rejection of the egalitarian and humanist values of the modern moral order. Indeed, Taylor notes how both of these reactions resulted in the totalitarian challenges of communism and fascism to liberal democracy in the twentieth century, with the latter emerging victorious. Consequently, the modern moral order based on liberal democracy has, for Taylor, given a set of basic values that can be used to reject any attacks on them, be it Al Qaeda and the strike on the World Trade Centre or the practitioners of genocide in the Balkans or Africa.[217] Against such atrocities the appeal is made, he continues, to 'our own integrity and goodness' in upholding such values. Taylor realises that this can also lead to a feeling of superiority where there is an instinctive lashing out at the threat which

[212] Michael Billig, *Banal Nationalism*, London, Sage, 2001, pp. 1–4.
[213] Taylor, *Modern Social Imaginaries*, p. 178.
[214] Taylor, *Modern Social Imaginaries*, pp. 179–180.
[215] Taylor, *Modern Social Imaginaries*, pp. 180–181.
[216] Taylor, *Modern Social Imaginaries*, p. 181.
[217] Taylor, *Modern Social Imaginaries*, p. 182.

results in scapegoating and violence, which was typical of Latin Christendom in the vilification of Jews and witches, and which Taylor suggests is still present today. He realises that this is the dark side to the modern Western social imaginary where it connects with a sense of civilisational superiority.[218]

This then leads him to consider the relation of a social imaginary to 'what Marxists call ideology, a distorted false consciousness of our situation'.[219] Taylor argues that his use of the term social imaginary includes this notion of false consciousness in that the imaginary can be false and a distortion of reality. As an example, he cites the notion of ourselves as equal citizens in a democratic society, which can disguise the fact that there are people who are excluded from this process whilst living in that society. Indeed, he admits that it is a regular occurrence that actually lived social imaginaries are 'full of ideological and false consciousness', but he argues that they are never simply this because their falsity is never total. Consequently, the social imaginary operates with a 'constitutive function' where some people are experiencing democratic rule even if others are not. Taylor contends, then, just as in any form of human imagination, the social imaginary itself can be both an essential constituent of the real and a fiction that can result in oppression. So by his own admission, Taylor is using a Marxist understanding of society here in terms of the 'reality' of false consciousness. However, it is interesting to note that Marx himself never used the term false consciousness, although it has been utilised by certain writers in the Marxist tradition.[220] The danger in clinging to a notion of false consciousness is that it can all too easily lead to elitism or the Leninist substitutionism that Taylor consistently berates Marxism for. As E.P. Thompson points out, this arises from understanding class as a static category where one group appears to have a true consciousness and sets about imposing it on another, which in Lenin's case is the vanguard against the working class.[221] Given Taylor's worry about such substitutionism it is surprising to see him retain false consciousness as an aspect of his social imaginary. For Marx, of course, the edict to follow to avoid this elitism was that '"the emancipation of the working class must be the act

---

[218] Taylor, *Modern Social Imaginaries*, pp. 182–183.
[219] Taylor, *Modern Social Imaginaries*, p. 183.
[220] See Joseph McCarney, 'Ideology and False Consciousness' available at http:marxmyths.org/joseph-mccarney/article.htm, p. 1.
[221] E.P. Thompson, 'Class and Class Struggle', in Peter Joyce (ed.), *Class*, Oxford & New York, Oxford University Press, 1995, p. 134.

of the workers themselves"', and maybe that is precisely why he never used the term.[222]

Secularism

Taylor concludes *Modern Social Imaginaries* by considering the meaning of secularity in relation to the modern social imaginary.[223] Whilst he recognises there has been a diminution in the presence of religion in the public sphere, although this is not total as the US case illustrates, he thinks that belief and unbelief can and do exist as alternatives.[224] Such a secularity of public space involves a freeing of politics from religion and the founding of a society on itself, whilst at the same time opening a new space for religion in public life.[225] Taylor argues that modern democracies in particular are founded on a common will that claim to be based on popular sovereignty.[226] Part of accepting the legality of this common will is being governed by decisions that one does not agree with. Taylor contends that what bonds people to act in this way with a strong common purpose or value is what he defines as a '"political identity"'.[227] Expanding on this further, he says that in democratic societies, for example, a political identity involves having freedom both for the majority and the dissenting minority.[228] For Taylor, the answer, valid or not, to the question of how a decision which goes against a person serves their freedom, lies in the fact that they have ongoing rights enshrined in law as part of a society and a collective agency with which the members identify.[229] When this form of identity breaks down, democratic regimes begin to lose their legitimacy and risk the possibility of rebellion. On this basis, Taylor notes that in the appeal to popular sovereignty there resides the '"republican"' and '"national"' variant, even though at times they are often combined.[230] The republican variety was inspired by the ancient republics and was invoked by the American and French Revolutions. The national variant developed both positively and negatively out of democracy in that there

[222] Karl Marx, *Critique of the Gotha Programme*, in Karl Marx & Frederick Engels, *Selected Works*, Volume 3, Moscow, Progress Publishers, 1983, p. 20.
[223] Taylor, *Modern Social Imaginaries*, p. 185.
[224] Taylor, *Modern Social Imaginaries*, p. 187.
[225] Taylor, *Modern Social Imaginaries*, pp. 187–188.
[226] Taylor, *Modern Social Imaginaries*, p. 188.
[227] Taylor, *Modern Social Imaginaries*, pp. 188–189.
[228] Taylor, *Modern Social Imaginaries*, p. 189.
[229] Taylor, *Modern Social Imaginaries*, p. 190.
[230] Taylor, *Modern Social Imaginaries*, pp. 190–191.

was a reference back to a pre-existing cultural or ethnic nation.[231] What becomes defended and realised in the national state is not simply a person's freedom as a human being, but the guaranteed expression of a common cultural identity. Taylor notes how this form of identification with a regime was possible in premodern times as with the king or hierarchical orders, but in the democratic age the difference is that people do this as free agents, which is why the common will confers legitimacy.[232] Taylor notes that whether such claims are founded in actuality is dependent on the state being imagined as such by its citizens. He also realises that to ask who exactly the state is for is answered by the notion of political identity, which is distinct from the identities of its members, and will be far richer and more complex. Taylor now thinks it is possible, therefore, to see the space for religion and God in the modern state acting strongly in the political identity.[233] This can take the form of people fulfilling God's will in setting up a polity and following its edicts as many Americans have done during and beyond the revolutionary period. Additionally, a person's national identity can be related to God if they see themselves defined by their piety and faithfulness, and this has particularly arisen amongst those who are surrounded by nonbelievers, but which can degenerate into forms of chauvinism when taken to the extreme, as the example of Northern Ireland can testify. For Taylor, then, the secularity of the contemporary world means that God is not necessarily absent from public space, but is crucial for the personal identities of individuals and groups, and offers a possible defining constituent of political identities.[234] So modernity is secular, not in the sense of the absence of religion, but rather that religion takes a different place now that all social action occurs in profane time.[235] Secularity is simply another aspect of the social imaginary of Western modernity that has helped to construct this civilisation and from which local particularities can emerge.[236] Consequently, Taylor's 'foundational hunch' is that instead of speaking about modernity as a single process taking similar forms through the state, market, science and technology, he thinks we should speak of '"multiple modernities"' that are 'different ways of erecting and animating institutional forms that are becoming inescapable'. Taylor has

[231] Taylor, *Modern Social Imaginaries*, p. 191.
[232] Taylor, *Modern Social Imaginaries*, p. 192.
[233] Taylor, *Modern Social Imaginaries*, p. 193.
[234] Taylor, *Modern Social Imaginaries*, pp. 193–194.
[235] Taylor, *Modern Social Imaginaries*, p. 194.
[236] Taylor, *Modern Social Imaginaries*, p. 195.

therefore outlined the social imaginary of the modern West with Europe at its centre as one form, rather than *the* form, among the multiform world that, he hopes, can emerge in order and peace.

Conclusion

In this extensive examination of Taylor's latest major and stimulating work, I have tried to show some of the tensions in his argument and the persistence of certain Marxist ideas in his writings. In his notion of the self, he reiterates his earlier arguments on how the self should be understood socially. Additionally, he rejects the Robinsonade argument that the modern individual is the starting point for understanding the self, but again without any reference to Marx. The tensions arise in his depictions of the evolution of the social imaginaries, where the role of class struggle is either in the background or mostly non-existent, which leads almost to a top-down account of historical development. In response to this in the next Chapter, I begin to emphasise the importance of class struggle in the making of working class identity, and show how dynamic class formations can develop into aesthetic selves that can offer the possibility of transcending capital, whilst also responding to Taylor's persistent charge that Marxism is the enemy of freedom.

Chapter Seven

The Aesthetic Self

Art exists within reality, has its function in it, and is also inherently mediated with reality in many ways. But nevertheless, as art, by its very concept it stands in an antithetical relationship to the status quo.[1]

One of Taylor's major criticisms of Marxism that he developed as long ago as the 1970s, as I pointed out at the beginning of Chapter One, is that if it is to be a more relevant theory, it must say something extra about the personal level of the individual.[2] Taylor states that the reason this issue has been so absent is that the Marxist movement has focused on other questions such as when the revolution will take place or why it has not yet and so on.[3] Instead, he thinks the focus should change to offer a 'Marxist theory of art, human aesthetic experience and moral experience' that he detects in the history of humanist Marxism based on a theory of liberation and which, if taken further, 'could become something interesting'.[4] He argues that within such a theory there is 'almost a vision of man, social man, as a kind of artist, expressing himself in a society which has overcome alienation'.[5] In communism, he notes, 'all the capacities humans have to control their lives are put to the service of their expressive drives and aspirations'.[6] However, despite these positive statements, he regards classical Marxism as positing the unrealistic and even 'unliveable' notion of 'generic man, harmoniously united, in

[1]   Theodor Adorno, 'Extorted Reconciliation: On Georg Lukcs' *Realism in our Time*', in *Notes to Literature*, Vol. 1, New York, Columbia University Press, 1991, p. 224.
[2]   Charles Taylor, 'Marxist Philosophy', in Brian Magee (ed.), *Men of Ideas: Some Creators of Contemporary Philosophy*, London, BBC Publications, 1978, p. 52.
[3]   Taylor, 'Marxist Philosophy', p. 52.
[4]   Taylor, 'Marxist Philosophy', pp. 53 & 57.
[5]   Taylor, 'Marxist Philosophy', p. 48.
[6]   Taylor, 'Marxist Philosophy', p. 49.

contest with nature'.[7] For Taylor, this can only be an 'utterly empty freedom'. Indeed, he berates such a situationless notion of freedom for its destructiveness in making Marxist societies preoccupied with constructing the foundations of socialism at the expense of true freedom. Such a situationless freedom results in a 'characterless' self that has no defined purpose.[8] The claims for this self to be rational or creative are, for Taylor, too indeterminate to be meaningful. He argues that he is not saying that Marx should have offered a blueprint for a free society which is itself a contradiction, but Marx should have talked in "general terms how we envisage men's situation will have changed, what constraints, divisions, tensions, dilemmas, struggles and estrangements will replace those we know today".[9] He does note the positive aspects of revolutionary struggle where "behind the barricades, there is a real liberation of expression, a field for creative action, the breaking down of barriers, a real participatory democracy", but in the "image of the revolution triumphant" all these aspects are "thought away".[10]

The first response to Taylor's challenge to Marxism must be met by putting his own question back to him. What picture can he give us of his own situated self? How is freedom situated and organised in his preferred society where his ideal self might flourish? Taylor has certainly made a major contribution to our understanding of identity, but his deficiencies, many of which have been outlined in previous Chapters, will be further exposed here. I will do so by responding to Taylor's charge that a Marxist approach necessarily involves a negation of freedom, which, as we have seen, has been a recurring theme in his writings from the 1970s to the present. In doing so, I will show how his situated or '"characterful" self' is as 'characterless' as the self he mistakenly derides Marxism for, given his failure to see the need for transcending capital.

The second response to make to Taylor's challenge relates to understanding properly Marx's notion of communism as:

> not a *state of affairs* which is to be established, an *ideal* to which reality [will] have to adjust itself. We call communism the *real*

---

[7] Charles Taylor, *Hegel*, Cambridge, Cambridge University Press, 1975, p. 558.
[8] Taylor, *Hegel*, p. 561.
[9] Taylor, *Hegel*, p. 558.
[10] Taylor, *Hegel*, p. 559.

movement which abolishes the present state of things. The conditions of this movement result from the now existing premise.[11]

Taylor's challenge, then, is somewhat disingenuous because communism is not some end state, but a process which emanates from the dialectical contradictions of capital in the here and now. What is therefore a more legitimate response to his challenge is to identify intimations of this 'real movement', given that Marx's own intimations of communism derive from his analysis of capitalism and are therefore rooted in reality. To this end, I will defend a conception of the aesthetic self that is dialectical in its mediation between universals and particulars. I argue that it is in movements and ideas that oppose capital, and in their desire for a more humane world, that we can see the realm of the aesthetic emerging. To do this, I give an outline of the development of the self through class struggle in history from the early making of the working class identified by E.P. Thompson, through to the pioneering work of the Italian Autonomist Marxist movement particularly in the form of Antonio Negri and, more recently, his collaborative work with Michael Hardt.[12] As I pointed out in previous Chapters, Taylor's discussion of the self is woefully inadequate due to its lack of attention to class struggle, and the above writers, in contrast, put the latter at the centre of their analysis for understanding how subjects antagonistically constitute themselves in society. I begin by considering the supposedly negative relationship that Taylor persistently posits between Marxism and freedom.

Marxism and Freedom

One of Taylor's main concerns in relation to the unfreedom he detects in Marxism relates to the issue of democracy. As we saw in the Introduction in his response to Berlin's comments, and also in the last Chapter, Taylor did not speak in general about the question of democracy in relation to Marxism, but simply held up Leninism as an example where Marxism has gone badly wrong in this area. However, in his 1989 retrospective essay, he does expose the anti-demo-

---

[11] Karl Marx & Frederick Engels, *The German Ideology*, in Karl Marx & Frederick Engels, *Collected Works*, Volume 5, London, Lawrence & Wishart, 1976, p. 49. Term in square brackets in the original translation.

[12] For an historical overview of this movement see Steve Wright, *Storming Heaven: Class Composition and Struggle in Italian Autonomist Marxism*, London, Pluto, 2002. Cf. Harry Cleaver, *Reading Capital Politically*, London, AK Press, 2000, Introduction.

cratic nature of Marxism in the roots of Marx's own theory. Taylor depicts Marx as being part of the Rousseauean tradition that posits a general will around which everyone can unite in a common purpose and gives them a single identity.[13] For Taylor, this tradition has an inadequate conception of freedom because as it manifests itself in Marxism, it means that an individual, which was a 'self-creating' subject, loses its individuality and becomes a 'social subject' as a species-being. For Taylor, Marx's notion of species-being creates the conditions of its own existence and of human society as a whole. Taylor calls this the self-determining notion of freedom. Marxism, by holding on to the self-determining notion of freedom inevitably becomes authoritarian[14] leading to the imposition of a general will upon any differences that might be aired in society. Positing unanimity as freedom, as Taylor thinks Marx does, inevitably leads to Leninist substitutionism where a vanguard rules in the name of the proletariat as a 'super-subject' that is mistakenly assumed to have its own will.[15] Moreover, such a conception of freedom leads to centralisation because decentralisation raises the prospect of different wills as exemplified in the early years of the Soviet Union where instances of the desire for workers' control were severely resisted. Taylor sees Soviet Marxism and Leninism in particular as clear evidence for the emasculation of any independent points of view. For Taylor, this has disastrous consequences because the life-blood of citizen self-rule is dependent on vibrant decentralised 'foyers of self-control'.[16] These 'foyers' are not only eliminated but they are also stopped from being created anew as the political culture of self-rule is subordinated to the dictates of the party.

In contrast, Taylor stresses a 'civic humanist tradition of freedom' (stemming from Tocqueville and leading to Hannah Arendt) as a more realistic basis for a self-governing society. This model sees society as a participatory community where institutions and laws give structures to the form of this participatory life, and are seen as a common repository of the human dignity of all the participants. In this tradition, freedom can be defined as having a place in the 'ongoing order of political rule' within a framework of common understandings. Freedom in this model therefore presupposes some things that

[13] Charles Taylor, 'Marxism and Socialist Humanism', in Robin Archer *et al* (eds.), *Out of Apathy: Voices of the New Left Thirty Years On*, London, Verso, 1989, pp. 64–65.
[14] Taylor, 'Marxism and Socialist Humanism', pp. 65–6.
[15] Taylor, 'Marxism and Socialist Humanism', p. 66.
[16] Taylor, 'Marxism and Socialist Humanism', p. 67.

are not entirely under the control of the common will and which are to be respected. Conflicts over ideas, interests and so on, are assumed to continue and actually offer the vibrancy to a participatory society, which ensures the airing of different opinions and the winning of arguments through reason and persuasion. For Taylor, the socialist movement therefore needs a humanism that offers models of self-rule that recognise conflict and difference whilst also affirming common rule and human dignity. Additionally, such humanism needs to move beyond self-expression and offer another model of freedom. Taylor argues that it is this Tocquevillean model of self-rule that allows for and contains conflict within its structures.[17] Decentralised rule is therefore a priority because difference is subsumed under a centralised system.[18] Moreover, a proper socialist humanism must understand people as bearers of rights that exist over and against society and any Rousseauean notion of the general will. So the Marxist humanism built on the Rousseauean notion of freedom is a complete disaster for democracy in the long run, and therefore far inferior to the civic humanism of the Tocquevillean model.

Taylor is certainly correct to note that the issue of democracy sits problematically in Marx's thought and in the history of Marxism. Alan Gilbert, for instance, has valuably mapped out the difficulties that have to be faced in sustaining democracy, such as the tendency towards elitism and authoritarianism, while also noting the radical democratic credentials of Marx and even some Marxist movements.[19] Ironically, such a contrast occurs in Taylor's own analysis here. Taylor himself had previously (in 1978) noted the incredible democratic credentials of Marx and then argued that 'there's no doubt…of Marx's view that what ought to follow from a revolution is a democratic, self-managing society'.[20] As evidence for this, he points to the example of Marx's comments on the Paris Commune of 1871 which, in Taylor's own words, 'had on paper a more radical, basic democracy than exists in any western society today'.[21] Marx therefore endorsed a decentralised form of political organisation

---

[17]   Taylor, 'Marxism and Socialist Humanism', pp. 72–3
[18]   Taylor, 'Marxism and Socialist Humanism', p. 73.
[19]   Alan Gilbert, 'Political Philosophy', in Terrell Carver (ed.), *The Cambridge Companion to Marx*, Cambridge, Cambridge University Press, 1991, p. 191.
[20]   Taylor, 'Marxist Philosophy', p. 56.
[21]   Taylor, 'Marxist Philosophy', pp. 56–57.

that Taylor himself had previously approved.[22] The democratic credentials of this form of organisation are worth remembering. Marx
supported the idea of universal suffrage for the election of municipal
councillors who were subject to recall and were to be paid working
class wages. The Communes were to extend to the local level and
delegates elected there sent to the national assembly to put forth the
interests of their own communities. Democracy was to be extended
to the judiciary in that magistrates and judges would be elected.
Religion, far from being allowed to impose a universal education
over all communities, was to be disestablished and left as a private
matter for individuals themselves. Even the police was to be turned
into a people's militia and again be democratically accountable to
the Commune. All these indications of how a socialist society might
be organised hardly imply the imposition of a Rousseauean general
will upon people's freedom. The 'foyers of self-control' that Taylor
desires could be accommodated within this political structure. Now
it can obviously be agreed that such self-rule was severely crushed in
Stalinist states, as Taylor rightly points out, but it cannot hide the
basic fact that, given his recommendations above, Marx himself
would not be in favour of such authoritarianism. Additionally, to
equate Marx's position with Rousseau is also problematic. Rousseau
was hostile to decentralised decision-making because he was wor-
ried that particular wills would be in opposition to the general will of
the whole assembly.[23] Marx, in contrast, is allowing local concerns to
be expressed in their own community and in relation to a national
assembly. Marx is therefore advocating political structures within
which differences can be aired and democratic decisions made.

　　The latter point relates to a further issue for Taylor, namely,
whether Marx is assuming away conflict after capitalism. In 1978,
Taylor initially states that it would be 'unfair' to suggest that Marxists assume away all conflict after capitalism, but he then goes on to
say that Marxists 'do foresee certain kinds of conflict', and then qualifies this by saying they 'do believe that the really deep conflicts,
those which make people take up cudgels against each other, are
grounded in economic exploitation and will disappear'.[24] By 1989,
Taylor becomes even more adamant and apportions to Marx the
idea that *all* conflict will end after capitalism. The evidence centres

[22]　Karl Marx, *The Civil War in France*, in Terrell Carver (ed.), *Later Political
　　　Writings*, Cambridge, Cambridge University Press, 1996, pp. 184–89.
[23]　Jean–Jacques Rousseau, *The Social Contract*, Harmondsworth, Penguin,
　　　1987, p. 73.
[24]　Taylor, 'Marxist Philosophy', p. 51.

on Marx's comment in the 1859 'Preface' to *A Contribution to a Critique of Political Economy*. Marx states there that the 'bourgeois mode of production is the last antagonistic form of the social process of production'.[25] He goes on to add that it is 'antagonistic not in the sense of individual antagonism but of antagonism that emanates from the individuals' social conditions of existence'. It is clear then that antagonisms do remain in communism, but Taylor rejects the idea that antagonisms in the material conditions of production will disappear, as Marx believes.[26] As an example, Taylor supposes a society in which all the means of production are socially owned, but suggests that antagonisms will still exist between say those in the export trade compared to those in local markets or those who want to develop one region compared to those in another region. This, though, is not the antagonism that Marx is talking about at all. He is talking about the exploitative relationship between capital and labour through the pumping out of surplus value. That antagonism will be at an end in communism, according to Marx. There are bound to be conflicts of interest about how we do things, but it will not be done through the subordination of labour to capital and through the expropriation of surplus value.

Taylor also seems to forget that one of the greatest constraints on our freedom is the tyranny of necessary labour and the incessant pumping out of surplus value that a vampire-like capitalism consistently requires. Marx's desire is that necessary labour should be dramatically reduced in communism to allow creative development to flourish and radical democracy to succeed. The space opened up here would allow time for individuals to engage in debate and offer alternative conceptions of the good life - the type of activity Taylor himself would endorse. This is precisely Marx's point. Individuals could become multifaceted as captured in his dictum that in communism we can 'hunt in the morning, fish in the afternoon, rear cattle in the evening, criticise after dinner ... without ever becoming hunter, fisherman, shepherd or critic'.[27] The images may not be totally relevant to today, and they are a reflection that Marx is rooting his analysis in the 'real movement' of communism in his time, but the sentiment clearly is. The 'real movement' of communism suggests the possibility of openness where difference is tolerated through the

[25] Karl Marx, 'Preface' to *A Contribution to the Critique of Political Economy*, Moscow, Progress Publishers, 1977, p. 21.

[26] Taylor, 'Marxism and Socialist Humanism', p. 75.

[27] Marx & Engels, *The German Ideology*, p. 47.

institutions of radical democracy, and individuals have the ability to develop themselves in many different directions. Despite all this, Taylor could point to the passage in the *Economic and Philosophical Manuscripts* where Marx describes communism as 'the genuine resolution of the conflict between ... man and man'.[28] So is Marx actually assuming away conflict after capitalism? The 'conflict' Marx is referring to here is, as he himself says, 'human self-estrangement'. In communism, humans attempt to appropriate their essence and eschew the antagonisms of class subordination that emanate from capitalism. For Marx, such an appropriation is 'as varied as the determinations of the human essence and activities'.[29] With self-estrangement at an end, we are allowed to develop ourselves freely and in many different ways, which may still certainly lead to disagreements about what we consider *our* conception of the good life to be, but this will be done where the antagonistic basis to production has been overcome.

It can also be pointed out that while Taylor wants people to be more contemplative about their lives and relations to others, he neglects to stipulate just how this can be done. One positive aspect of Marx's emphasis on the reduction of necessary labour is that it allows more free time for deliberation. As we saw previously, Taylor argued that in the affirmation of ordinary life individuals are juggling competing demands in terms of their family, job and so on. How can such individuals find the time for the level of contemplation that Taylor would desire given all of those demands? In particular, Taylor does not pay enough attention to what is a largely unavoidable fact for the majority of people: the necessity to sell their labour-power to satisfy their needs that is rooted in exploitation.[30] Marx's focus on this antagonism revealed the requirement to abolish the wage relation and so end this form of conflict by also reducing the need for necessary labour. That form of conflict will be over but other conflicts will remain, even those which may make people take 'cudgels against each other', which can occur for many different reasons and not just those related to 'economic exploitation'.

This leads on to a further problem that Taylor has with Marxism as a supposed enemy of freedom, which relates to the issue of ecology. Taylor argues that Marx's argument that humans as species-beings

---

[28]   Karl Marx, *Economic and Philosophical Manuscripts*, in Karl Marx, *Early Writings*, Harmondsworth, Penguin 1992, p. 348.

[29]   Marx, *Economic and Philosophical Manuscripts*, p. 351. n. 5.

[30]   Cf. Nicholas H. Smith, *Charles Taylor. Meanings, Morals and Modernity*, Cambridge, Polity, 2002, p. 182.

making over nature as they desire, can only result in environmental disaster.[31] For Taylor, Marx's seemingly instrumental approach to nature would lead to its destruction. Marx and the Marxist tradition are therefore deeply flawed in positing a decrease in necessary labour by these means. Again, there is little doubt that Taylor is pinpointing a problem that subsequent Marxists have attempted to address given the upsurge in ecological awareness. For writers such as Rudolf Bahro, for instance, Marx is dismissed out of hand because of his seemingly destructive attitude towards nature through his emphasis on the expansion of the productive forces.[32] Other Marxists, such as Ted Benton, although still critical of Marx's seeming instrumentalism towards nature, have recognised how Marx's arguments are 'unclear' on this issue.[33] Taylor, though, seems to be clearly aligning himself with Bahro's position and therefore assumes that Marx sees nature as a passive and infinitely manipulable source for the satisfaction of human needs with little concern for its devastation. However, the ambiguity noted by Benton certainly displays the possibility for a more sympathetic and immanent interpretation of Marx on this issue. Indeed, there is certainly clear textual evidence to support the idea that Marx *is* aware of the damage that can be done to the environment, and can be seen as proposing a more harmonious relationship between humanity and nature.[34] Just two examples will suffice. First, in a discussion of the effects of pollution in a river, Marx notes how the essence of the freshwater fish is the water of the river which is its medium of existence, but he argues that this essence is destroyed once the river is made to serve industry and pollution occurs.[35] Such sentiments hardly suggest an instrumentalist view of nature and instead indicate a sensitivity to preserving the natural environment.

Second, Marx showed how capitalism itself had no respect for nature, be it human or non-human, in its rapacious expansion of the productive forces in the 'unashamed, direct, brutal' pursuit of surplus value.[36] Capitalism turns everything into a commodity:

[31] Taylor, 'Marxism and Socialist Humanism', p. 65.
[32] Rudolf Bahro, *From Red to Green*, London, Verso 1984, p. 143.
[33] Ted Benton, 'Marxism and Natural Limits: An Ecological Critique and Reconstruction', *New Left Review*, 178, 1989, pp. 58–60.
[34] Lawrence Wilde, *Ethical Marxism and its Radical Critics*, London, Macmillan, 1998, Ch. 7.
[35] Marx & Engels, *The German Ideology*, p. 58; Wilde, *Ethical Marxism*, p. 124
[36] Karl Marx & Friedrich Engels, *The Communist Manifesto*, Harmondsworth, Penguin, 1987, p. 82; Wilde, *Ethical* Marxism 1998, p. 127.

humans, nonhuman animals and nature, whereas communism is concerned with developing a more harmonious relation between production and nature in the pursuit of reducing necessary labour. It is therefore ironic that that when Taylor considers this issue again when writing in 1991, he approvingly mentions Marx's tirade against the commodification that results from capitalist technological development.[37] Additionally, on the issue of technology itself, Taylor argues that we need to put technology 'in the service of an ethic of benevolence towards real flesh and blood people', but how is this inimical to Marx's position?[38] If Marx is raging against capital for treating people and things merely instrumentally then the use of technology in society must not be merely instrumental as well. Instead, the ethic Taylor thinks should be driving the use of technology would be hugely appropriate in communism. Once again, Taylor is too quick to dismiss Marx on this issue without giving due concern to a more sympathetic interpretation of his arguments. Taylor can consistently hold up the stultified system of Soviet Marxism as a caveat against realising communism, but only by ignoring the more humanist side of Marx's writings.

With a Marxism offering radical democratic structures and a sensitivity to ecological issues, the next bone of contention relates to the economy. One would think that given Taylor recognises how the market, and the bureaucratic nature of the state for that matter, produce atomisation and alienation, then he would want to develop ways of transcending these forms of organisation. Marx's suggestion, given his understanding of the co-operative nature of human beings, was to bring the economy under the control of the associated producers, but for Taylor, this is dismissed as 'illusory'.[39] His evidence for this is the collapse of the old Communist regimes of Eastern Europe and the Soviet Union in particular.[40] He argues that the communist ideal that a society can be run on the basis of a single principle such as planning under the general will is dead, but he suggests that this must also apply to the single principle of the free market. In contrast, Taylor contends that we need to 'combine in some non-self-stultifying fashion a number of ways of operating, which are jointly necessary to a free and prosperous society but which also

---

[37] Charles Taylor, *The Ethics of Authenticity*, Cambridge, Mass, Harvard University Press 1991, pp. 6–7.
[38] Taylor, *Ethics*, p. 107.
[39] Taylor, *Ethics*, p. 109.
[40] Taylor, *Ethics*, pp. 109–110.

tend to impede each other'.[41] These ways are 'market allocations, state planning, collective provision for need, the defence of individual rights, and effective democratic initiative and control'. Taylor argues that whilst the market cannot be abolished, it is also the case that markets should not exclusively dominate economic organisation.[42] Whilst restricting markets can be costly, allowing them free reign can be 'fatal'. He therefore proposes a sort of balancing act between these modes of economic and political organisation he mentions above. Consequently, he contends that there can never be one single solution in governing contemporary society. For Taylor, we simply have no other alternative but to live with the bureaucratic state and the market despite their tendency to cause atomism and instrumentalism. Indeed, Taylor thinks their eternal existence 'has a lot to do with the unending, unresolvable nature of our cultural struggle'. And what of the fate of those suffering the glaring and growing inequalities of wealth throughout the world that are the outcome of this process?[43] Taylor advocates a maximin strategy that is intended to help those at the bottom but without any reductions in the income of high earners.[44] So Taylor's emphasis on freedom is the freedom to let the rich get richer, a policy that has been pursued with messianic vigour particularly in the UK and US with the net result of increasing rather than decreasing inequality.[45] Moreover, the consequences of such disparities in inequality have ramifications for Taylor's emphasis on recognition as a crucial aspect of the self. In his impressive study, *The Impact of Inequality*, Richard Wilkinson's research utilising evidence from all round the world, refutes the idea that it is acceptable to let the rich minority accrue as much wealth as they want as long as those at the bottom achieve improvement as well.[46] Such an argument does not take into account that a lack of social status, or recognition in Taylor's own term, causes major

---

[41]   Taylor, *Ethics*, p. 110.
[42]   Taylor, *Ethics*, p. 111.
[43]   See Alex Callinicos, *Equality*, Cambridge, Polity, 2000, Ch 1.
[44]   Interview with Hartmut Rosa & Arto Laitinen, 'On Identity, Alienation, and the Consequences of September 11th', in Arto Laitinen & Nicholas H. Smith (eds.), *Perspectives on the Philosophy of Charles Taylor*, Helsinki, Acta Philosophica Fennica, The Philosophical Society of Finland, Vol 71, 2002, p. 173. Cf. Ruth Abbey, 'Introduction: The Thought of Charles Taylor' in Ruth Abbey (ed.), *Charles Taylor*, Cambridge, Cambridge University Press, 2004, p. 26. n. 1.
[45]   See Callinicos, *Equality*, Chs. 1 & 4.
[46]   Richard G. Wilkinson, *The Impact of Inequality: How to Make Sick Societies Healthier*, London, Routledge, 2005.

psychological damage to those at the bottom of society as Wilkinson's study clearly proves.

Taylor also posits a false dichotomy in his discussion of economic organisation here. If all that was on offer was central planning of the old Soviet type and unfettered markets then maybe his via media between the two would be acceptable, but this is to ignore the possibility of democratic planning systems that allow people increased participation in production, consumption and distribution.[47] Moreover, Taylor makes no mention of the power of transnational corporations to manipulate markets and the governments of nation states themselves for that matter, through threats of capital flight or lack of investment. Similarly, the consolidation of the ownership of the means of production into these monoliths is not even acknowledged, and even when he does consider the effects of globalisation in relation to his Canadian homeland, the power of transnational corporations is absent from his analysis.[48] Moreover, his answer to the rapacious nature of international competition is simply to utilise the state to make sure citizens of a society are well positioned in the global market.[49] He has seemingly left behind any class analysis that exposes the truths of capitalist production that result in huge inequalities and alienation, which not only exposes the weakness of his position, but also displays the persistent relevance of Marxism as a critique of capitalism.

To display further how Taylor does not see that only by transcending capital can we eliminate atomism and alienation, we can consider his discussion of authenticity and retrieval in relation to the self.[50] Taylor argues that the first consideration of authenticity and retrieval centres on 'the conditions of human life that must condition the realisation of the ideals in question', and the second emanates from 'what the effective realisation of the ideals would amount to'. Taylor offers the example of medical care and the relationship between practitioner and patient.[51] The first consideration above leads Taylor to argue that we are encumbered, dialogical selves, living our lives in a temporal narrative in which our past informs our future. It follows then that for the second consideration, the proper

---

[47]   See, for example, Pat Devine, *Democracy and Economic Planning*, Cambridge, Cambridge University Press, 1988.
[48]   Charles Taylor, 'Globalisation and the Future of Canada', *Queen's Quarterly*, 105/3, 1998.
[49]   Taylor, 'Globalisation and the Future of Canada', p. 333.
[50]   Taylor, *Ethics*, p. 105.
[51]   Taylor, *Ethics*, pp. 107–108.

treatment of a human being needs to respect these aforementioned aspects of the self. The practitioner needs to understand the patient as a person, and relate the treatment to his or her narrative life through an ethic of benevolence served by technology. This is in contrast to an instrumentalist approach which, Taylor argues, should be rejected for ignoring this human and ethical dimension, and for seeing technology as an ever-expansive form of control imposed over nature. Taylor contends that the fact that these two frameworks of instrumentalism on the one side, and human benevolence on the other, means that we will therefore always be engaged in a 'probably unending struggle' in a 'battle for hearts and minds'. Indeed, he notes how this battle of ideas itself will be bound up with political struggles about different forms of social organisation, which he sees as inevitable given the atomism and instrumentalism that emerges from our institutions.

Taylor is clearly correct here but ignores the fact that capitalism by its nature is a system of commodification, which he himself deplores, and as such it veers away from this humanistic approach and towards instrumentalism. Health care is an excellent example of this with the state's pursuit of efficiency acting as a smokescreen for cuts, intensification of workloads, and the setting of targets, all of which undermine any notion of an ethic of benevolence in patient care. Moreover, it is often against these pressures that dedicated medical staff attempt to hold on to the benevolent ethical and more human practitioner-patient approach. Obviously, Taylor thinks this can be solved within the capitalist system, and the advent of welfare states in the twentieth century is clear evidence of this, but he seriously underestimates the instrumentalism that is at the core of capitalist ideology and which has resulted in the attack on the institutions of the welfare state. Capitalism does not have a human face, and the neo-liberal attack on those institutions that make it appear human, only further exposes its inhumanity.[52]

It is clear, then, that Taylor remains locked within the logic of capital, and his claims about the unfreedom of Marxism have been countered on a number of fronts. Ironically, it is Taylor's situated self that seems 'characterless' given his inability or unwillingness to address the fact that the alienating and exploitative operations of the capitalist system suggest it should be overthrown. As Marx points out, 'the entire movement of history is therefore both the *actual* act of creation of communism' and 'for its thinking consciousness, the *compre-*

[52]   Alex Callinicos, *An Anti-Capitalist Manifesto*, Cambridge, Polity, 2003, p. 26.

hended and *known* movement of its *becoming*'.[53] Marx is therefore emphasising how 'communism is at once real and directly bent towards action' in the here and now on the basis of transcending capital through class struggle.[54] On that basis, I now want to examine the development of the identity of the aesthetic self.

Class and Identity

In Chapter One on the self and in the discussion of modern social imaginaries in the previous Chapter, I emphasised the important role of class and class struggle in the formation of identity and used it as part of my critique of Taylor's notion of the self. I now want to offer a brief account of working class identity through the main stages of struggles in the formation and continued, for now, existence of capitalism. The reason for this is to try and understand the changing formation of working class identity and its relevance for a twenty-first-century Marxism in the day-to-day dialectical process of antagonistically transcending capital. To know where we might be going we need to know where we have come from. As I mentioned at the beginning of this Chapter, to do this I want to draw on those writers in the Marxist tradition that have focused on subjects constituting themselves through class struggle, most notably E.P. Thompson, and the Autonomist Marxism of Antonio Negri and Michael Hardt. In relation to Hardt and Negri in particular, they are valuable in the sense that they are suggesting radical ways of envisaging identity formation that I interpret, with some amendments, as part of the development of the aesthetic self.

Taking Thompson as our starting point, his *Making of the English Working Class* is an attempt to 'rescue' from the 'enormous condescension of posterity' the story of those who were actively resisting the exploitative nature of the emerging capitalist system towards the end of the eighteenth century.[55] Thompson shows how, during the period 1780-1832, different groups such as artisans, outworkers and labourers, may have had different experiences specific to their own occupations, but they also came to 'act, think, and feel, not in the old modes of deference and parochial seclusion, but in class ways'.[56] In

[53] Marx, *Economic and Philosophical Manuscripts*, p. 348.
[54] Marx, *Economic and Philosophical Manuscripts*, p. 349.
[55] E.P. Thompson, *The Making of the English Working Class*, Harmondsworth, Penguin, 1970, p. 13.
[56] Thompson, *Making of the English Working Class*, pp. 937–938. Historically Thompson's seminal account of the formation of the working class as an

doing so, they were forging 'new solidarities' that gave them a heightened sense of commitment to a movement, which expressed their own class objectives and went beyond the revolt of the crowd. Chartism was the outcome of these differing and similar experiences and the tensions between them were partly to blame for the movement's failure, and it is from this that Thompson re-emphasises his dynamic notion of class in arguing that a 'new phase of class relationships and institutions commenced'. Additionally, in a later essay, he argues that the new form of class relationship that emerged here was reformism, as the main class institutions of the Labour Movement — trade unions, trades councils, the co-operative movement, etc. — were created and had to be accommodated by the bourgeois-democratic state.[57] As Ellen Meiksins Wood also notes, the defeat of Chartism was an 'epochal watershed in the transformation of working-class militancy from a political to an "economistic" consciousness' and ushered in an era of bourgeois democracy.[58] However, the 'defeat' should be put in perspective given that 'no period of British history [had] been as tense, [and] as politically and socially disturbed' as the 1830s and 1840s.[59] The same, of course, could also be said across Europe, which was being haunted by the spectre of communism culminating in the revolutions of 1848. It is in relation to this that one of the most important figures of Autonomist Marxism, Antonio Negri, could say that June 1848 with the uprisings on the streets of Paris was the moment when the 'modern industrial proletariat first discovered its class autonomy, its independent antago-

---

actor on the stage of history does need a caveat. Following in the footsteps of Thompson, Peter Linebaugh has inverted the title of Thompson's book by suggesting it is more correct to say the making of the '"working class in England"' rather than the making of the English working class. His reason for this relates to the incredible international basis of the London working class in the 1790s in that many had been slaves or transported to colonies, fought in foreign wars, or been members of the labour force of mercantilist expansion. There was therefore an international and multiethnic aspect to the working class in its making. See Peter Linebaugh, *The London Hanged. Crime and Civil Society in the Eighteenth Century*, Harmondsworth, Penguin, 1991, pp. 415–416. See also Peter Linebaugh and Marcus Rediker, *The Many-Headed Hydra. Sailors, Slaves, Commoners, and the Hidden History of the Revolutionary Atlantic*, Boston, Beacon Press, 2000.

[57] E.P. Thompson, *The Poverty of Theory and Other Essays*, London, Merlin, 1978, pp. 280–281.

[58] Ellen Meiksins Wood, *The Pristine Culture of Capitalism*, London, Verso, 1991, p. 74.

[59] Eric. J. Hobsbawm, *Industry and Empire*, Harmondsworth, Penguin, 1983, p. 77.

nism to the capitalist system'.[60] For Negri, the fact that these
revolutions were defeated does not alter the fact that the working
class was achieving a political identity. This was further affirmed
with the Paris Commune of 1871, the defeat of which led to the realisation for greater political organisation and which eventually led to
the Russian Revolution of 1917, where the working class now
appeared as an *'independent* variable in the process of capitalist
development, even to the extent of imposing its own political autonomy'.[61] Negri refers to this stage of working class development as
the era of the 'professional worker'[62]. This era was typified by the
emergence of formidable mass trade unions and the Factory Movement that were asserting their own control over the process of production.[63] Negri denotes this process of new formations in working
class identity as a 'class composition', which capital then attempts to
attack and decompose.[64] Historically, therefore, there is a constant
're-making of the working class' as it takes on new forms in its struggle
against capital.[65] In the case of the 'professional worker', capital's
aim was to break any alliances between workers' vanguards and the
proletariat, and to use Taylorist and Fordist managerial techniques
involving time and motion studies to strictly control the work process and deskill the labour force.[66] The result of this was to bring
forth a new 'class composition' of what Negri calls the 'mass worker'
of assembly line production that was typical of major car manufac-
turers such as Ford in Britain and Fiat in Italy.[67] Economically, this
era is typified by an interventionist state using Keynesian demand
management to ensure productivity and social welfare, which
reflects the power of the working class against capital. As the 'mass
worker' grows in strength and engages in the insubordination of
labour through the refusal of work and making excessive wage

[60] Antonio Negri, 'Keynes and the Capitalist Theory of the State post-1929', in
      his *Revolution Retrieved*, London, Red Notes, 1988, p. 9.
[61] Negri, 'Keynes and the Capitalist Theory of the State', p. 10.
[62] Antonio Negri, 'Interpretation of the Class Situation Today:
      Methodological Aspects', in Werner Bonefeld, Richard Gunn and Kosmas
      Psychopedis (eds.), *Open Marxism. Volume II. Theory and Practice*, London,
      Pluto, 1992, pp. 75–76.
[63] Negri, 'Keynes and the Capitalist Theory of the State', p. 10.
[64] Negri, 'Keynes and the Capitalist Theory of the State', p. 11 & his
      'Archaeology and Project: The Mass Worker and the Social Worker', in
      Revolution Retrieved, p. 209.
[65] Negri, 'Archaeology and Project', p. 209.
[66] Negri, 'Keynes and the Capitalist Theory of the State', p. 11.
[67] Negri, 'Interpretation of the Class Situation', pp. 76–77.

demands, capital then again responds by attempting to decompose the power of the 'mass worker', which ushers in the era of the 'social worker'.[68] The inclusive policies of Keynesianism are now abandoned in favour of the market and a rampant individualism that typified Thatcherism and Reaganism. Monetary policies are implemented to force down real wages and draconian measures used to curb the powers of trade unions. The locus of production is decentralised and dispersed away from the industrial factory and there is a rapid development of the service sectors of the economy. Capital also seeks maximum geographical flexibility through multinational operations in order to overcome the rigidities of working class resistance. For Negri, the 'mass worker' was based in the factory but the 'social worker' is now based in the whole of society which now 'becomes an enormous factory',[69] or, in Mario Tronti's terms, a 'social factory'.[70] The era of the 'social worker' is typified by automation and computerisation and 'immediately productive labour loses its centrality in the process of production' as labour becomes 'completely abstract, immaterial, intellectual'.[71]

Negri has developed this understanding of working class identity in the era of the 'social worker' more recently in his collaboration with Michael Hardt in *Empire* and *Multitude* where they place a particular emphasis on the importance of immaterial labour.[72] Hardt and Negri see the new age of Empire as being an age of 'immaterial labour' which is labour that 'produces an immaterial good, such as a service, a cultural product, knowledge or communication' and which is mostly present in the service sectors of the economy.[73] They note two forms of immaterial labour. The first relates to the increasing computerisation of society in which most jobs in dominant countries require some knowledge of computer technology.[74] They argue, endorsing the work of Robert Reich, that this form of immaterial labour means that humans are actually beginning to think like computers and engage in symbolic-analytical work that involves

---

[68]   Negri, 'Interpretation of the Class Situation', p. 77.
[69]   Antonio Negri, *The Politics of Subversion*, Cambridge, Polity, 1988, p. 204.
[70]   Mario Tronti, 'Social Capital', *Telos*, 17, 1973.
[71]   Negri, 'Interpretation of the Class Situation', p. 77.
[72]   Michael Hardt and Antonio Negri, *Empire*, Harvard, Harvard University Press, 2000 & *Multitude*, London, Hamish Hamilton, 2005.
[73]   Hardt & Negri, *Empire*, p. 290.
[74]   Hardt & Negri, *Empire*, p. 291.

problem-identification and problem-solving.[75] Following Reich, they suggest that this form of immaterial labour has the 'highest value' in global competitive capitalism, but will also result in jobs with 'low value' and low skills such as word-processing and the simple entering of data. For Hardt and Negri, this indicates the onset of a clear division of labour in immaterial production.

The second form of immaterial labour relates to what they call '*affective labour*' which involves the use of contact and interaction to cause an affect in another person.[76] This type of labour can be found in the caring services, and in the work of legal assistants, flight attendants and fast food workers, for instance, where it creates social networks and forms of community, or what they refer to as 'biopower'. They also add that a tendency towards immaterial labour can be found in industrial production, which has moved from Fordist forms of organisation to Toyotism, and involves just-in-time methods of producing with informational links with market demand.[77] Hardt and Negri argue that in all of these forms of immaterial labour lies social interaction and cooperation, which is not imposed from above but is present in the labouring activity itself.[78] They suggest that this therefore calls into question Marx's understanding of labour-power as variable capital that is activated only by something outside, namely, capital. Whilst they admit that value still needs to be produced by humans, they suggest that this outside other is 'not necessarily provided by capital and its capacities to orchestrate production'. On that basis, they feel confident enough to assert that immaterial labour with its emphasis on 'cooperative interactivity through linguistic, communicational and affective networks' can offer the 'potential for a kind of spontaneous and elementary communism'. However, they argue later in *Multitude*, their sequel to *Empire*, that their notion of immaterial labour is not meant in any way to 'lessen the hierarchy and command in the workplace'.[79] In

---

[75] Hardt & Negri, *Empire*, pp. 291–292 & *Multitude*, p. 108. Robert Reich, *The Work of Nations: Preparing Ourselves for 21st Century Capitalism*, New York, Knopf, 1991, p. 177.

[76] Hardt & Negri, *Empire*, pp. 292–293 & *Multitude*, p. 108.

[77] Hardt & Negri, *Empire*, p. 290.

[78] Hardt & Negri, *Empire*, p. 294.

[79] Hardt & Negri, *Multitude*, p. 111. This responds to Paul Thompson's criticism that Hardt and Negri are guilty of mistakenly supporting management theorists and their endorsement of a knowledge economy, where power lies with the workers who are seen to be free from capitalist control. See Paul Thompson, 'Foundation and Empire: A Critique of Hardt and Negri', *Capital & Class*, 86, 2005, pp. 83 & 84–86.

Multitude, the importance of immaterial labour itself is reiterated and they argue that it now has a qualitative hegemonic position in the global economy, just as industrial labour had 150 years ago.[80] They contend that it is always the case that one form of labour in any economic system will have dominance over other forms of labour, because it acts as a vortex that causes other forms of labour to adopt its own qualities.[81] Industrial labour was therefore hegemonic in the nineteenth and twentieth centuries, even though quantitatively it was smaller compared to other forms of production such as agriculture. Additionally, it was all pervasive in forcing not only other forms of labour such as agriculture, mining etc., into its vortex of industrialisation, but social institutions such as the family, school and the military. Hardt and Negri recognise that whilst labouring practices did differ from those in industry in some respects, there was a commonality also in certain forms of labour. They argue that this multiplicity and commonality aspect is what interests them most.

Hardt and Negri are quick to add here that what is immaterial in immaterial labour is the product of labour not the labour itself, because the latter is material as it involves the use of the brain and body.[82] It is at this point that they recognise a certain ambiguity of the term immaterial labour and suggest that it may be better to understand this new hegemonic form of labour as 'biopolitical labour', which is 'labour that creates not only material goods but also relationships and ultimately social life itself'. On this basis, they suggest that distinctions between the economic, political, social and cultural are becoming increasingly difficult to maintain, but they also recognise that even biopolitics contains ambiguities and complexities, which makes them re-emphasise that the best way to grasp this new form of economic transformation that is taking place is through the notion of immateriality. Immaterial labour means that all societies need to 'informationalise, become intelligent, become communicative, become affective'.

In relation to affective labour Hardt and Negri note how, when it becomes part of waged labour, it can become increasingly alienating because it involves the selling of the ability to make human relationships, which is a very intimate activity, to the power of the boss or

---

[80]   Hardt & Negri, *Multitude*, p. 109.
[81]   Hardt & Negri, *Multitude*, pp. 107–108.
[82]   Hardt & Negri, *Multitude*, p. 109.

client.[83] They therefore argue that the notion of alienation, which they suggest 'was always a poor concept for understanding the exploitation of factory workers', is now a 'useful conceptual key' for understanding exploitation in this realm of affective labour. However, Hardt and Negri do not explain why they think Marx's notion of alienation is inadequate for grasping the exploitation of factory workers, but I would argue that the theory clearly exposes the dehumanising effects of factory labour that Marx depicted in his writings, and that still resonate in their power today. Instead, then, we should retain Marx's theory of alienation in relation to factory labour alongside the alienating affects in the realm of immaterial labour, and in conjunction with the theory of fetishism for a proper understanding of how capital attempts to negate every aspect of our identity.

Hardt and Negri develop further their examination of class identity by proffering a new class composition of the social worker that now takes the form of what they call the multitude.[84] They argue that the multitude is a class concept and as such this necessitates a discussion of the nature of class.[85] Hardt and Negri point out that the two dominant theories in relation to class are between unity, which is associated with Marx and his notion of the proletariat confronting capital, and plurality which is associated with liberal positions that stress the multiplicity of classes and also differences in relation to race, gender and so on. Hardt and Negri agree that both of these apparently contradictory understandings are true and so therefore choosing between either one or the other can only lead to a dead end.[86] Instead, then, they argue that to escape this dichotomy requires understanding class politically. In doing so they argue, in a similar fashion to E.P. Thompson, that 'class is determined by class struggle' and whilst classes can be constituted in many ways, such as hair colour, for example, the only classes that are really important are 'those defined by the lines of collective struggle'. Class itself therefore is not defined by certain empirical differences, but is formed through collective resistance to power. Similarly, they assert that race as a political concept is not determined by skin colour or ethnicity, but by the collective struggle against racial oppression.

---

[83] Hardt & Negri, *Multitude*, p. 111.
[84] Hardt & Negri, *Empire*, p. 60 & *Multitude*, p. 103.
[85] Hardt & Negri, *Multitude*, p. 103.
[86] Hardt & Negri, *Multitude*, p. 104.

Hardt and Negri also understand class as a political concept in a second way, namely that it contains not only the present lines of class struggle but future lines as well. On this basis, they propose that a theory of class must 'identify the existing *conditions* for potential collective struggle and express them as a political *proposition*'. So 'class is really a constituent deployment, a project' and they suggest that this is the way we should understand Marx's argument about the tendency in capital for classes to converge in binary opposition to capital, not as a given fact, but as a possibility. This is also why Marx talks of different classes of labour and capital whilst proposing the possibility of the uniting of all struggles in the proletariat as a class. For Hardt and Negri, it is this political project that divides Marx's notion of a binary class to that of the class pluralism of liberalism.[87] It is here that they want to overcome the dichotomy between economic and political struggles because the latter obscure a proper understanding of class relations.[88] They argue that class is a 'biopolitical' concept that is both economic and political, which means that labour must be understood as 'human creative capacities in all their generality' and not simply as waged labour. Consequently, they define the multitude as the 'productive, creative subjectivities, of globalisation' which 'form constellations of singularities and events that impose continual global reconfigurations on the system'.[89] The struggle of the multitude therefore brings into being a new era of Empire, which is a sovereign power that governs the world and regulates global exchanges.[90] For Hardt and Negri, Empire is a new form of rule in which sovereignty has begun to take a global form given the declining sovereignty of nation states. Empire, unlike imperialism, has no boundaries or any centre of territorial power and the 'object of its rule is social life in its entirety'.[91] The multitude itself is therefore '*within* Empire and *against* Empire', and its constituent movement is one of negative antagonism and 'creative positivity'.[92] They argue that the internal presence of the multitude in Empire is not dialectical in terms of a negative producing a positive, but is instead an 'absolutely positive force' that offers an 'alternative paradigm', and 'pushes the dominating power toward an abstract and empty unifi-

---

[87]   Hardt & Negri, *Multitude*, pp. 104–105.
[88]   Hardt & Negri, *Multitude*, p. 105.
[89]   Hardt & Negri, *Empire*, p. 60.
[90]   Hardt & Negri, *Empire*, pp xi–xii.
[91]   Hardt & Negri, *Empire*, p. xiv.
[92]   Hardt & Negri, *Empire*, p. 61.

cation'.[93] For Hardt and Negri, the multitude has a 'deterritorialising power' that both supports Empire, whilst at the same time implying its abolition. Empire may appear to have power over the multitude but it is parasitic on the productive capacity of the latter, just as Marx had said that capital is vampire-like in that dead labour lives by sucking the blood of living labour.

Hardt's and Negri's haste to dispense with the dialectic does run into difficulties here, given I am emphasising the dialectics of the self. They describe the presence of the multitude in Empire as being negatively antagonistic and positively creative which is indicative of the movement of the dialectic, but they insist against this that the negating influence of the multitude is absolutely positive and not part of the process of negation. However, their reference back to Marx and the vampire nature of capital undermines such an argument. The dialectic between living labour and dead labour is that living labour is turned into dead labour (negative) whilst at the same time trying to assert its own essence (positive) through the negation of capital. Against their attempt to reject the dialectic, a legacy of Negri's preference for Spinoza over Hegel,[94] I retain it for understanding new class formations that I will develop shortly through the notion of the aesthetic self.

In developing their argument further in *Multitude*, Hardt and Negri say explicitly that they want to 'repropose Marx's political project of class struggle'.[95] In that sense, what they seek is not just identifying who the multitude is, but rather identifying what the multitude can become. They therefore offer a definition of the multitude by referring to it as all those who work under the rule of capital, and refer to its potentiality as the class of people who refuse the rule of capital.[96] This allows them to make a distinction between the multitude and the working class, as the latter is based on exclusion and hence is a restrictive concept. They argue that the working class has been understood limitedly as referring only to industrial labour, and more widely as referring to all waged labourers, which leads to the exclusion of the non-waged. On this basis, the working class has been given a privileged position in the struggle against capital with other classes following in its wake. For Hardt and Negri, this is no

[93] Hardt & Negri, *Empire*, p. 62.
[94] On the importance of Spinoza for Negri see Antonio Negri, *The Savage Anomaly. The Power of Spinoza's Metaphysics and Politics*, Minneapolis, University of Minnesota Press, 1991.
[95] Hardt & Negri, *Multitude*, p. 105.
[96] Hardt & Negri, *Multitude*, p. 106.

longer the case because there is no priority in any of the forms of labour existing today. All forms of labour not only produce in common but also share the common potential to rebel against capital.[97] They are quick to point out that they are not saying that industrial labour is unimportant, what they are saying is that it does not hold a privileged position in relation to other classes in the multitude.[98] The multitude is therefore an 'open and expansive concept' and overcomes the exclusivity of the working class as industrial labour. In this way, various types of labour are now in a position to 'communicate, collaborate and become common'. Hardt and Negri are again quick to add that their emphasis on this commonality of labour as a basis for the construction of the multitude does not result in the exclusion of those who are not engaged in wage labour such as the poor, the unemployed, and the homeless and so on.[99] They argue that these classes are part of the multitude because they all engage in social production. For Hardt and Negri, the poor are certainly victims of global capital in the way they are deprived of resources with which to live a decent life, but they are also 'powerful agents' in their involvement in service work, agriculture and mass migration. The poor are depicted as being incredibly resourceful even when they do not earn a wage precisely because they have to be so in order to survive.[100] They are therefore part of the circuits of social and biopolitical production, and in the dominant countries of the twentieth century poor people's movements have become united in calling national governments to account for their plight.[101] So Hardt and Negri argue that there is not a qualitative difference between the poor and waged workers because all are engaged in social production, and hence this gives a shared common experience for the multitude as a whole.[102]

The focus on class struggle in relation to identity formation that I have been discussing, and which is largely absent from Taylor's account, reveals the antagonistic basis to the development and continued existence of capital. From Thompson's path-breaking early work, through to the innovative interpretations of Hardt and Negri, albeit with some amendments by me, a vibrant understanding of identity for Marxism in the twenty-first century has developed that

[97] Hardt & Negri, *Multitude*, pp. 106–107.
[98] Hardt & Negri, *Multitude*, p. 107.
[99] Hardt & Negri, *Multitude*, p. 129.
[100] Hardt & Negri, *Multitude*, p. 131.
[101] Hardt & Negri, *Multitude*, pp. 129 & 135.
[102] Hardt & Negri, *Multitude*, pp. 134–135.

is a far cry from Taylor's accusation of a 'characterless' self. A radical understanding of identity is being forged through material and immaterial labour and the encompassing but varied development of the multitude. To expand on this further, I now want to give some instances of how the aesthetic self emerges in its dialectical struggles against capital. In doing so, we will be not only transcending Charles Taylor, but also transcending the constraints of capital itself.

Transcending Capital

To even utter these two words invites mocking laughter at best and instant dismissiveness at worst, but following Marx's edict on communism being a process, we need to look in the here and now for the dialectical movement of the aesthetic self within the multitude. The reasons why should be obvious. The juggernaut of capital powers on sundering all before its wake producing exploitation, instrumentalism, wars, insecurity, poverty, exclusion, and alienation to name but a few. For the ideologues of capital these realities become hidden behind a language of flexibility, choice, efficiency, expanding 'democracy' and 'freedom', competition, wealth creation, and an understanding that this is the only system possible. As Harold Pinter pointed out in his acceptance speech when receiving the prestigious Nobel Prize for literature, an event largely ignored by the British media for the obvious reason that it was largely an attack on US and UK foreign policy, the lust for power and its maintenance by politicians means truth is the first casualty as they offer us a 'vast tapestry of lies, upon which we feed'.[103] Iraq and weapons of mass destruction: a lie.[104] That Iraq had a relationship with Al Qaeda and shared responsibility for the atrocity in New York of September 11th 2001: a lie. Bush and Blair, the people responsible for these lies and the subsequent slaughter of thousands, stayed in office hardly troubled by a weak political opposition within their respective countries, coupled with a largely compliant and subservient mainstream media. The capitalist show must go on with its theatre of blood. Iraq and the pursuit of oil as an adjunct of intended US hegemonic dominance, backed up by a 'bleating little lamb tagging behind it on a lead' in the guise of Blair, is of course only one issue.[105] Twenty-first

[103] Harold Pinter, 'Art, Truth and Politics', *The Guardian*, December 8, 2005.
[104] Jonathan Freedland, 'Yes, they did lie to us', *The Guardian*, June 22, 2005. Henry Porter, 'It's clear: The case for war was cooked up', *The Observer*, November 5, 2006.
[105] Pinter, 'Art, Truth and Politics'.

century capital and its acolytes are dripping in blood from head to foot for all the obvious reasons mentioned above. The rapacious nature of global capital that Marx noted as long ago as 1848 is worth restating here to show his continued relevance for today:

> The need of a constantly expanding market for its products chases the bourgeoisie over the whole surface of the globe. It must nestle everywhere, settle everywhere, establish connexions everywhere. The bourgeoisie has through its exploitation of the world market given a cosmopolitan character to production and consumption in every country ... [and] compels all nations, on pain of extinction, to adopt the bourgeois mode of production ... In one word it creates a world after its own image.[106]

And so capital has gone on trying to create the world in its own image, but in doing so it has had to respond to working class resistance as I outlined previously. The class struggle that we are told by political elites is over instead goes on and on, and just as Marx emphasised the international basis to this struggle through his clarion call for all workers of the world to unite, so too has the response to global capital taken new forms of confrontation. On that basis, I want to mention the presence of aesthetic selves that have and are dialectically emerging in, against and potentially beyond capital in all the realms of everyday life.

What in recent times has been a defining and inspiring example of those who oppose the logic of capital, and has caused so many problems for the neo-liberal Mexican state, is that of the Zapatistas. Their insurgent actions in December of 1994 when they broke through the cordon of the state army caused tremors on the financial markets as 'capital fled'.[107] In terms of the aestheticisation of the self, the Zapatistas are interesting in that Subcomandante Marcos uses stories and poems to articulate the suffering and hope of the Mexican peasants and their relation to other struggles around the world. For example, Marcos has conversations with the character of Durito, a beetle, who acts as his 'superadvisor'.[108] In one instance, Durito informs Marcos that neo-liberalism 'is not a theory to confront or explain the crisis. It is the crisis itself made theory and economic doc-

[106] Marx & Engels, *The Communist Manifesto*, pp. 83–84.
[107] John Holloway, 'Zapata in Wall Street', in Werner Bonefeld & Kosmas Psychopedis (eds.), *The Politics of Change. Globalization, Ideology and Critique*, Houndmills, Palgrave, 2000, p. 173.
[108] Subcomandante Marcos, *Ya Basta. Ten Years of the Zapatista Uprising*, Oakland and Edinburgh, AK Press, 2004, p. 106.

trine ... In the end, pure theoretical shit'.[109] With neo-liberalism identified, Marcos and Durito lie down together as night approaches in the Lacandon jungle, contemplating how this 'shit' can be overcome.[110] When Durito asks Marcos what he intends to do, the latter replies: 'win'. As Olga Taxidou points out, Marcos' '"literary" style is one that fuses the aesthetic with the polemic, the private with the public', and overcomes the possible divide between intellectuals and activists to re-affirm the belief that 'literature could be anything other than political'[111] The aesthetic self, then, is not an elitist self or a de-politicised self as the latter example of the Zapatistas can testify, and aligned with these forms of an aesthetic self are *all* those who, as Hardt and Negri point out, refuse the rule of capital.

One particular manifestation of aesthetic selves is encapsulated by Paul Kingsnorth's inspirational book, *One No, Many Yeses*, in which he gives a first-hand account of the development of the global anti-capitalist movement.[112] Kingsnorth relates his involvement in the major protests of the movement after the Zapatista uprising, and its baptism in the battle of Seattle against the World Trade Organisation in 1999 reflects its varied nature.[113] When Kingsnorth considers the 'no' that all these disparate groups, made from the bottom up, with no leaders and no manifestos, are asserting, he suggests that the two most common are the negative epithets of the anti-capitalist and anti-globalisation movement based around the positive principles or 'yeses' of 'democracy, diversity, decentralisation, sovereignty and access'.[114] Kingsnorth repeats again and again that the strength of the movement lies in the fact that there is no manifesto, but he then sets out his own based around the aforementioned principles over some six pages.[115] This is why writers such as Alex Callinicos suggest that to develop a strategy and propose an alternative is determined by clearly identifying who the enemy is.[116] The strength of

---

[109] Marcos, *Ya Basta*, p. 106.

[110] Marcos, *Ya Basta*, pp. 106 & 108.

[111] Olga Taxidou, 'Reviews' of Subcomandante Marcos, *Shadows of Tender Fury. The Letters and Communiques of Subcomandante Marcos and the Zapatista Army of National Liberation*, New York, Monthly Review Press, 1995 & *Zapatistas! Documents of the New Mexican Revolution*, New York, Autonomedia, 1994, *Common Sense*, 18, 1995, p. 84.

[112] Paul Kingsnorth, *One No, Many Yeses. A Journey to the Heart of the Global Resistance Movement*, London, Free Press, 2003.

[113] Kingsnorth, *One No, Many Yeses*, pp. 61–62.

[114] Kingsnorth, *One No, Many Yeses*, pp. 70–71 & 319.

[115] Kingsnorth, *One No, Many Yeses*, pp. 321–326.

[116] Callinicos, *An Anti-Capitalist Manifesto*, p. 14.

this global movement has certainly been its disparate nature as Kingsnorth highlights above, but it is important to recognise that it is the capitalist system that should be the target and its overthrow should be the aim. In that sense, this global movement can best be described as anti-capitalist even if there are many different strategies put forward to overcome such a system.[117] Indeed, the global anti-capitalist movement in its many forms displays the democratisation of the aesthetic self by forming new ways of thinking and organising.[118] It is the dialectical movement on the path to transcending capital. That such a global movement involving millions of people exists at a time of a supposed triumphant capitalism is truly astonishing. So against the dead-behind-the-eyes mantra of 'there is no alternative' is the life-affirming cry of 'Another world is Possible'. Consequently, the dialectical impact of the global forces that manifest themselves through foreign direct investment, global finance, global media and the sundering of human relationships to the commodification of consumerism, bring forth those who oppose such forces.[119] The information age that Hardt and Negri see as crucial in relation to new sites of class struggle, means the global links of resistance to capital brings people together to realise that they are not on their own in their resistance to capital. Global Exchange, the international human rights organisation for example, is committed to promoting social, economic and environmental justice around the world.[120] It runs campaigns against the heinous practices of the transnational corporations and corrupt governments. Similarly, Corporate Watch challenges the professed beneficial ethos of many transnational corporations such as Wal-Mart for instance, to expose them for the authoritarian, exploitative firms they really are. Outside the formal, bourgeois media, which accepts capitalism as the only system possible and reports it in that way, there are those who are developing networks of communication to subvert the status quo.

So the forces of globalisation bring in their wake aesthetic selves that attempt to negate the stultifying hegemony of capitalism. Wal-Mart, for example, one of the biggest corporations in the world,

[117] For a useful overview of these varied strategies see Callinicos, *An Anti-Capitalist Manifesto*, Ch. 2.
[118] See for example, Notes from Nowhere (ed.), *We are Everywhere: The Irresistible Rise of Global Anti-capitalism*, London, Verso, 2003.
[119] Leslie Sklair, *The Transnational Capitalist Class*, Oxford, Blackwell, 2001, pp. 296 & 299.
[120] See www.globalexchange.org

has engaged in a number of nefarious practices that resulted in the International labour Rights Fund filing lawsuits against it for their use of sweatshop labour in a number of countries throughout the world.[121] This has led to a major international campaign against the organisation linking workers and activists on a huge scale. Resistance to the power of corporate capital is therefore present and growing out of the increase in globalisation itself. At the time of writing, organised labour unions from the US, Britain, and Germany are in the process of developing the first global super-union with more than six million members to combat the 'power of global capitalism'.[122] The union aims to respond to the ways in which transnational corporations can trade off workers and countries against each other by creating solidarity agreements. This is in recognition by union officials that given the nature of global capital a trade union acting in one country is no longer viable. Whether this initiative will work or even come to fruition is, at this time, unclear, but it is a further indication of the development of aesthetic selves in their struggles against capital.

The political and economic aspects of a development of the aesthetic self are accompanied by the cultural manifestations, which also point to a rejection of capital. A whole counter-culture is offering the possibility for a flourishing of aesthetic selves that are being educated to question the system rather than accept it. For example, the resurgence of documentary making for the cinema from those who oppose the rule of capital and the neo-liberal agenda in particular is further evidence of the development of the aesthetic self. The campaign against Wal-Mart mentioned earlier, has been translated into a documentary that exposes the malpractices within the organisation and, in particular, its authoritarian stranglehold on its workforce.[123] Similarly, the excellent film documentary *The Corporation* considered the ramifications of the fact that corporations have the same legal status as human beings.[124] On that basis, the film engaged in a psychological test on the actions and operations of major corporations and concluded, perhaps unsurprisingly, that they are psychopathic. These fact-based analyses of the evils of

[121] www.globalexchange.org/campaigns/corpaccount/walmart.html

[122] Oliver Morgan, 'Birth of the first global super-union', *The Observer*, 31 December, 2006.

[123] *Wal-Mart: The High Cost of Low Price*, directed by Robert Greenwald, USA, 2005.

[124] *The Corporation*, directed by Jennifer Abbot & Mark Ahbar, Other English Language, 2003.

corporate capitalist power are also supplemented by 'fictional' accounts such as, for example, the filming of John Le Carré's novel *The Constant Gardner*, which exposes the corrupt practices of the pharmaceutical industry in league with corrupt members of the British political elite using the poor people of African countries as guinea pigs for medical experimentation.[125] Additionally, the film itself begins by the main female character Tess, played by Rachel Weisz, in the midst of assorted journalists, challenging Ralph Fiennes' Justin, a junior British diplomat, over the Iraq war to the utter bewilderment and boredom of the rest of the press pack who have obviously accepted the Blairite mantra that it is time to move on. Similarly, the corruption and lies of the Bush administration over the Iraq war, a diversionary tactic to detract attention from the failure to capture Osama bin Laden and the Bush's family business links with the Saudi Bin Laden Royal family, were also brought to millions of people through Michael Moore's controversial, but inventive documentary *Fahrenheit 9/11*.[126] As one critic pointed out, the film 'made populist dissent the stuff not merely of websites or print journalism but big Hollywood box office'.[127] Moore's film was also particularly important as it exposed how the mainstream American media were complicit in spreading lies and deceit to ensure public support for the war and the neo-liberal agenda of the Bush regime.

To cite these examples is not to ignore the fact that this movement of the aesthetic self is at the margins, that it is an outsider arguing against the grain of the accepted wisdoms of capitalist ideology. That is fairly obvious. Rather, the point is that despite the perceived ideological predominance of capital's hegemony there are millions of people throughout the world who are prepared to question it. The fact that the whole of the system is geared towards continuing capital's existence through accumulation and the pursuit of profit means that such questioning is truly remarkable and deserves to be recognised as such.

Given the preceding discussion, then, what intimations from the here and now might we glean about the possible development of the aesthetic self in a process of transcending capital? The aesthetic self

---

[125] *The Constant Gardener*, directed by Fernando Meirelles, Rest of the World, 2005.

[126] *Fahrenheit 9/11*, directed by Michael Moore, USA, 2004. Cf. Craig Unger, *House of Bush House of Saud: The Secret Relationship Between the World's Two Most Powerful Dynasties*, London, Gibson Square Books, 2007 for more details on the links between the two families.

[127] Peter Bradshaw, 'Review' of *Fahrenheit 9/11*, *The Guardian*, July 9, 2004.

is emerging in the demand for radical democratic structures that give real meaning to his or her own life in developing and encouraging a vibrant political community. The questioning of market competition and an emphasis on democratic and cooperative forms of economic organisation, linked to reductions in labour time through ecologically sensitive technological production, could lead to a real flourishing of the aesthetic self. The aesthetic self emerges in his or her immediate community, but ultimately transcends that community, and the nation, to engage with aesthetic selves in the world. With greater time for contemplation, the aesthetic self could have increased time for moral deliberation and recognise that, in a de-fetishised world, his or her actions are inextricably linked with others globally. Mutual respect and recognition are the bywords for the operations of everyday life through the auspices of global citizenship and global democracy. As Hardt and Negri rightly argue, 'the possibility of democracy on a global scale is emerging today for the very first time'.[128] Freed from a capitalist system which rules through the instrumentalised and fetishised forms of exchange value, the aesthetic self 'strives not to remain something' he or she 'has become, but is in the absolute movement of becoming' in the 'working out of ... creative capacities' with the 'development of all human powers as such the end in itself'.[129] All this is possible because a reduction in necessary labour time to a minimum allows the 'artistic, scientific, etc. development of the individuals in the time set free'.[130] The 'true realm of freedom' is where 'the development of human powers' is an end in itself and lies beyond the realm of natural necessity.[131] Just how and in what ways these powers manifest themselves is open to debate, but the desire for the contemplative life for *all* suddenly becomes a possibility beyond the stringencies of capital, but not within it as Taylor suggests. A more direct democracy stands in opposition to representative democracy, participatory economic organisation is positively contrasted with the vagaries of the market, and the social conditions of production could be used to benefit the majority rather than a minority transnational capitalist class.[132] For bourgeois apologists of capital, of course, such hopes must be curtailed immediately. However, the

[128] Hardt and Negri, *Multitude*, p. 1.
[129] Karl Marx, *Grundrisse*, Harmondsworth, Penguin, 1973, p. 488. Cf. Terry Eagleton, *The Ideology of the Aesthetic*, Oxford, Blackwell, 1990, p. 226.
[130] Marx, *Grundrisse*, p. 706.
[131] Karl Marx, *Capital*, Volume 3, Harmondsworth, Penguin, 1991, p. 959.
[132] See Sklair, *The Transnational Capitalist Class*.

aesthetic self in its manifest forms is positing a different world, a world that challenges and transcends the supposedly 'everlasting truths'[133] of capitalism, a world where:

> in the place of the old local and national seclusion and self-sufficiency, we have intercourse in every direction, universal interdependence of nations. And as in material, so also in intellectual production. The intellectual creations of individual nations become common property. National one-sidedness and narrow-mindedness become more and more impossible, and from the numerous national and local literatures, there arises a world literature. [134]

It is from the haunting spectre of the humanist Marxist tradition that such a world can become a real possibility.

---

[133] A dictum Marx attributes to the 'vulgar economists' of the nineteenth century. See, Karl Marx, *Capital*, Volume 1, Harmondsworth, Penguin, 1988, p. 175. n. 34.

[134] Marx & Engels, *The Communist Manifesto*, p. 84.

Bibliography

Works By Charles Taylor Cited

'Marxism and Humanism', *New Reasoner*, 2, 1957.

'The Ambiguities of Marxist Doctrine', *The Student World*, 2, 1958.

'Marxism and Empiricism', in Bernard Williams & Alan Montefiore (eds.), *British Analytical Philosophy*, London, Routledge & Kegan Paul, 1966.

'From Marxism to the Dialogue Society', in Terry Eagleton & Brian Wicker (eds.), *From Culture to Revolution*, London & Sydney, Sheed & Ward, 1968.

'Socialism and Weltanschauung', in Leszek Kolakowski & Stuart Hampshire (eds.), *The Socialist Idea: a Reappraisal*, London, Weidenfeld & Nicholson, 1974.

Hegel, Cambridge, Cambridge University Press, 1975.

'Marxist Philosophy', in Brian Magee (ed.), *Men of Ideas: Some Creators of Contemporary Philosophy*, London, BBC Publications, 1978.

'Atomism', in *Philosophy and the Human Sciences: Philosophical Papers II*, Cambridge, Cambridge University Press, 1985.

'Marxism and Socialist Humanism', in Robin Archer *et al* (eds.), *Out of Apathy: Voices of the New Left Thirty Years On*, London, Verso, 1989.

Sources of the Self: The Making of the Modern Identity, Cambridge, Cambridge University Press, 1989

The Ethics of Authenticity, Cambridge, Mass, Harvard University Press, 1992.

'Charles Taylor Replies', in James Tully (ed.), *Philosophy in an Age of Pluralism: The Philosophy of Charles Taylor in Question*, Cambridge, Cambridge University Press, 1994.

'The Importance of Herder' in his *Philosophical Arguments*, Cambridge, Mass, & London, Harvard University Press, 1997.

'The Politics of Recognition', in *Philosophical Arguments*, Cambridge, Mass, Harvard University Press, 1995.

'Globalisation and the Future of Canada', *Queen's Quarterly*, 105/3, 1998.

'Modes of Secularism', in Rajeev Bhagarva (ed.), *Secularism and its Critics*, Delhi Oxford University Press, 1998.

'A Catholic Modernity?', in James. L. Heft (ed.), *A Catholic Modernity?* Oxford, Oxford University Press, 1999.

'Concluding Reflections and Comments', in James L. Heft (ed.), *A Catholic Modernity?*, Oxford, Oxford University Press, 1999.

Varieties of Religion Today. William James Revisited, Cambridge, Mass & London, Harvard University Press, 2002.

Modern Social Imaginaries, Durham & London, Duke University Press, 2004.

'A Place for Transcendence?', in Regina Schwartz (ed.), *Transcendence. Philosophy, Literature and Theology Approach the Beyond*, New York & London, Routledge, 2004.

Other Works

Abbey, Ruth. *Charles Taylor*, New Jersey, Princeton University Press, 2000.

Abbey, Ruth. 'The Articulated Life: An Interview with Charles Taylor', *Reason in Practice*, 1, 3, 2001.

Abbey, Ruth. 'Introduction: The Thought of Charles Taylor', in Ruth Abbey (ed.), *Charles Taylor*, Cambridge, Cambridge University Press, 2004.

Abbey, Ruth. 'The Primary Enemy? Monotheism and Pluralism' in James Boyd White, (ed.), *How Should We Talk about Religion?*, South Bend, Indiana, University of Notre Dame Press, 2004.

Abbey, Ruth. 'Turning or Spinning? Charles Taylor's Catholicism: A Reply to Ian Fraser', *Contemporary Political Theory*, 5, 2, 2006.

Abbot, Jennifer & Ahbar, Mark. (Directors), *The Corporation*, Other English Language, 2003.

Adorno, Theodor. *Minima Moralia. Reflections from Damaged Life*, London, Verso, 1978.

Adorno, Theodor. *Negative Dialectics*, London, Routledge, 1990.

Adorno, Theodor. 'Trying to Understand *Endgame*', in *Notes to Literature*, Vol. 1, New York, Columbia University Press, 1991.

Adorno, Theodor. 'Extorted Reconciliation: On Georg Lukács' *Realism in our Time*', in *Notes to Literature* Vol. 1, New York, Columbia University Press, 1991.

Adorno, Theodor. 'Theses upon Art and Religion', in *Notes to Literature* Vol. 2, New York, Columbia University Press, 1992.

Adorno, Theodor. 'On Proust', in *Notes to Literature* Vol. 2, New York, Columbia University Press, 1992.

Adorno, Theodor. *Aesthetic Theory*, London, Athlone, 1997.

Adorno, Theodor. & Horkheimer, Max. *Dialectic of Enlightenment*, London, Verso, 1992.

Anderson, Benedict. *Imagined Communities*, London and New York, Verso, 1991.

Archer *et al*, Robin (eds.), *Out of Apathy: Voices of the New Left Thirty Years On*, London, Verso, 1989.

Aveling, J.C.H. *The Jesuits*, London, Blond & Briggs, 1981.

Bahro, Rudolf. *From Red to Green*, London, Verso 1984.

Benton, Ted. 'Marxism and Natural Limits: An Ecological Critique and Reconstruction', *New Left Review*, 178, 1989.

Beja, Morris. *Epiphany in the Modern Novel*, London, Peter Owen, 1971.

Benjamin, Walter. 'Theses on the Philosophy of History' in Walter Benjamin, *Illuminations*, Hannah Arendt (ed.), London, Fontana, 1992.

Benjamin, Walter. 'The Task of the Translator', in Walter Benjamin, *Illuminations*, Hannah Arendt (ed.), London, Fontana, 1992.

Benjamin, Walter. 'On Some Motifs in Baudelaire', in Walter Benjamin, *Illuminations*, Hannah Arendt (ed.), London, Fontana, 1992.

Benjamin, Walter. 'One Way Street', in Walter Benjamin, *One-Way Street and Other Writings*, London, Verso, 1997.

Berlin, Isaiah. 'Introduction', to James Tully (ed.), *Philosophy in an Age of Pluralism: The Philosophy of Charles Taylor in Question*, Cambridge, Cambridge University Press, 1994.

Bernstein, J.M. *The Fate of Art. Aesthetic Alienation from Kant to Derrida and Adorno*, Cambridge, Polity, 1992.

Billig, Michael. *Banal Nationalism*, London, Sage, 2001.

Bloch, Ernst. *Atheism in Christianity*, New York, Herder & Herder, 1972.

Bloch, Ernst. *A Philosophy of the Future*, New York, Herder & Herder, 1970.

Bloch, Ernst. *On Karl Marx*, New York, Herder and Herder, 1971.

Bloch, Ernst. *The Principle of Hope*, 3 Volumes, Oxford, Basil Blackwell, 1986.

Bloch, Ernst. *Literary Essays*, California, Stanford University Press, 1998.

Brace, Laura. *The Politics of Property: Labour Freedom and Belonging*, Edinburgh, Edinburgh University Press, 2004.

Bradshaw, Peter. 'Review' of *Fahrenheit 9/11*, *The Guardian*, July 9, 2004.

Breuilly, John. 'Reflections on Nationalism', *Philosophy and Social Science*, 15, 1, 1985.

Burns, Robert A. *Roman Catholicism After Vatican II*, Washington, D.C, Georgetown University Press, 2001.

Calhoun, Craig. 'Nationalism and Ethnicity', *American Review of Sociology*, 9, 1993.

Callinicos, Alex. *Equality*, Cambridge, Polity, 2000.

Callinicos, Alex. *An Anti-Capitalist Manifesto*, Cambridge, Polity, 2003.

Cleaver, Harry. *Reading Capital Politically*, London, AK Press, 2000.

Colum, Padraic. 'Padraic Colum on Joyce and Dublin', in Robert H Deming (ed.), *James Joyce. The Critical Heritage*, Volume 1 — 1902–1927, London, Routledge, 1970.

Costello, Peter. *James Joyce. The Years of Growth*. 1882–1915, London, Kyle Cathie, 1992.

Clary, E. G. & Snyder, M. 'A Functional Analysis of Altruism and Prosocial Behaviour: The Case of Volunteerism', *Review of Personality and Social Psychology*, 12, 1991.

Collier, Andrew. *Christianity and Marxism. A Philosophical Contribution to their Reconciliation*, London, Routledge, 2001.

Connolly, William E. 'Catholicism and Philosophy: A Nontheistic Appreciation' in Ruth Abbey, (ed.), *Charles Taylor: Contemporary Philosophy in Focus*, Cambridge, Cambridge University Press, 2004.

Deane, Seamus. 'Introduction' to James Joyce, *Finnegans Wake*, London, Penguin, 1992.

Pat Devine, *Democracy and Economic Planning*, Cambridge, Cambridge University Press, 1988.

Eagleton, Terry. *The Ideology of the Aesthetic*, Oxford, Blackwell, 1990.

Eagleton, Terry. *Sweet Violence. The Idea of the Tragic*, Oxford, Blackwell, 2003.

Eagleton, Terry. *After Theory*, London, Penguin, 2004.

Eagleton, Terry. *The English Novel. An Introduction*, Oxford, Blackwell, 2005.

Ellman, Richard. *James Joyce*, Oxford, New York, Toronto, Melbourne, Oxford University Press, 1983.

Engels, Frederick. Letter to Conrad Schmidt August 5, 1890 in Karl Marx & Frederick Engels, *Collected Works* Vol 49, London, Lawrence & Wishart, 2002.

Flanagan, O. *Self Expressions: Mind, Morals and the Meaning of Life*, New York, Oxford University Press, 1996.

Frank, Joseph. 'Spatial Form in Modern Literature' in *The Widening Gyre*, New Brunswick, N.J., Rutgers University Press, 1963.

Frank, Joseph. 'Spatial Form: Some Further Reflections', *Critical Inquiry*, V, Winter, 1978.

Fraser, Ian. 'Two of a Kind: Hegel Marx, Dialectic and Form', *Capital & Class*, 61, 1997.

Fraser, Ian. *Hegel and Marx: The Concept of Need*, Edinburgh, Edinburgh University Press, 1998.

Freedland, Jonathan. 'Yes, they did lie to us', *The Guardian*, June 22, 2005.

Geoghegan, Vincent. *Ernst Bloch*, London, Routledge, 1996.

Geoghegan, Vincent. 'Bloch: Postsecular Thoughts', in Lawrence Wilde (ed.), *Marxism's Ethical Thinkers*, London, Palgrave, 2001.

Geras, Norman. 'The Controversy About Marx and Justice', *New Left Review*, 150, 1985.

Geras, Norman. 'Bringing Marx to Justice: An Addendum and Rejoinder', *New Left Review*, 195, 1992.

Gernet, Jacques. *China and the Christian Impact. A Conflict of Cultures*, Cambridge, Cambridge University Press, 1985.

Gethin, Rupert. *The Foundations of Buddhism*, Oxford and New York, Oxford University Press, 1998.

Gilbert, Alan. 'Political Philosophy', in Terrell Carver (ed.), *The Cambridge Companion to Marx*, Cambridge, Cambridge University Press, 1991.

Gombrich, Richard. 'Introduction: The Buddhist Way' in Heinz Bechert, & Richard Gombrich, (eds.), *The World of Buddhism*, London, Thames & Hudson, 1984.

Greenwald, Robert. (Director), *Wal-Mart: The High Cost of Low Price*, USA, 2005.

Habermas, Jürgen. *The Theory of Communicative Action Vol. 1. Reason and the Rationalisation of Society*, Cambridge, Polity, 1984.

Habermas, Jürgen. *The Philosophical Discourse of Modernity*, Cambridge, Polity, 1992.

Habermas, Jürgen. *The Structural Transformation of the Public Sphere*, Cambridge, Polity, 1992.

Habermas, Jürgen. *Justification and Application*, Cambridge, Polity, 1993.

Hardt, Michael. and Negri, Antonio. *Empire*, Harvard, Harvard University Press, 2000.

Hardt, Michael. and Negri, Antonio. *Multitude*, London, Hamish Hamilton, 2005.

Hastings, Adrian. (ed.), *Modern Catholicism. Vatican II and After*, London & New York, SPCK & Oxford University Press, 1991.

Haughton, Rosemary Luling. 'Transcendence and the Bewilderment of Being Modern', in James L. Heft (ed.), *A Catholic Modernity?*, Oxford, Oxford University Press, 1999.

Heft, James. L. 'Introduction' to James. L Heft (ed.), *A Catholic Modernity?* Oxford, Oxford University Press, 1999.

Hill, Christopher. *The World Turned Upside Down*, London, Penguin, 1991.

Hitchens, Christopher. *The Missionary Position: Mother Theresa in Theory and Practice*, London, Verso, 1995.

Hjort, Mette. 'Literature: Romantic Expression or Strategic Interaction', in James Tully (ed.), *Philosophy in an Age of Pluralism: The Philosophy of Charles Taylor in Question*, Cambridge, Cambridge University Press, 1994.

Hobsbawm, Eric J. *Industry and Empire*, Harmondsworth, Penguin, 1983.

Hobsbawm, Eric J. *Nations and Nationalism Since 1780*, Cambridge, Cambridge University Press, 1993.

Hohendahl, Peter Uwe. *Prismatic Thought. Theodor W. Adorno*, Lincoln & London, University of Nebraska Press, 1995.

Holloway, John. 'Zapata in Wall Street', in Werner Bonefeld & Kosmas Psychopedis (eds.), *The Politics of Change. Globalization, Ideology and Critique*, Houndmills, Palgrave, 2000.

Holloway, John. *How to Change the World Without Taking Power*, London, Pluto, Expanded Edition, 2005.

Holstun, James. *Ehud's Dagger. Class Struggle in the English Revolution*, London & New York, Verso, 2000.

James, C.L.R. 'Letters to Literary Critics', in Anna Grimshaw (ed.), *The C.L.R. James Reader*, Oxford, Blackwell, 1992.

Jarvis, Simon. *Adorno. A Critical Introduction*, Cambridge, Polity, 1998.

Jay, Martin. *The Dialectical Imagination. A History of the Frankfurt School and the Institute of Social Research 1923–1950*, London, Heinemann, 1973.

Jay, Martin. *Adorno*, Cambridge, Mass, Harvard University Press, 1984.

Joyce, James. *Stephen Hero*, Theodore Spencer, Rev. John J. Slocom and Herbert Cahoon, London, Cape, 1956.

Joyce, James. *A Portrait of the Artist as a Young Man*, London, Folio Society, 1965.

Joyce, James. *Ulysses*, London, Penguin, 1992.

Joyce, Stanislaus. *My Brother's Keeper: James Joyce's Early Years*, New York, Viking Press, 1958.

Kerr, Fergus. *Immortal Longings*, London, SPCK, 1997.

Kiberd, Declan 'Introduction' to James Joyce, *Ulysses*, London, Penguin, 1992.

Kingsnorth, Paul. *One No, Many Yeses. A Journey to the Heart of the Global Resistance Movement*, London, Free Press, 2003.

Lacouture, Jean. *Jesuits*, London, Harvill Press, 1996.

Lamotte, E. 'The Buddha, His Teachings and His Sangha', in Heinz Bechert, & Richard Gombrich, (eds.), *The World of Buddhism*, London, Thames & Hudson, 1984.

Langbaum, Robert. 'The Epiphanic Mode in Wordsworth and Modern Literature', in Wim Tigges (ed.), *Moments of Moment. Aspects of the Literary Epiphany*, Amsterdam-Atlanta, GA, Rodopi, 1999.

Lefebvre, Henri. *Critique of Everyday Life*, Volume 1, London & New York, Verso, 1992.

Lenin, V.I. 'What the Friends of the People Are', in *Collected Works*, Volume 1, Moscow, Progress Publishers, 1963.

Levin, Harry. *James Joyce: A Critical Introduction*, London, Faber & Faber, 1960.

Linebaugh, Peter. *The London Hanged. Crime and Civil Society in the Eighteenth Century*, Harmondsworth, Penguin, 1991.

Linebaugh, Peter. and Rediker, Marcus. *The Many-Headed Hydra. Sailors, Slaves, Commoners, and the Hidden History of the Revolutionary Atlantic*, Boston, Beacon Press, 2000.

Löwy, Michael. *Redemption and Utopia. Jewish Libertarian Thought in Central Europe. A Study in Elective Affinity*, Stanford, Stanford University Press, 1992.

Lukács, Georg. *History and Class Consciousness*, London, Merlin, 1990.

Manser, Gordon. & Cass, Rosemary Higgins. *Voluntarism at the Crossroads*, New York, Family Service Association of America, 1976.

Marcos, Subcomandante. *Ya Basta. Ten Years of the Zapatista Uprising*, Oakland and Edinburgh, AK Press, 2004.

Marcuse, Herbert. *One Dimensional Man. Studies in the Ideology of Advanced Industrial Society*, London, Routledge, 1999.

Martin, Mike W. *Virtuous Giving*, Bloomington & Indianapolis, Indiana University Press, 1994.

Marsden, George. 'Matteo Ricci and the Prodigal Culture', in James L. Heft (ed.), *A Catholic Modernity?* Oxford, Oxford University Press, 1999.

McCarney, Joseph. 'Ideology and False Consciousness' available at http:marxmyths.org/joseph-mccarney/article.htm.

Marx, Karl. Letter to Arnold Ruge, 1843 in David McLellan (ed.), *Karl Marx. Selected Writings*, Oxford, Oxford University Press, 2000.

Marx, Karl. *Critique of Hegel's Doctrine of the State*, in Karl Marx, *Early Writings*, Harmondsworth, Penguin, 1992.

Marx, Karl. *A Contribution to the Critique of Hegel's Philosophy of Right: Introduction*, in Karl Marx, *Early Writings*, Harmondsworth, Penguin 1992.

Marx, Karl. *Economic and Philosophical Manuscripts*, in Karl Marx, *Early Writings*, Harmondsworth, Penguin, 1992.

Marx, Karl. *Theses on Feuerbach*, in Karl Marx & Frederick Engels, *Collected Works*, Volume 5, London, Lawrence & Wishart, 1976.

Marx, Karl. *The Eighteenth Brumaire of Louis Bonaparte*, in Karl Marx, *Surveys from Exile*, Harmondsworth, Penguin, 1973.

Marx, Karl. *Grundrisse*, Harmondsworth, Penguin, 1973.

Marx, Karl. 'Preface' to *A Contribution to the Critique of Political Economy*, Moscow, Progress Publishers, 1977.

Marx, Karl. *Capital*, Volume 1, Harmondsworth, Penguin, 1988.

Marx, Karl. *Capital*, Volume 3, Harmondsworth, Penguin, 1991.

Marx, Karl. *The Civil War in France*, in Terrell Carver (ed.), *Later Political Writings*, Cambridge, Cambridge University Press, 1996.

Marx, Karl. *Critique of the Gotha Programme*, in Karl Marx & Frederick Engels, *Selected Works*, Volume 3, Moscow, Progress Publishers, 1983.

Marx, Karl. & Engels, Frederick. *The German Ideology*, in Karl Marx & Frederick Engels, *Collected Works Vol. 5*, London, Lawrence & Wishart, 1976.

Marx, Karl. & Engels, Friedrich. *The Communist Manifesto*, Harmondsworth, Penguin, 1987.

Menke, Christoph. *The Sovereignty of Art. Aesthetic Negativity in Adorno and Derrida*, Cambridge, Mass & London, MIT Press, 1998.

Meirelles, Fernando. (Director), *The Constant Gardener*, Rest of the World, 2005.

Mészáros, István. *Marx's Theory of Alienation*, London, Merlin, 1970.

Mitchell, David. *The Jesuits. A History*, London, Macdonald Futura, 1980.

Monroe, Kristen Renwick. *The Heart of Altruism. Perceptions of a Common Humanity*, Princeton, Princeton University Press, 1996.

Moore, Michael. (Director), *Fahrenheit 9/11*, USA, 2004.

Morgan, Michael L. 'Religion, History and Moral Discourse', in James Tully (ed.), *Philosophy in an Age of Pluralism: The Philosophy of Charles Taylor in Question*, Cambridge, Cambridge University Press, 1994.

Morgan, Oliver. 'Birth of the first global super-union', *The Observer*, 31 December, 2006.

Mount, Joan. 'Why Donors Give', *Nonprofit Management & Leadership*, 7, 1, 1996.

Muggeridge, Malcolm. *Something Beautiful for God: Mother Theresa of Calcutta*, London, Fontana, 1971.

Negri, Antonio. 'Keynes and the Capitalist Theory of the State post-1929', in Antonio Negri, *Revolution Retrieved*, London, Red Notes, 1988.

Negri, Antonio. 'Archaeology and Project: The Mass Worker and the Social Worker', in Antonio Negri, *Revolution Retrieved*, London, Red Notes, 1988.

Negri, Antonio. *The Politics of Subversion*, Cambridge, Polity, 1988.

Negri, Antonio. *The Savage Anomaly. The Power of Spinoza's Metaphysics and Politics*, Minneapolis, University of Minnesota Press, 1991.

Negri, Antonio. 'Interpretation of the Class Situation Today: Methodological Aspects', in Werner Bonefeld, Richard Gunn and Kosmas Psychopedis (eds.), *Open Marxism. Volume II. Theory and Practice*, London, Pluto, 1992.

Nichols, Ashton. *The Poetics of Epiphany. Nineteenth-Century Origins of the Modern Literary Moment*, Tuscaloosa & London, University of Alabama Press, 1987.

Nicholsen, Shierry Weber. *Exact Imagination, Late Work on Adorno's Aesthetics*, Cambridge, Mass, & London, MIT Press, 1997.

Notes from Nowhere (ed.), *We are Everywhere: The Irresistible Rise of Global Anti-capitalism*, London, Verso, 2003.

Olafson, F.A. 'Comments on *The Sources of the Self*', *Philosophy and Phenomenological Research*, LIV (I), 1994.

Ollman, Bertell. *Alienation*, Cambridge, Cambridge University Press, 1976.

Ollman, Bertell. 'Toward a Marxist Theory of American Patriotism: How "They" Murder Us, and What We Can Do About It', available at http://nyu.edu/projects/ollman/docs/patriotism_content.php

Partsch, Susanna. *Paul Klee*, Cologne, Midpoint Press, 2001.

Piliavin, J.M. & Charng, H.W. 'Altruism: A Review of Recent Theory and Research', *Annual Review of Sociology*, 16, 1990.

Pinter, Harold. 'Art, Truth and Politics', *The Guardian*, December 8, 2005.

Porter, Henry. 'It's clear: The case for war was cooked up', *The Observer*, November 5, 2006.

Proust, Marcel. *Swann's Way. In Search of Lost Time*, Volume 1, London, Vintage, 2002.

Rabinbach, Anson. "Why were the Jews Sacrificed?' The Place of Antisemitism in Adorno and Horkheimer's *Dialectic of Enlightenment*', in Nigel Gibson and Andrew Rubin (eds.), *Adorno: A Critical Reader*, Oxford, Blackwell, 2002.

Redhead, Mark. *Charles Taylor. Thinking and Living Deep Diversity*, Lanham, Rowman & Littlefield, 2002.

Reich, Robert. *The Work of Nations: Preparing Ourselves for 21ˢᵗ Century Capitalism*, New York, Knopf, 1991.

Reynolds, Mary T. *Joyce and Dante. The Shaping Imagination*, Princeton NJ, Princeton University Press, 1981.

Roberts, John Michael. & Crossley, Nick. 'Introduction' to John Michael Roberts & Nick Crossley (eds.), *After Habermas. New Perspectives on the Public Sphere*, Oxford, Blackwell, 2004.

Roberts, Julian. *Walter Benjamin*, London, Macmillan, 1982.

Rorty, Richard. *Contingency, Irony and Solidarity*, Cambridge, Cambridge University Press, 1989.

Rorty, Richard. 'Taylor on Truth', in James Tully (ed.), *Philosophy in an Age of Pluralism: The Philosophy of Charles Taylor in Question*, Cambridge, Cambridge University Press, 1994.

Rosa, Hartmut. 'Goods and Life-Forms: Relativism in Charles Taylor's Political Philosophy', *Radical Philosophy*, 71 (May/June), 1995.

Rosa, Hartmut. & Laitinen, Arto. 'On Identity, Alienation, and the Consequences of September 11ᵗʰ', in Arto Laitinen & Nicholas H. Smith (eds.), *Perspectives on the Philosophy of Charles Taylor*, Helsinki, Acta Philosophica Fennica, The Philosophical Society of Finland, Vol 71, 2002.

Rousseau, Jean-Jacques. *The Social Contract*, Harmondsworth, Penguin, 1987.

Schervish, Paul G. & Havens, John J. 'Social Participation and Charitable Giving: A Multivariate Analysis', *Voluntas*, 8, 3, 1997.

Shea, William M. '"A Vote of Thanks to Voltaire"' in James L. Heft (ed.), *A Catholic Modernity?* Oxford, Oxford University Press, 1999.

Shields, Susan. 'Mother Theresa's House of Illusions. How She harmed her Helpers as well as those they "Helped"', *Free Inquiry* 18, 1, 1997/98.

Skinner, Quentin. 'Who are "We"? Ambiguities of the Modern Self', *Inquiry*, 34, 1991.

Skinner, Quentin. 'Modernity and Disenchantment: Some Historical Reflections', in James Tully, (ed.), *Philosophy in an Age of Pluralism*, Cambridge, Cambridge University Press, 1994.

Sklair, Leslie. *The Transnational Capitalist Class*, Oxford, Blackwell, 2001.

Smith, Nicholas H. *Charles Taylor. Meanings, Morals and Modernity*. Cambridge, Polity, 2002.

Spence, Jonathan D. *The Memory Palace of Matteo Ricci*, London, Faber & Faber, 1985.

Steiner, George. 'Introduction' to Walter Benjamin, *The Origin of German Tragic Drama*, London, Verso, 1998.

Stout, Jeffrey. 'Review' of *A Catholic Modernity?*, *Philosophy in Review*, 21, 6, 2001.

Stuart, Elizabeth. *Spitting at Dragons. Towards a Feminist Theology of Sainthood*, London & New York, Mowbray, 1996.

Tadié, Jean-Eves. *Marcel Proust. A Life*, Harmondsworth, Viking, 2000.

Taxidou, Olga. 'Reviews' of Subcomandante Marcos, *Shadows of Tender Fury.The Letters and Communiques of Subcomandante Marcos and the Zapatista Army of National Liberation*, New York, Monthly Review Press, 1995 & *Zapatistas! Documents of the New Mexican Revolution*, New York, Autonomedia, 1994, in *Common Sense*, 18, 1995.

Thompson, E.P. *The Making of the English Working Class*, Harmondsworth, Penguin, 1970.

Thompson, E.P. *The Poverty of Theory and other Essays*, London, Merlin, 1978.

Thompson, E.P. *Customs in Common*, London, Merlin, 1991.

Thompson, E.P. 'Class and Class Struggle', in Peter Joyce (ed.), *Class*, Oxford & New York, Oxford University Press, 1995.

'Class and Class Struggle', in Peter Joyce (ed.), *Class*, Oxford & New York, Oxford University Press, 1995

Thompson, Paul. 'Foundation and Empire: A Critique of Hardt and Negri', *Capital & Class*, 86, 2005.

Tronti, Mario. 'Social Capital', *Telos*, 17, 1973.

Turner, 'Denys. Religion: Illusions and Liberation', in Terrell Carver (ed.), *The Cambridge Companion to Marx*, Cambridge, Cambridge University Press, 1991.

Unger, Craig. *House of Bush House of Saud: The Secret Relationship Between the World's Two Most Powerful Dynasties*, London, Gibson Square Books, 2007.

van Beeck, Franz Joseph, S. J. *Catholic Identity After Vatican II. Three Types of Faith in the One Church*, Chicago, Loyola University Press, 1995.

Walzer, Michael. *The Revolution of the Saints*, Harvard, Harvard University Press, 1965

Warner, Michael. *The Letters of the Republic*, Cambridge, Mass, Harvard University Press, 1990.

Wheen, Francis. *Karl Marx*, London, Fourth Estate, 1999.

White, Stephen K. 'Weak Ontology and Liberal Political Reflection', *Political Theory*, 25, 4, 1997.

White, Stephen K. *Sustaining Affirmation. The Strengths of Weak Ontology in Political Theory*, Princeton & Oxford, Princeton University Press, 2000.

Wilde, Lawrence. *Ethical Marxism and its Radical Critics*, London, Macmillan, 1998.

Wilde, Lawrence. (ed.), *Marxism's Ethical Thinkers*, Basingstoke, Palgrave, 2001.

Wilkinson, Richard G. *The Impact of Inequality: How to Make Sick Societies Healthier*, London, Routledge, 2005.

Williams, Paul with Tribe, Anthony. *Buddhist Thought*, London & New York, Routledge, 2000.

Wolin, Robert. *Walter Benjamin. An Aesthetic of Redemption*, New York, Columbia University Press, 1982.

Wood, Ellen Meiksins. 'The Separation of the Economic and the Political in Capitalism', *New Left Review*, 127, 1981

Wood, Ellen Meiksins. *The Pristine Culture of Capitalism*, London, Verso, 1991.

Woodrow, Alain. *The Jesuits. A Story of Power*, London & New York, Geoffrey Chapman, 1995.

Wright, Steve. *Storming Heaven: Class Composition and struggle in Italian Autonomist Marxism*, London, Pluto, 2002.

Zinn, Howard. *A People's History of the United States. 1492–Present*, Essex, Pearson, 2003.

Zuidervaart, Lambert. *Adorno's Aesthetic Theory. The Redemption of Illusion*, Cambridge, Mass & London, MIT Press, 1993.

Index